LAWYERS AND LAWBREAKERS

LAWYERS AND LAWBREAKERS

Dick Hamilton

'A third observation no less obvious to me is that the people of the North of England are more litigious than in the south parts, which was likeways told me by the Judge. This humour is the same in the North of Scotland. It seems the distance and difficulty to obtain justice promotes the desire of it.'

Sir John Clerk, *Journal*

DORSET PRESS
New York

Originally published as *Foul Bills and Dagger Money*
Copyright © 1979 Dick Hamilton

This edition published by Dorset Press,
a division of Marboro Books Corporation.
Reprinted by arrangement with
Macmillan Publishing Company,
a division of Macmillan Inc.
1991 Dorset Press

ISBN 0-88029-653-4

Printed in the United States of America

M 9 8 7 6 5 4 3 2 1

To
each great Circuiteer
past, present and future
and the long-suffering spouse
thereof

CONTENTS

LAWYERS AND LAWBREAKERS

Alfred and Afterwards

'Since histories must be in the past, then the more
past the better.'
Thomas Mann, *The Magic Mountain*

As far as most people are concerned, English history starts
with Alfred the Great. It is said that in his reign a man could
leave a bag of gold by the wayside and find it there on his
return, which is much too good to be true. It is believed that he
burnt the cakes, but that charming legend was first attributed
to St Neot. And it is recorded in *The Mirror of Justices* that he
hanged 44 judges in a single year, which makes a rousing start
to any legal history.

But this too is a legend. *The Mirror of Justices* was written in
the 13th century, and has been described by an eminent legal
historian as 'a puzzling mixture of sense and nonsense.' It
includes a list of legal abuses, the most colourful of which is: 'It
is an abuse that rape should extend to others than virgins.'
Another is that: 'It is an abuse to answer or appear by
attorney,' which is an affront to every member of the Bar. This
book is a history of the Northern Circuit, a legal terrain
created for the Judges of Assize and recognised by every
member of the Bar. It came into existence 200 years after
Alfred's reign, which is a useful time to begin because the
seeds of the future are to be seen sprouting in Saxon soil. He
combined the laws of Wessex, Kent and Mercia, the three
great territories of England, and chose the best of them to
make up 'the common law'.

Alfred took a keen interest in the way his judges performed
their duties, as a Saxon biographer describes, but he did not go
to the extent of hanging them:

If the judges acknowledged they had given judgment because they knew no better, he discreetly and moderately

1

reproved their inexperience and folly in terms such as these:

'I wonder truly at your insolence, that whereas by God's favour and mine, you have occupied the rank and office of the wise, you have neglected the studies and labours of the wise. Either, therefore, at once give up the discharge of the temporal duties which you hold, or endeavour more zealously to study the lessons of wisdom. Such are my commands.'

He cared deeply about justice; one of his laws is taken from Exodus: 'Judge thou very fairly. Do not judge one judgment for the rich and another for the poor; nor one for the one more dear and another for the one more hateful.'

His next law is just as appealing: 'A man can think on this one sentence alone, that he judges each one rightly; he has need of no other law-books.'

Saxon law-books can hardly have been elaborate, for the laws were very simple. They stated clearly what people were not to do, and fixed the penalties for doing it. For instance: 'If anyone in lewd fashion seizes a nun either by her clothes or her breast without her leave, the compensation is to be double that we have established for a lay person.'

Compensation was much more important than punishment in Saxon Law. If a man killed another, the dead man's kinfolk might seek revenge, but could be appeased if the blood-money was paid. As a proverb ran: '*Buy off* the spear from thy side, or endure it.'

Almost everything had its price: 'A dog biting or rending a man to death, 6 shillings the first offence, 12 shillings the second, 30 shillings for the third offence.'

Compensation worked on a sliding scale. For injury causing the loss of:

a thumbnail or nostril	3 shillings
a thumb	20 shillings
an eye	50 shillings

The same principle applied to killing:

a churl or labourer	200 shillings
a bishop	1200 shillings
an archbishop	3600 shillings

2

Almost every crime could be paid for in cash; only for conspiring against the King's life, for arson and for theft was death the inevitable penalty.

Each county had its Shire Court, which sat twice a year, and each shire had its smaller units called 'hundreds'—the name survives in 'the Chiltern Hundreds'. Each Hundred Court was held once a month. It was a regular system of justice, a firm foundation on which the Normans were to build, and one of its most typical features was Trial by Ordeal.

Every nation in the world has at some time used Trial by Ordeal. 'Ordeal' means 'judgment', and the Saxons saw Trial by Ordeal as a deeply religious ceremony, it being God's judgment. Before undergoing the rite a man had to fast for three days and then attend Mass. When administering the Sacrament, the priest gave him a solemn oath to swear:

I charge you by the Father and the Son and by the Holy Ghost, and by your Christianity which you have received, and by the holy cross on which God suffered, and by the holy gospel and the relics which are in this church, that you should not dare to partake of this sacrament nor to go to the altar if you did this of which you are accused, or knew who did it.

The most famous ordeal was the Ordeal of Iron, when the accused had to take a red-hot iron in his hand, weighing one pound, and carry it a distance of nine paces. The church would be lined with men who had come to see the ordeal fairly performed. They too had fasted and were sprinkled with holy water. They kissed the Gospel and made the sign of the cross. The ordeal took place at the time of the Sacrament. From a stake in the church a distance of nine feet was measured off with three marks. At the first mark from the stake the accused had to set his right foot; at the second, his left; and at the third, as he completed the distance of nine feet, he could throw down the iron and hasten to the altar. There his hand would be bound up with clean linen. If in three days it had healed cleanly, he was innocent; if it was festering, he was guilty, and would be hanged.

There was a different version of this ordeal where the accused had to walk across red-hot ploughshares. King Edward the Confessor accused his mother of committing adultery with the Bishop of Winchester; she passed the ordeal successfully.

There was also the Ordeal of Hot Water, which had particularly strong religious undertones; it combined the fires of hell with the waters of the flood. The accused had to plunge his hand into a cauldron of boiling water and pull out a piece of stone or another object from the bottom of the cauldron. Then his hand would be bound up and inspected in three days to see how it had healed.

If the offence was particularly serious—treason, for instance—the ordeal became a 'three-fold ordeal', as it was called. The accused would have to plunge not only his hand but his arm up to the elbow into the boiling water or, if he were carrying the red-hot iron, it would weigh not one pound but three pounds.

The Ordeal of Cold Water was generally reserved for the most ordinary people and took place either in a pond or in a well, as near to the church as possible. The accused was given holy water to drink and lowered by a rope gently into the water, so as not to make a splash. If he sank, he was deemed innocent; if he floated, he was guilty. This may seem the wrong way round but during the ceremony God was asked to accept the innocent into the water and cast out the guilty. This is the oath St Dunstan (patron saint of the blind) used to utter at Canterbury: 'Let not the water receive the body of him who, released from the weight of goodness, is upborne by the wind of iniquity!'

These were the three most common kinds of ordeal. Early court records show them in practice at York Assizes in 1208: 'Robert Kipperkarl of Moreby is suspected of robbery by the jurors and four villages. And he was indicted at these Assizes. And therefore let him purge himself by the judgment of water.' If the ordeal proved him guilty of robbery, he would have been hanged. Generally speaking, the Ordeal of Hot Water was for men, and of the Iron for women, as a juicy case shows at Hereford in 1207: 'The whole neighbourhood suspected Marion of procuring her husband's murder, because she had committed adultery with a great many men, and after his death all his goods went missing from the house. 'She was obviously the main suspect and had to undergo the ordeal of iron.

4

Henry Blund was her husband's servant and had often been present when the adulterers were in the house, but after the murder he was missing when the hue and cry was started, which was always regarded as very suspicious. He was accused of consenting to the murder and had to undergo the Ordeal of Water. As a mere servant, he would probably have the Ordeal of Cold Water.

Two of the adulterers fled and the court ordered their arrest; they would certainly face the ordeal when they were caught. Geoffrey of Norfolk was found in possession of the dead man's bow and arrows, which would have implicated him too, if the evidence had not shown that he had been handed them during the hue and cry to help catch the criminals.

The court records of Trials by Ordeal never state what the result was, perhaps because it was so obvious that if the accused failed the ordeal, he would automatically suffer the penalty for the crime. They simply say: 'Let him have the water,' which sounds as uneventful as offering him a cup of cocoa.

These were the most common kinds of Trial by Ordeal but there were others. There was the Corsnaed, or 'sacred mouthful', where a man had to eat a piece of bread containing a feather or some other foreign body. The only recorded instance of it is where Godwin, the father of King Harold of England, was accused at dinner of murdering his brother Alfred (not the same person as King Alfred). 'May this bread choke me if I am guilty!' cried Godwin. It did.

There was also the Bier Rite, which is better remembered as the superstition that if a murderer passed the body of his victim, its wounds would start to bleed again. There are no records of it in English legal history but, in 1634, four hundred years after Trial by Ordeal had been abolished, there was a case at Durham when a man was accused of strangling his kinsman. A bloodstained length of cord was found in his pocket which matched the marks on the dead man's neck and he was the last man to be seen with the deceased whilst he was still alive, so that there was already a strong case against him. Nevertheless, they asked him to touch the body and, when he did, blood ran out of its mouth, ears and nose. The jury must have been very impressed by that evidence, since the old superstitions still survived.

Trial by Ordeal lasted for several centuries in England; King Canute was only one of several kings whose laws dealt with it. But in 1215, the same year as Magna Carta, the Pope decided that the clergy should not undergo Trial by Ordeal. It was no great loss, because it was falling into disuse; too many people were cheating when they took it. Four years later Henry III sent a message to the judges who were going the Northern Circuit in Cumberland, Westmorland and Lancaster, that trial by ordeal was abolished, and it has never been practised since.

But there was another way in which guilt or innocence could be proved physically, and that was Trial by Battle. Although Trial by Ordeal goes back as far as one can trace into the Saxon darkness, it was the Normans who brought Trial by Battle into England after 1066. It may seem no more civilised than Trial by Ordeal, but it was, for its conditions were most carefully regulated. As little as possible was left to chance; it was as much an improvement as a boxing match with a referee is over a bar-room brawl.

Trial by Ordeal was a religious rite and Trial by Battle was much the same. The accused swore on the Bible that he was not guilty of the offence. Before the fight commenced each champion appeared shaven-headed, bare-legged and bare-armed; he knelt before the judge and handed him his glove with a penny in each finger, in honour of the five wounds of God. The contestants were then taken to separate churches to pray that God would grant the victory to the man who was in the right.

It is natural to think of its taking place between two knights in shining armour, galloping towards each other and splintering lances, then fighting it out with battle-axes and spiked clubs. It was usually much less elaborate; sometimes the contestants were armed only with wooden clubs and sandbags, and fought it out, drably dressed without armour, until one of the two lay dead.

The extent to which they made sure the contestants were equally matched was almost laughable. In the XIIIth century a contest took place near Otterburn in Northumbria, almost on the Scottish border, where one of the two was a one-eyed man; he was able to insist that his opponent lost an eye before they began the fray. It also mattered how many teeth he had—not the molars, those back teeth which merely grind

6

tough food—but the sharp incisors which counted as a weapon. Here too he could insist on being equally matched.

Once the battle started, even the king himself could not stop it; it went on until one of the men was dead, or cried 'craven', the word of a coward who had had enough and craved mercy. If the accuser cried 'craven', he lost his case, and was treated as a perjurer for bringing a false claim; he was condemned to wear the calfskin garments of cowardice for the rest of his life, so that his disgrace could be known. But if the accused cried 'craven', he was guilty and could be hanged. So the battle went on until it was finished. But if night drew on and the stars came out, the battle was over. If the accuser had not won by then, he had lost, and was a perjured man.

Here is an example of Trial by Battle at Carlisle in 1292: 'Gilbert the Goose' (the goose-herd, perhaps) accused Hugh Bolare of stealing his ox at the Court of Robert le Brus. Hugh claimed that he had bought the ox quite honestly from William the Long but William denied selling it to him, so, to resolve that important question, the Court ordered that William and Hugh should settle the matter in Trial by Battle. William beat Hugh, so Hugh was hanged. Not everybody would or could fight their own battles and so champions were used by them to fight their battles. It is not clear in what sort of cases they were allowed to do so—not in criminal cases, perhaps, but in other kinds of cases.

Monks certainly used to hire champions to fight their battles for them, for priests were not always the doughtiest warriors. An unsuccessful champion was in the same position as his master; his defeat made him a perjurer and perjurers were liable to have their right hand cut off. In 1220 there was an Elias Piggun who lost and had his foot cut off instead. The name is worth noting; 'Piggun' is almost certainly the same word as 'pugilist', and Elias was therefore simply 'Elias the Champion'. He may have thought himself hardly treated but this was not the view of the King's council who decided his fate: 'It is considered that he do lose his foot, and be it known that by the action of the King's council he is dealt with mercifully, for by law he had deserved a worse punishment.'

The worst fate lay in store for William Pygun, another pugilist, who was a monk at St Albans at this time, or rather 'not a monk so much as a twisting fiend', as they described him.

7

He forged some deeds with the Abbey's official seal and took bribes from an enemy of the monks, for which he was transferred to the priory at Tynemouth. It was a punishment quite often inflicted and its rigours in winter must have been severe indeed.

The prior at Tynemouth had a dispute with Simon of Tynemouth about some 'corrodies', a sort of life subscription which people could pay for board and lodging at a monastery. Monasteries sold these rights to raise ready cash and Simon claimed he had paid his money but had not been granted his rights. The quarrel ended in Trial by Battle, the monastery being represented by William Pygun, now described as 'a great boxer', and 'our great champion'. But he lost, and from then on the monks had not a good word to say for him. The startling description of his fate at Tynemouth may well have come from the pen of the great mediaeval historian Matthew Paris, who wrote most of the *Deeds of the Abbots of St Albans* from which it comes.

THE FRIGHTFUL DEATH OF WILLIAM PYGUN

It happened one night that William was sitting on the lavatory at the rear of the dormitory. He forgot the early service and went on sitting there, drunk and bloated with the food he had gorged himself on. He began to nod off to sleep and his snores were loud and disgusting. Gradually he passed from drunkenness into sleep and from sleep into expected death. It may have been due to the cold weather but I prefer to think it was the vengeance of God. For when his frightful snoring had stopped, a voice was clearly heard in the privy, where he sat dying, bellowing: 'Get him, Satan, get him!'

This was clearly heard by those monks who were in the dormitory at the time because they were not in the choir and who had stayed behind for that reason. And that was the disgraceful way in which this wretch lost his life whilst he was using the lavatory. When his dead body was found the following day they were all so outraged that it was only with reluctance that they granted him Christian burial. However, to avoid a scandal, the monks were prepared to turn a blind eye to it out of respect for their monastic order and habits.

By the XIIIth Century, when William Pygun died, Trial by Battle was falling into disuse; Trial by Jury was becoming more popular. It had certainly become quite forgotten by 1571 when a dispute arose over an estate in Kent, and the parties claimed Trial by Battle, 'not without great consternation among the lawyers'. It was adjourned to be fought in Tothill Fields not far from Westminster Hall but Queen Elizabeth let it be known that she disapproved of it and the case was settled behind the scenes. The 4000 spectators who gathered to see the battle went home disappointed; so did the fencing-master who was to have been the plaintiffs' champion. He begged to be allowed to 'show some pastime', with perhaps just a few parries and thrusts to show what he could do, but his opponent did not oblige him.

Trial by Battle seems to have taken the form that its fighters preferred. In 1602 Thomas Musgrave and Lancelot Carleton agreed 'The true trial of such controversies as are between them' to be held near Carlisle. They were to use traditional Border equipment such as steel bonnets, Scotch daggers, and so on. There is no record of the fight taking place, but so many quarrels were settled on moonless nights in Border country that it is only surprising that they agreed to meet fairly in broad daylight. Most Border quarrels were settled treacherously on moonless nights.

Another case arose between two northern families, the Claxtons and the Lilburns, who were violently disputing the right to an estate at a village with a name which matched their obstinate aggressiveness—Thickley Punchardon. They came to Durham Assizes in 1638 and demanded Trial by Battle. Mr Justice Berkeley was so taken aback that he did what any judge would have done in the circumstances—he adjourned the case. It was adjourned several times further but a year later he found the case still confronting him. This time he questioned the champions on each side to ask whether they were not hired for money, which was still not an accepted practice, and they admitted that they were. So he adjourned the case for further consideration.

Charles I was very much against the battle taking place but the law did not allow him to override the wishes of the contestants. Many of the senior judges then put their heads together to see if there was not some special legal way of stopping the proceedings, but found none. However, the Civil War then broke out and the case was never heard of again.

One hundred and fifty years went by. In 1817, two years after the cannons roared at Waterloo, a man was charged at Warwickshire Assizes with murdering a girl and was acquitted. Her brother sprang up in Court and accused the Defendant afresh. 'Not guilty,' he answered coolly, and threw his glove to the floor; 'and this I am ready to defend with my body.' These were the ancient words of Trial by Battle.

The judges were acutely embarrassed but as the girl's brother was restrained by people in court from picking up the glove, the challenge was never accepted.

Two years later Lord Chancellor Eldon moved in the House of Lords that Trial by Battle should be abolished. One would have thought they would have been glad to abolish it but, according to a biography of Lord Eldon, 'The Lords seem to have been struck dumb with astonishment for, without another word being uttered, the bill was agreed to.' Thus, in 1819, Trial by Battle was abolished. It was the last of the primitive forms of trial to survive and its passing has not been lamented. Still, as a bishop has observed, 'Trial by Battle is, I need hardly say, a deeply rooted institution of fallen humanity.'

Trial by Battle and Trial by Ordeal were thought to be governed by the will of God. And when a suspect took sanctuary, divine and human rights overlapped. It may seem like an easy escape for a criminal, but it was not. When he fled to a church he was immediately presumed to be guilty and his stay inside the church was limited. By one of the laws of King Alfred: 'If anyone takes sanctuary running or riding, no-one is to drag him out for seven days, if he can live in spite of hunger, unless he fights his way out.' There is a sanctuary-knocker on the door of Durham Cathedral, by which he would claim to be let in and inside the church he might find a seat set aside for him in the choir or near the altar; such frith-stools ('chairs of peace') are still to be seen at Beverley and Hexham.

When a suspect fled to a church, he had either to give himself up and stand trial or, if he admitted the crime, to leave the country within two days, going into exile from the nearest port. If he managed to escape to sanctuary after he had been captured or condemned, he could stay there 40 days, until the judges or the coroners came. But if he refused to leave, what then? No layman could make him—'this would be horrible and unhallowed,' says Bracton, a Norman writer on law. Only a member of the clergy could force him to go; if, however, he could not be forced out, he could stay almost indefinitely, '40 days, and for a year and for two years, if this be the pleasure of the malefactory.'

There must be a limit to the time even the hardest criminal would wish to stay within a sanctuary, but the rights of sanctuary had to be protected. In 1014 AD, Ethelred ordered compensation to be paid to the church whose sanctuary was violated, whether by fighting or by robbery, or—somewhat startlingly—by unlawful sexual intercourse. The Saxons laid down a fixed list of penalties for this, of course. For violating a 'chief minster', such as York, the penalty was £5; less for 'a rather smaller minster', and less again for a 'still smaller minster'—a mini-minster, perhaps. At the bottom end of the scale came a 'field-church', where the penalty was 30 shillings.

Sanctuary was therefore not the perfect haven for a criminal. Nor, for that matter, was it an unmixed blessing for a town to be one of those 'liberties' where the King's writ did not run and criminals might remain indefinitely. Hexham was one of them, described as 'an asylum of thieves and robbers, the greatest offenders to the Crown and their country daily removing thither upon trust of refuge, to the great comfort and encouragement of many of the vilest and worst subjects and offenders in the northern parts.'

In Lancashire, Henry VIII allowed only Manchester and Lancaster to retain such 'liberties', but Manchester found they attracted more undesirable characters than it could cope with. Six years after Henry VIII's statute was passed, Manchester obtained permission to send its refugees to Chester; since then it has ceased to be a 'Centre of Sinners'. At least, a *History of Lancashire* says so.

Trial by Ordeal fell into disuse long before being abolished. Obsolete laws often linger on unnoticed for centuries, until they are repealed in a flurry of legislative spring-cleaning. Sometimes, like Trial by Battle in 1817, they emerge from a forgotten crypt, clanking their chains, and are then exorcised as soon as possible. The right of sanctuary was still used up to the time that James I abolished it entirely. But there was one

11

Saxon practice which continued vigorously into Victorian times and that was the 'deodand'.

When an object caused a fatal accident, it had to be forfeited: *deo dandum*, 'to God it had to be given'. As an old rhyme ran:

> *Whatever moved to do the deed*
> *Is deodand and forfeited.*

Thus the thing expiated its crime. At the Yorkshire Assize in 1218: 'A youth named Alan fell on his scythe and died. No-one is suspected. Verdict, misadventure. The scythe is given to the lepers.' Though the scythe in this case was given to charity, it could have been sold to purchase masses for the soul of the deceased but such money was usually given to the King.

Coroner's juries had to assess the money value of the thing to be forfeited, which became less and less as time went on. The deodand system might have expired out of sheer indifference had it not been for the invention of steam engines. Today, steam engines have great nostalgic charm and symbolise the solid craftsmanship of the Industrial Revolution, but to unimaginative juries they were frightful juggernauts whose owners should be made to pay for unleashing them. When the railway engines *Merlin* and *Basilisk* collided on the Grand Junction Railway in 1838, killing a driver, both of them were ordered to be forfeited as deodands. When, in the following year, the steamship *Victoria* blew up on the Thames near Shadwell, killing a foreman, the boiler and engine were declared deodands, and the ship owners were on risk for the sum of £1500.

Extraordinary legal manoeuvres took place to avoid such forfeitures, sometimes successfully, but the powerful railway companies were not amused and Parliament abolished the whole silly system in 1846. This was the last of the Saxon practices to survive. With the coming of the Normans, justice became more efficient, and the curtain is about to rise on the Northern Circuit.

TWO

The Circuits Begin

*'This gives me an opportunity of bringing in a
succinct little account of the Conquest, which will
be beneficial to the lower classes. The editor
peremptorily insists upon that kind of thing.'*
Anthony Trollope, *The Three Clerks*

The circuits came about quite naturally. From Saxon times the
King's Court used to travel the country and the names of its
edicts showed where the royal caravanserai had rested: the
Constitutions of Clarendon, the Assizes of Northampton, the
Statute of Merton. When the Court heard cases, the King like
Solomon sometimes pronounced judgment, but more often he
was content to preside and let his nobles decide the result,
much as a judge leaves it to a jury.

It was all rather haphazard but William the Conqueror was
formidably efficient. He sent his officials throughout England
to compile the Domesday Book for tax purposes and thus the
Exchequer was the first government department to exist on its
own. But judges also could visit the people. When Henry I
sent out his staff to gather in revenue, they were his commissioners; when he sent them out to hear cases, they were his
justices, and the seeds of the circuit system were sown. By the
royal edict of 1166 called the 'Assize of Clarendon' Henry II
ordered two judges to cover 18 counties in a single 'circuit'. In
1176 he sent the judges on six different circuits which covered
the country, and this was the Northern one: Warwickshire,
Richmondshire (now part of Yorkshire), Copeland (now
West Cumberland), Westmorland, Northumberland and
Cumberland. Warwickshire was soon allotted to the Midland
Circuit, and the Northern Circuit came to include Cumberland, Lancashire, Northumberland, Westmorland, Yorkshire
and, much later, Durham. In 1876 its territory east of the
Pennines became the new North-Eastern circuit but there has

been a Northern Circuit since 1176. It is now 800 years old.

In that first year of 1176 each of the six circuits were assigned three judges apiece. The Northern Circuit had Robert de Vaux, the Sheriff of Cumberland. Sheriffs were often made judges in their own counties, until it was realised that it was rather like letting shady financiers audit their own accounts. The second judge was the great lawyer Rannulph de Glanville; the third was the obscure Robert Pikenot, about whom nothing is known. He certainly never sat as a judge on any other occasion. They had their strict instructions to follow, beginning with the question of Trial by Ordeal.

They had for instance to regulate the harbouring of strangers, because it was an important security provision in a simple society; nobody was to give hospitality to a stranger without very good reason, and then only for one night.

Item: let nobody either in a town or in a village give hospitality to any for more than one night in his house, whom he ought not to have unless the guest has a reasonable excuse, which the master of the house should explain to his neighbours; and when he departs he can be received by the neighbours for a day.

And the judges had instructions about criminal trials. For example, if anyone had openly admitted his guilt of murder, burglary, robbery or forgery, he was not allowed to deny it thereafter. Modern trials would be much shorter if that rule was still in force.

They also had demolition work to see to: 'Let the justices see that the castles are knocked down and thoroughly demolished'. Castles were not pretty tourist attractions in those days but strongholds of power which threatened royal authority, as King Stephen had learnt to his cost; a famous passage in the *Anglo-Saxon Chronicle* describes what happened in 1137:

The Barons were all untrue to their oaths and broke their promises, because each of them built his own castle and kept it in defiance of the King; they filled the land with castles. They terrorised the unfortunate inhabitants of the places in which their castles were, and when the castles were completed they manned them with fiends and villains.

14

When they thought that anybody still had anything left worth having, they threw them into prison at any time of the day or night, whether they were men or women, for the sake of their gold or silver, and tortured them unspeakably; no martyrs ever suffered worse. They strung them up by their feet, and choked them with thick smoke; they hanged them up by their thumbs or heads, and applied flames to their feet.

With others they tied cords tightly round their heads and increased the pressure until they suffered cerebral damage. As a different form of torture they put others into dungeons containing snakes, adders and toads. Others they put into a torture-chamber, being a short narrow shallow chest with sharp stones in; they squashed people inside so as to break all their bones . . . They starved thousands of people to death . . . This went on for 19 years during Stephen's reign, getting worse every day.

So the castles were razed, as the King commanded. After the frightful anarchy of Stephen's reign, any system of law was better than none and it is why the justices had to take action in 1176.

The justices went on circuit again in 1177, and perhaps also in 1178, but in that year:

. . . the King, pausing in England, asked the justices he had appointed there whether they had well and fairly treated the men of the realm; and when he learnt that the country and its population was overburdened by such a large number of justices, *there being 18.* . . .

he consulted with the wise men of his court, and appointed five judges to stay within the King's Court and hear cases, 'so that'—since he did not usually try the cases himself—'if any issue comes before the judges which they cannot themselves decide, it shall be put forward for the King's hearing'.

It meant that there were five judges in London ready to consider difficult problems. This may have been the origin of the King's Bench; all the judges were professional lawyers, which was not true of the itinerant justices, who included sheriffs and knights who lived in or near the Circuit territory.

A further assize took place in 1189, when the country was

divided into four circuits: north, south, east and west. The Northern Circuit consisted of 'Nottinghamshire, Derbyshire, Warwickshire, Northumberland, Westmorland, Cumberland, "Inter Ribble and Mersey" (South Lancashire), and Lancaster.' As it included part of the Midlands, six judges were appointed to it this time: Godfrey of Luci, later Bishop of Winchester; John Cumin, later Archbishop of Dublin; Hugh of Gaerst; Rannulph de Glanville again; Willian of Bendinge, the Sheriff of Dorset and Somerset; and Alan of Furnell, later Bishop of Oxford. Since that date judges have been out every year on circuit to some part of the country. The regular circuits had begun.

The later Circuits, however, were usually six in number, so that the Northern Circuit lost its Midland counties and for most of its history consisted of Lancashire, Cumberland, Westmorland, Yorkshire, Durham and Northumberland.

Many people can still remember what happened at the assizes: A Rolls-Royce drew up outside the law courts in a provincial town and the High Court judges emerged, fully robed, to be greeted by the High Sheriff, the Lord Mayor and a fanfare of trumpets. It was an important event and deserved to be, for was not the royal court, in the person of the judges, visiting the provinces to do justice there? Anybody could take a case to London if he liked, but with the assizes, justice came to him.

'Assize' is a curious word. A Frenchman says, 'Asseyez-vous' when he asks someone to sit down and an assize was an edict of the King when he sat with his council; it also meant the sitting of the judges in court. The phrases 'Assize of bread' and 'Assize of wine', which occur in old records, can be ignored; in this book assizes will be used only to describe the visits of the judges.

The judges on circuit had many things to do besides hearing cases. Demolishing castles was one of them and settling a clergyman's strike was another. This occurred because Geoffrey of York, the Archbishop, was a particularly proud prelate, with a flair for enraging his juniors. In 1193 Richard I was held captive in an Austrian castle and a king's ransom had to be raised for his release. Up and down the country the clergy were required to contribute one quarter of their incomes, and did so; but in York they refused, accusing the

16

Archbishop of trying to destroy the freedom of their church. They had a further source of grievance because he wanted to appoint his own choice as Dean, so they went on strike. They refused to hold any services in the Minster, they silenced the bells, stripped the altars of their hangings, locked the Archbishop's stall in the choir and barred his private door into the building.

He ordered them to resume their normal duties, and they refused, so he appointed other clergy to carry out their duties. They in turn complained to the Pope, who appointed Simon of Apulia, their own choice, to be the Dean. The struggle was not yet over: the Archbishop ordered his men to seize the property of the canons, who complained to the Archbishop of Canterbury. Finally, the itinerant justices were appointed to settle the dispute. They ruled that the Archbishop was in the wrong and all his men who had seized the canon's property were thrown into prison.

So the itinerant justices had always more to do than hear law-suits; but they never had more to do than when there was a 'General Eyre' every seven years or so, for they had then to act as judges, inspectors and auditors. An Eyre had nothing to do with an Eyrie, eagle-like though its gaze was; the word comes, much altered, from the Latin word 'iter', a journey, which also gives rise to the word 'itinerant'. The judges on circuit were always itinerant justices, but they were only 'Justices in Eyre' every seven years or so and were particularly formidable.

They examined every detail of local administration; they detected embezzlement and oppression by the sheriffs; and they wrung such massive fines out of almost everybody who appeared before them that the Eyre was a major source of royal revenue. It was said that in 1233 the men of Cornwall fled into the woods for fear of them.

Many of the records of the General Eyres still survive. They are only minutes of the proceedings written in Medieval Latin, but still they give a vivid impression of what went on.

On the second Monday after Easter 1256, the Northumberland Assizes began at Newcastle with the proclamation of the King's writ:

The King to all Archbishops, Bishops, and all other faithful subjects of the Counties of Northumberland, Cumberland,

Westmorland, and Lancaster, Greeting. Know ye that we have constituted our well beloved and faithful the Abbot of Peterborough, Roger de Thurkelby, Nicholas de Hadlon, and John de Wyvule, our Justices Itinerant, this time to take common pleas in the counties aforesaid. Witness the King at Woodstock this Twentieth day of February.

If the weather was fine, the Eyre could be held near a bridge, or at the market cross; but if it rained some large hall could be used, or a church; York Minster was used for the Assizes in 1238. The Court would probably sit every day for a fortnight, Sundays included.

First came the 'apologies for absence' (*essoins*) which had to be made if the absentee was not to be fined. At the Yorkshire Assizes of 1218–19, an accused person sent the splendid apology that he had gone to the Crusades. A list follows of those who were *attorned* (appointed) to attend on behalf of others; these attorneys developed in time into the advocates' profession. Priors, for instance, usually appointed their cellarers to handle their cases, not from that acquaintance with ardent liquors which has marked the careers of some attorneys, but from the practical business experience they had with the outside world.

Then the cases were heard. At this General Eyre of 1256 there were no Trials by Ordeal—they were abolished in 1219. However, William, son of John of Newton, claimed Trial by Battle against Patrick Herring for attacking him with an axe at Stamford on St Margaret's Day but unfortunately omitted to raise the hue and cry immediately after the incident. This rendered his claim invalid. However, the court had a public duty to inquire into every breach of the King's peace, but the jurors decided that Patrick had indeed wounded William deeply with the axe. The result was that Patrick was put into prison for doing it, but as William's claim was invalid he was put into prison for making a 'false claim'. No wonder people hated the Eyre.

Most of the civil cases were actions of *mort d'ancestor* and *novel disseisin*, property claims of rather specialised interest; but in one case the jury's decision was wrong. Some men, armed with bows and arrows and axes, smashed the plaintiff's weir in the Tyne. The jury ordered the defendants to rebuild

18

it, and awarded the plaintiff 40 shillings damages. But the judges intervened; if the weir was rebuilt, the plaintiff could not have compensation for its total loss as well, so they ordered instead that the defendant should pay 40 shillings to the plaintiff who could rebuild his own weir.

There were several cases about mill-ponds interfering with water supplies and a number of cases of false imprisonment, especially when high-handed sheriffs exceeded their powers. In a claim for false imprisonment, the plaintiff had to prove that he had no effective means of escape, as one case shows:

> Agnes Bertram, John of Kirkby and Walter le Carect were required to be present to answer the claim of Richard, son of William of Ponte, that they had imprisoned him and ill-treated him against the peace, etc. They kept him in prison for two days, as a result of which he claims that he has suffered damages to the value of 20s.
>
> Agnes and the others are present, and deny that they used any force on him or caused him any loss; they did not ill-treat him or imprison him, as he claims. When Richard was asked what prison they kept him in, he says they shut Agnes' doors, so that he could not leave the Hall. But since Richard was not imprisoned in any prison, nor in irons, nor shut in, even in the Hall—and the evidence is that there were several ways he could have got out of the Hall—there is judgment for the Defendants, and Richard is fined for a false claim.

Any flaw in the pleadings was enough to wreck a case. Pollock and Maitland, the distinguished legal historians, said that a litigant who hoped to get to the end of his case without being fined was something of an optimist, 'for he was playing a game of forfeits.' In another case of false imprisonment, Alan of Calverley claimed that *two men* took him and put him in York Castle prison for four days, but his evidence was *the keeper of the castle* did it, albeit on behalf of the other two. So his case failed through that error and he was fined.

The records do not show how much he was fined; they simply say he was 'in mercy', a phrase which occurs in almost every case. It was certainly more merciful for the judges to fine Alan than to put him in prison and they would inquire what his means were before fixing the sum he was to pay; but he would probably find that his pockets had been lightened most unsympathetically.

In Anglo-Saxon times the law's chief concern was to fix penalties for each offence: 6 shillings for a dog's first bite, 12 for the second, and so on. But in the XIIIth Century, the law was obsessed with correct procedure. When a crime was committed, the hue and cry had to be raised in the nearest village and that village, with the three others nearest it, had to pursue and catch the criminal. Failure always led to a fine. For instance, when in 1256 Alan of Rascawe struck Richard Whirlpippin, a minstrel, on the head with a shovel, killing him, Alan ran away, which proved his guilt conclusively, and he failed to attend court at the due time, which made him an outlaw. So he forfeited his possessions, valued at sevenpence. His own village of Birtley did not catch him, so *they* were fined; and the three neighbouring villages of Chipchase, Barrasford and Gunnerton failed to pursue him, so *they* were fined too.

Anybody who was in a house at night when a crime was committed was automatically the first suspect and had to attend court; so did the victim, if he could. But it was easier to make the rules than to keep them:

Unknown criminals burgled the house of Alan of Newton, and tied him up and took away his goods. Nobody knows who they were. Alan was bound over to attend because he was tied up in that house, but is not present, and his sureties to attend were Elias Tod of Newton and Reginald son of Bernard of Hespol, so he will be fined. The town of Newton did not make pursuit, so they will be fined.

'Unknown criminals burgled' was a phrase frequently used, thanks to the Border raiders who came into England by night, tied up the household and were back in Scotland with their spoils before the hue and cry was raised. There were plenty of other bolt-holes called 'liberties' where the King's writ did not run and criminals could remain at liberty. There was the See of Durham, Hexham, Tynedale, Carham, and the little shires of Norhamshire, Islandshire and Bedlingtonshire; the most notorious of all was Tynemouth, where criminals took refuge at the Sanctuary Cross. That is why few criminals were caught in Northumberland; but stern justice awaited those who were:

The jurors report that Gilbert of Niddesdale, a stranger, fell in with a hermit called Semannus of Bottlesham. They went together onto a moor where Gilbert seized the hermit, beat him, wounded him, and sent him away half dead, and stole his clothes and one penny. Then he fled. Ralph of Beleford (being in the King's service) met him as he was running away, captured him, accused him of being a criminal, and took him to Alnwick.

The hermit came to Alnwick, and said he had robbed and beaten him, as already mentioned, and Gilbert admitted it to the bailiff and the man of Alnwick. The King's servant made the hermit cut off his head.

The sheriff and the coroner, being asked what right he had to cut his head off, say that *it is customary within the county* that whenever someone is caught red-handed his head is cut off immediately, and the person who complains of being robbed of his goods can have the property of the deceased.'

Even when a criminal was caught red-handed, the King's bailiff or coroner had to be present when he admitted his crime and was executed.

Villagers were hardly reluctant to execute a criminal on the spot, since they were fined every time he escaped. A criminal did not exactly escape justice when he took sanctuary, because he had to swear to go into exile (*abjure the realm*), and his goods were confiscated; but the community was still fined:

John of Craumford fled to the church of Bamburgh and admitted he was a robber, and promised to go into exile in the presence of William of Bamburgh, then the coroner. He had no possessions. The evidence is that the whole town accused him of robbery, wanting him arrested, but he managed to escape to the church, as already mentioned; so the town will be fined. And the 12 jurors concealed the matter, so they will be fined.

Even when nobody was to blame for an accident, people were punished for not coming to court:

An unknown stranger was found dead in the fields at Colwell, torn limb from limb by dogs. Reginald, a shepherd from Colwell, was the first to find him; he is present and is not suspected. Nobody knows who killed him. The villages of Colwell, Swinburn and Barrasford were not fully represented at the inquest, so they are to be fined.

So many people were 'in mercy' when the Eyre was held that one might wonder if true clemency survived at all. But pardons were granted several times. Peter Grapir of Colwell shot an arrow at a pigeon, and missed—it killed a man by accident. Peter then ran away and, like all fugitive criminals, became an outlaw. He was later pardoned in a ceremony, not unlike the reading of marriage banns in church, when the congregation has three opportunities 'to speak now or forever hold their peace.' The victim's relatives were given three chances to declare that they wished to sue Peter but none of them wanted to, so he was acquitted and granted a full pardon.

It was a pity that Peter ever ran away, because the law recognised justifiable homicide, as a colourful example shows:

The jurors report that Thomas of Gunnerton, a mad priest, went by night whilst possessed by the devil to the house of Hugh of Burton, and found everybody asleep inside. He wanted to get into that house where Hugh and the family lay, so he broke three planks in the wall and tried to get in.

Gilbert of Dutton, Hugh's servant, heard the noise and thought burglars were trying to get in; as the priest was poking his head into the house, trying to get in, Gilbert struck him on the forehead with a yoke, killing him outright. Gilbert was bound over to attend and is present and admits it, so he is kept in custody, and the matter has to be investigated.

Later, the jurors and the neighbouring villages gave evidence that he did not strike the blow unlawfully, particularly because he took him for a burglar, so he was acquitted.

A case of justifiable homicide at the Northumberland Assizes in 1279 is too remarkable to be omitted:

An unknown woman, a witch, entered the house of John of Kerneslawe at the hour of vespers, and sprang at him; he crossed himself at the time when the Benedicite was being said. In defending himself, as if against the devil, John struck her with a staff, and killed her. Later, by the decision of all the clergy, her body was burnt.

After this incident John went mad. But when he regained his sanity he remembered what had happened and, being afraid of getting into trouble he fled into the See of Durham. He is not suspected of any felony, so he can come back, if he likes, but his goods must be confiscated because he ran away. The goods are worth £4 5s.

In criminal cases jurors had to note carefully what sort of weapon was used and the size of the wound. If a female victim suffered a miscarriage and the foetus was fully formed and already animated, it counted as homicide of the unborn child. A cattle thief knocked down a woman and she miscarried. The foetus was only one inch long, so it remained theft, not homicide.

There were many cases to be heard at the General Eyre in 1256. When they were over men came forward from the different towns to show how they had performed their duties, such as inquiring into fatal accidents: 'Thomas the son of Thomas fell from a plum tree and died immediately. The first person to find him is present and is not suspected, nor is anyone else. Verdict, misadventure. There is nothing to be paid on account of the tree.'

The primitive system of the deodand—something 'given to God'—flourished when it led to a death. Even if an accident was entirely the fault of the deceased, the forfeiture might still take place:

Gilbert Colt, a servant of the parson of Brombury, was driving a cart with a cask of wine, but being extremely drunk fell under the cart, which ran over him. Nobody is suspected. Verdict, misadventure.

Value of the wine, the oxen and the cart 8 marks 2 shillings, for which the sheriff must answer.

Only the wheel made direct contact with him, but the horse, the cart and its load had added to its weight and impetus and had to be forfeited too. There was plenty of variety in these fatal accidents. People fell from their horses into the Tyne and drowned; the horses were valued and forfeited and the money given to the King. Some were crushed by mill-stones, or fell into vats of boiling water in tanneries; the mill-stones and vats had to be forfeited too. But some people flouted the law.

23

Walter of Newcastle was in a rowing boat so overloaded with its catch that it sank and he was drowned. However, the boat's Flemish owner immediately fled to sea and escaped having to forfeit the value of the boat.

The saddest case at this Eyre was a suicide:

Richard of Newton, a parish priest, Master of the Hospital of St Margaret of Westgate, went to bed at the same time as the brothers of that establishment in the dormitory, and when they went to matins they sent him back to bed because he said he was feeling ill. As soon as they returned Richard went back into the room and hanged himself from one corner.

William, the baker at the hospital, was the first to find him; he is present and is not suspected, nor is anybody else. Verdict, suicide.

He had no possessions of his own.

The jurors' reports about fish-ponds and weirs may be less exciting than cases of sudden death but they can light up a whole landscape and reveal a great deal about everyday life. It is time for the men of Newcastle to step forward and address the Judges:

As far as the King's revenue is concerned, they say at Newcastle for 15 days before the Purification of the Blessed Mary, and for 15 days afterwards, the Constable of the Castle can take for his own use, if he wants to, 100 haddocks if they can be caught, for sixpence. And likewise during the whole year he can take one cod, or one conger eel or one ray for one penny, if three or more are found in one catch, provided however that the fisherman can have one first choice. He can also take on credit 40 pence of bread, ale, fish and meat for 40 days only. And as long as he is entitled to this, he cannot take more on credit.

As far as encroachments on royal land are concerned, they say that the Prior of Durham, after the last circuit of the justices, built 26 houses in the town of South Shields, and two furnaces and four breweries on the shore of the Tyne, and made fish-ponds in that river up to the centre of the stream and beyond towards Newcastle, to the damage and nuisance of the whole town of Newcastle, but it is not known how much loss the King has suffered as a result.

They have also to report that the highways are out of repair, a matter which was also the concern of the itinerant justices in 1256:

The jurors report that the roads out of Newcastle have got much worse on the way to Corbridge because of ditches and mines, and travellers by night are in great danger, because the land has been undermined in many places by them, so as to cause an obstruction to the highway. There must be an inquiry.

Almost everything came within the scope of the Eyre. When a man married a ward of court without permission, they looked into it; when wine was sold contrary to the regulations, they looked into it; the offenders could be placed in the pillory. Little escaped their scrutiny. In a case of treasure trove the long arm of the law reached out after nearly a quarter of a century:

. . . And the jurors say that Simon the son of Folentinus and Robert Brand found this treasure some 22 years ago. And they say that since the treasure was found they have enjoyed a much higher standard of living. Simon is present, so let him be put in prison. Robert is absent, so he must be arrested.

From town after town the men came to the Eyre to make their report, with every chance of being fined before the day is out. The men of Felton only needed to report one accidental death, but they had concealed it, so they were fined. The men of Alnwick correctly reported the incident of Gilbert of Niddesdale, who robbed the hermit and was beheaded, and an accident where a little girl fell into a cauldron of hot water and was scalded to death, so no fine had to be paid for those matters; but they had not pursued the culprits in a certain brawl, so they were fined for that. Only the men of Wark escaped penalty, getting off scot-free in more senses than one; the King of Scotland had his court there and though they attended the Eyre, they were only answerable to Scottish law.

After a furiously busy fortnight, the Eyre is finally over. The fines reach the tremendous total of £556 3s. 10d., though it will take at least 15 years for it all to be collected.

The judges head for home and the jurors may now return to their ordinary lives, Adam the Clerk, for instance, and Adam of Blakeden, to Newcastle. The men of Morpeth include William the Dyer and William the Tanner. William the Palmer and Thomas the Cook should bolt their doors at night against the border raiders, a source of great peril in Wark. Thomas the Serjeant can give William of Ridale sound legal advice as they ride back to Corbridge, and the soundest is to beware the greed of the sheriffs: unknown Scotsmen may take a man's money but they will not put him in prison as well. William Beaufiz has his house, and Dr Ivo his practice at Alnwick; his patients have claim on him now, till the next assizes are held.

The General Eyre is over and may not be repeated for another seven years. A juror's lot is unenviable at times like these but not as hard, surely, as that of the unknown, unnamed and unconsidered serfs.

THREE

The Jews at York

> 'I say this only, that usury is something *permitted*
> *through the hardness of men's hearts*; for since
> there must be borrowing and lending, and men are
> so hard of heart that they will not lend freely,
> usury must be permitted.'
>
> Francis Bacon, *Essays*

For a circuit historian, there is no difficulty in writing about the laws of King Alfred; they have all been preserved and are discussed in many books. There is no difficulty in setting out the beginning of the Circuit; it is contained in a royal decree and assize records date from the early XIIIth century. But these are merely minutes of the proceedings; their interest is not inexhaustible and they only provide flickering rush-lights in the darkness which surrounds the early years of the Northern Circuit.

Mediaeval times provide no books of Famous Trials. The bleak fact is that of the 800 years of circuit history, 450 must elapse before one finds a detailed account of a famous trial, that of the Lancashire Witches; 500 must elapse before the first visit of a judge which is worth describing, that of Judge Jeffreys; and 600 must elapse before the Circuit's own records begin, in the age of Boswell, who is virtually the first circuit figure of whom a full-length portrait may be drawn.

The monks' Latin chronicles throw the best light on to the XIIth and XIIIth centuries but only cast the law into deeper shadow. The Anglo-Saxon Chronicle reports battles and a new comet but never a court case; its only mention of the law is when a new king is crowned and vows to preserve 'the best laws that ever before were in the land', a very formal promise.

The Chronicle says nothing further about the law. But there is no need for this history of the Northern Circuit to be confined to the barristers alone; why should it make no mention of the judges who rode the Circuit and the cases they tried, or turn a blind eye to the times in which they arose? May it not, indeed, occasionally inquire whether justice was done, and spare a thought for the end-product of the law, those who went to prison? If, then, injustice sometimes plays a part in the history of the Circuit, there is no good reason for excluding a crime so monstrous that the judges were given special instructions from the King to deal with it, yet where no trial was held, for the criminals escaped justice altogether. It was an event of international importance and it happened when the Circuit was only 14 years old, in the year 1190.

The chain of events began on 3 September 1189, which is a magnificent day in legal history. When a layman speaks of 'time immemorial', he simply means the distant past, a period perhaps before the Battle of Waterloo. But the phrase has a much more precise meaning for a lawyer dealing with questions of rights of way or 'ancient lights'. There are various ways of establishing such rights; if someone wishes to prove they have existed since time immemorial, they have to be a good deal more ancient than he might suppose. They must date back to the coronation of Richard I—3 September 1189.

It was a splendid occasion. Westminster Abbey was full of bishops, earls and great dignitaries. Many abbots and priors were there. Roger of Wendover and Roger of Howden wrote accounts of the ceremony which bring the scene vividly to life.

At the great door of the Abbey, the Archbishops of Canterbury, Rouen, Trèves and Dublin, waited to meet Richard. Then the clergy went in procession to the high altar, followed by the barons and earls, bearing golden candlesticks, the King's cap and golden spurs, the royal sceptre and other insignia, and finally the golden crown studded with precious stones.

Last came Richard, walking under a silken canopy carried by two bishops. At the high altar he swore to honour God and the Holy Church, to do right and justice towards the people and to abolish all bad laws and wicked practices within the realm, if such there were, and set up good laws. When Baldwin, the Archbishop of Canterbury, had anointed him, the crown was set upon his head, the sceptre placed in his right hand, and the royal staff in his left, and he was led to Mass at the altar.

After the service he put on lighter robes, and went to dine with the archbishops and clergy. The citizens of London waited upon them at a magnificent banquet and the wine flowed like water.

Everything had gone smoothly so far, with nothing to strike the spark which was to become an inferno of racial intolerance; but while the king was yet at table a disturbance occurred outside the palace. He had banned all Jews and women from being present at the coronation in case they uttered magic incantations, which (says Matthew Paris) is just the sort of thing they do. But the Jews had come; Joce and Benedict of York were there, with others of the richest and most important Jews of the realm, bringing costly gifts as a mark of respect and in hope of royal favour. They were recognised, however, by the crowd who attacked them savagely, tearing their clothes and beating them out of the King's hall.

Benedict was so badly injured that his life was in danger and he was only saved from being torn limb from limb by being baptised a Christian in the nearby Church of the Innocents. King Richard was furious about these riots, not from any sympathy to the Jews, but because a fire which the mob started amongst Jewish houses in London spread to Christian houses too. He hanged three of the ring-leaders and sent for Benedict.

'Who are you?' he inquired.

'I am Benedict, your Majesty's Jewish subject from York.'

'I thought you told me he had become a Christian,' said the King, turning to the Archbishop of Canterbury.

'So we did, your Majesty,' he replied.

'What shall we do with him, then?' said the King.

'If he doesn't want to be a Christian,' said the Archbishop, 'the devil can have him!' Which was going a bit far—'more bluntness than was necessary,' says Roger of Howden.

Anyway, 'William', as Benedict had been christened, returned to his Jewish ways and died soon after. No Christian or Jewish cemetery would bury his body, 'since he had first turned Christian, and then returned to his Jewish depravity like a dog to his vomit.'

Such abusive expressions are to be found in all the monks' chronicles. Their hatred of the Jews seems hardly pious; so what had the Jews done to deserve it?

They first came to England after the Norman Conquest and gradually established themselves in London and various provincial towns, such as Bury St Edmunds, Lincoln, Winchester and York. They were in a curious position; they did not belong to the feudal system, holding no property under the King, but were deemed to be part of his own property and under his protection. They were not the only money-lenders in England—some Christians operated perhaps on an even larger scale—but they were thought of as such, for there was practically no other trade or calling they were allowed to follow. There were some distinguished Jewish doctors; some traders in corn, wool and cheese, and some goldsmiths, but by and large they were able to do nothing except lend money and were blamed for every misery which debt entails. It was hardly surprising that the Jews were so hated, when their name was a by-word for usury; that is the usual result when a group of people are associated with one particular activity. To take an absurd example, if income tax officials were recruited solely from the inhabitants of Bognor Regis, that amiable resort would soon be hated throughout the length and breadth of Britain.

And, being hated, prejudices buzzed around them like wasps round a jam-jar. Whatever else the Jews' faults may be, ritual murder is not one of them. But on several occasions when dead boys were found, people believed they had been kidnapped by the Jews, circumcised, and killed in a form of crucifixion. They were buried in cathedrals and minsters as Christian martyrs. It was quite ridiculous, but the Jews made popular scapegoats. But they were cat's-paws too, if one may mix metaphors, for when they gathered in debts, the King got his share of the money. 'Whereas,' stated Henry III in one of his decrees, 'loans at usury by Jews of our realm were wont to be made and allowed in the time of our ancestors, Kings of England, and *our ancestors had large profits thereby*,' they were very pleased to have the money. When Aaron of Lincoln died in 1185, he was perhaps the wealthiest private citizen in all England. All his property became vested in the Crown and the Exchequer had to set up a special department to deal with it; lists of his debtors take up page after page in the royal accounts.

This was the background to the trouble which broke out at London on King Richard's coronation day. It was important enough for him to send his Chief Justiciar, Rannulph de Glanville, to quell the riots, and the feeling ran so deep that the hanging of three of the rioters and the King's strict command that the Jews were to go unmolested were not enough to stop it.

Not long afterwards, Richard went to Normandy, where he and the King of France were planning the next Crusade. In his absence, more anti-Jewish demonstrations broke out at Norwich and Stamford, with killing and looting, often by those who were about to go on the Crusades; they needed money to pay for their expenses and counted on escaping justice once they had left the country.

'It was not from any religious feeling,' wrote William of Newburgh, 'but because the Christians were jealous of the Jews' success and had their tongues hanging out for their wealth. They thought they could pose before God as fearless enthusiasts in his service while they robbed and killed the Jews as enemies of Christ. They acted without the smallest grain of conscience but wallowed in their own greed. God cares little for justice of *that* kind.'

At Stamford, many Jews were attacked and fled into the castle where they were allowed to shelter and store their valuables; many others were killed and their homes ransacked. One thief sneaked away to Northampton, where a friend killed him for his share of the loot and dumped his body outside the walls of the town. Because a Jewish settlement was established there, people treated the victim as another martyr and kept solemn vigils at his tomb as a mark of respect. People flocked from near and far and nobody who hoped to see a miracle occur or to obtain some favour from the martyr came to the tomb empty-handed. Sensible people thought the whole thing ludicrous but the priests were happy enough to cash in on it. The Bishop, however, a man of complete integrity, got to hear of it and visited the spot; he swept away the relics of the so-called 'martyr', and banned further homage to the dead man.

Still, it was one more example of racial prejudice.

31

An uprising at Lincoln was unsuccessful but served as a warning to the Jews at York. The two most important members of the Jewish community there were Joce and Benedict. They owned spacious mansions, fit for a King—indeed, at this time, the Jews were the only private citizens who had houses made of stone. Benedict's fate in London has already been described but Joce escaped safely and resumed his business activities, lending money at the standard rate of twopence in the pound per week, which sounds modest enough but amounts to 43 per cent per year. Nevertheless, this was the rate of interest which the King expected the Jews to charge and he profited from it.

A number of noblemen, who had raised money on mortgages or given personal bonds to the Jews, were now in great financial difficulties, for the Jews were acting in the King's name and treasury officials were calling in the debts. The noblemen formed a conspiracy and an armed band of them smashed their way with crowbars into Benedict's house, where his widow and children were living. All the valuables were stolen, the roof was set on fire and everybody inside was murdered.

Joce, now the leader of the Jewish community, pleaded with the warden of the King's castle to be allowed to move into it with their belongings. Joce did so just in time—the mob attacked his house too and set it on fire; everyone inside it was slain or burnt to death.

Those inside the castle seemed safe for the time being but for some reason the warden had left it, and when he came back the Jews refused to let him in; they were afraid he might betray them to the mob outside. The warden complained to the Sheriff, who was furious at the Jews' arrogance and ingratitude for the privilege of being allowed inside. Besides, it was a royal castle, and he was afraid the King would have something to say about their being there.

So he decided to attack the castle. When he saw how enthusiastically the mob rallied to join in that plan, he had second thoughts; but it was too late by then. The besieged Jews had no provisions and might soon have been starved into surrender; they certainly had no weapons, for they were forbidden by law to carry any, and fought the attackers off desperately for several days with chunks of stone wrenched from an inner wall. One of them felled a fanatical white-robed hermit, who was urging the attackers on to victory; he was their only enemy to be killed and once siege engines were brought up against the Jews, the result was a foregone conclusion.

The besiegers spent the evening amusing themselves; there was no need to hurry now. Only despair kept the Jews resolute in their resistance. One was a distinguished foreign Rabbi on a teaching visit to England, who reminded them of the terrible heroism in 73 AD at the fall of Masada, the last Jewish fortress in Palestine to hold out against the Romans; when they could fight no more they all cut their throats, so that the Romans made their final assault on a stronghold eerily silent and found that everyone inside it was dead. They could not but admire the Jews' noble courage and strength of purpose.

This was the example the Rabbi urged them to follow; '. . . and since our Creator now claims back the life he gave us,' he said, 'let us deliver it into his hands willingly and with reverence.'

Not all the Jews agreed with him; some wanted to throw themselves upon the mercy of the mob outside, but Joce and those who chose death set fire to the castle and cut their throats. It became an inferno and those who decided to remain alive had to move as far from the flames as they could. When dawn broke they were seen standing on the battlements, weeping for the fate of their comrades; they begged the besiegers to spare their lives and let them be baptised into the church of Christ. They dropped some of the dead bodies from the walls, so that the besiegers could see for themselves what had happened.

Many of the Christians were appalled at what had happened and took pity on the survivors; but the ring-leaders, including Richard Malebysse—an 'evil beast' indeed, as his name means—felt not the slightest compassion for them. They coaxed the Jews out of the castle with promises and then slaughtered them on the spot. All round the castle lay the dead, perhaps only 150, perhaps as many as 500.

But the conspirators had not finished yet. They rushed to York Minster, where the Jewish money-lenders kept their records and burnt them in the centre of the church. Richard was in Normandy when the news came from York. He was outraged at the affront to his royal majesty, for after the disturbances in London he had promised the Jews peace and safety. But he was even more angry at the great loss to his revenue, for no copies had been kept of the money-lending transactions; the conspirators had succeeded in their aim, for there was no way of tracing their debts.

He sent his Chancellor, the Bishop of Ely, to punish the culprits. The Bishop was a man to be reckoned with; he took a small army with him and 60 pairs of fetters to bind the criminals who were caught. But Richard Malebysse and the six other chief conspirators had fled to Scotland and all the Bishop could do was to confiscate their estates. In Yorkshire alone the estates raised £59, a massive sum in an age when it cost all of 3 shillings to send a messenger to Normandy to give Richard I news of the massacre at York.

Before the Bishop left York, 50 of the burghers had been fined and the Sheriff was dismissed from office. The castle was repaired and may still be seen but the Jewish community there had almost ceased to exist. A few years later, when Richard was held prisoner by the Duke of Austria and a king's ransom was needed to buy his release, most of the Jewish communities had to make massive contributions but nothing was obtained from York, for there was nobody there who could pay.

The next visit of the assize judges came four years later in 1194. They had special instructions to find out who killed the Jews; anybody who had taken part was to be arrested and punished. They had also to find out how much anybody owed the Jews and collect the debts, and to find out what goods and estates the Jews possessed. But the scent had gone cold and they were no more successful than the Bishop of Ely.

Something had to be done about money-lending transactions. It was not good enough to keep the records in cathedrals, as had been a common practice, not least when the clergy had dealings with the Jews; from then on there had to be special registries where the debts were recorded in duplicate and kept in triple-locked chests, with a special Exchequer of the Jews set up. Treasury officials had only to look at the register to see what debts were still unpaid.

The early years of King John's reign were better for the Jews. He granted them his royal protection, though hardly in flattering terms: 'if I give my peace even to a dog,' he said, 'it must be kept inviolate.' He pardoned Richard Malebysse and his charter gave the Jews certain rights, though at a steep price. They could travel the country freely and could buy and purchase almost anything—not blood-stained clothing, for there were Fagins even then, dealing with criminals, nor church property, for monasteries sometimes pawned church plate and even the sacred relics of saints!

It would be naive, however, to think of the Jews as bleeding the Church to death, for the monasteries then enjoyed great power and wealth and many of their loans must have been ordinary business transactions.

This is not enough, therefore, to explain the waspish phrases about the Jews in the monks' chronicles. But in 1215 the Fourth Lateran Council gave an official Church pronouncement against heretics, largely aimed at the Saracens during the Crusades, and when the line was drawn between Christians and infidels, the Jews came on the wrong side of it.

Few monks missed a chance of damning the Jews. A good example can be found in the *Chronicles of Lanercost,* a charming abbey ten miles east of Carlisle: 'Concerning the Jews,' says the writer, 'I will relate an instance of their injustice occurring at this time, which may be of no small service to posterity against the crime of perjury and fraud.'

He explains that Marchby Priory in Suffolk, near Bury St Edmunds, used to share with the local inhabitants a right to pasture their cattle: 'But whereas avarice, which is in the minds of all men of the present day, endeavours to make all common lands private property,' the monastery sued its neighbours, having first bribed the judges, and the *jury* were wicked enough to give a verdict in favour of the monastery.

There seems to be a certain confusion of thought here; the monastery could be blamed, also the judges and possibly the jury; but the Jews had nothing to do with it at all. It is an extreme case of prejudice and it continues with a charming legend of a Phantom Jury.

After the monastery had won the case, 'the monks caused a great part of the land to be ploughed in token of their legal ownership. But, on the other hand, God did not allow his name to be usurped with impunity and he sowed the furrows of unrighteousness with the infamy of the act. For the 12 jurymen began to be steadily but gradually removed from the world, and ever as they were removed they were submitted to a terrible yoke. For during about two years afterwards there appeared in that country a fiery plough, glowing like hot brass, having a most foul fiend as driver, who drove the dead men, harnessed in that manner, to the ground where he had incited them to guile while living. Many persons beheld these wretches clearly, committed to the plough like oxen, always at the hour of noon, and this, I imagine, was done because it is at such an hour men most assiduously press litigation before the judges.'

The Chronicler had doubts about the truth of this legend, till he heard it confirmed by the lips of an unnamed nobleman who lived only three miles from the place in question; so it must be true.

The affairs of the Jews took a turn for the worse when King John returned from Ireland; he was short of funds, and had the Jews arrested until his coffers were filled; he was not the first nor the last English king to take such action. Tales of his torturing Jews by pulling their teeth out one by one to make them pay are probably like suggesting that income tax inspectors actually squeeze blood from stones, a slight exaggeration. Some of the poorer Jews were given the choice of paying the sums demanded, or going into exile.

When Henry III came to the throne in 1216 he was nine years of age. Thanks perhaps to his two regents, the Jews were not then harshly treated; they began to drift back to York and their community prospered once again.

But twenty years later, Henry married Eleanor of Provence, a spoilt child of 15, and perhaps the most unpopular queen England has ever had. Together they filled the court with favourites from abroad and showered money on futile military expeditions. It was sad company for Aaron of York to keep; he was Joce's son and became in turn one of the richest of his tribe; Henry appointed him Arch-Presbyter of the Jews of England, the highest honour open to him, when he presided over the Jewish Exchequer. But he bled him white, all the same; Aaron died in 1268 a ruined man.

It was hardly to be thought that Henry would leave the Jews with any spare cash when he was reduced to pawning the statue of the Virgin Mary from the Chapel-Royal at Windsor, and when he and his Queen had to cadge meals and presents from rich merchants in London. When she pledged her jewels with the Knights Templar, their son Edward went and snatched them back again, stealing £10,000 of their funds into the bargain. It was behaviour hardly commendable in a future king and when Edward I came to the throne in 1272 it was the beginning of the end for the Jews of England.

A Jew entering into a contract now often wrote a clause into it saying it was binding, 'unless I am cheated out of my property by any false accusation on the part of the King or Queen.' In Henry's reign, and Edward's, they were arrested time and time again, and made to pay more and more with the less and less they possessed. They were forced to wear a red badge on the chest to mark them out and were forbidden to charge any interest on the money they lent.

But Edward had discovered in his Gascon territories in France that more money was to be gained when Jews forfeited their estates than could be obtained gradually by taxing them. In June 1290, he gave the Sheriffs orders that all the registers of Jewish transactions should be sealed and a month later he announced the expulsion of the Jews from England. By November they had all gone, not to return for almost 400 years.

Thus ended a sequence of events which started at Richard I's coronation on 3 September 1189.

Save by the Jews themselves, the massacre at York in 1190 is virtually forgotten, but it was an event of international importance. It belongs to legal history because the assize judges were sent to do justice upon it and failed.

It is the worst thing that ever happened on the Northern Circuit.

37

FOUR

Foul Bills on the Border

'I curse them going, and I curse them riding; I
curse them standing, and I curse them sitting; I
curse them eating, I curse them drinking; I curse
them waking, I curse them sleeping; I curse them
rising, I curse them lying . . .'
The Archbishop of Glasgow's *Monition of Cursing*

In the early days of the Northern Circuit it was often reported
that unknown Scotsmen had burgled the homes of the English
living near the Border. Life was hard enough on outlying
farms when a stealthy footfall by night could mean a surprise
attack and the cry of an owl was the signal for a new atrocity.
But it was certainly worse when *known* Scotsmen came riding,
in broad daylight, to the sound of a trumpet if they willed,
fearing nothing and sparing nobody. It might be an act of
outright war for, once Edward I earned the nickname of 'the
hammer of the Scots', the Scots were ready to give as good as
they got; but lesser invasions were fearsome enough, when 300
clansmen rode.

Steady farming became a futile business when invaders
burnt the crops, so a race of Borderers grew up, almost
nomadic, ready to fight at a moment's notice. They raised their
own cattle, stole each other's and were an anarchy unto themselves. As it was said, 'the people of this country hath had one
barbarous custom among them; if any two be displeased, they
expect no lawyer but bang it out bravely.' Bravely, however,
was hardly the right word when feuds were settled with a shot
in the back.

By Tudor times the Border was an area of open quarrels and
secret intrigue, when spies rode backwards and forwards with
coded messages. The alehouses were full and the churches
empty; Bernard Gilpin, until 1583 the Rector of Houghton,
near Durham, found that the word of God was never heard in

38

the remote Northumberland valleys and made missionary journeys despite winter's iron clamp, when he had to keep moving throughout the night or freeze to death.

Sometimes his strength of character was all that kept rival gangs apart; he entered Rothbury church to find a glove hanging up there, as much a challenge to combat as a gauntlet flung on the floor. His sexton was too frightened to take it down, so Bernard Gilpin did and kept it inside his clothing until he entered the pulpit. 'I hear,' he said, 'that there is one amongst you who, even in this Sacred Place, hath hanged up a Glove to this Purpose and threateneth to enter into Combat with whoever shall take it down. Behold, I have taken it down myself.' He then denounced their barbarous feuds.

His efforts were not in vain; a thief stole his horse once, not knowing whose it was. When he found out, he brought it back hastily and begged his pardon and blessing, before Hell swallowed him up.

It used to be reckoned that if a man stood in fear of a deadly foe, he was safer with Bernard Gilpin than with an armed guard. But how could it be a God-fearing country when the wardens on each side of the Border, divided into three 'Marches' as the sections were called, gloried in what havoc they had done? Sir William Eure, for instance, Warden of the English East and Middle Marches, reported to the Duke of Suffolk in 1543 that he had burnt two Scots towns and their corn, stolen much goods and cattle, and taken some prisoners, 'which was a good exploit and an honest. As knowest the Holy Ghost, who ever preserve your grace.'

Each warden was governor in his own March and answered directly to the Crown; no scuffle took place on the Border without the warden sending in his report and when more money or men were needed to repair and guard a Border stronghold, it was to London that the English wardens wrote. Like game-wardens, they had to protect their charges against the raids by Scottish predators and like poachers, they raided Scotland, either in revenge for some Scottish inroad, or for the hell of it; and sometimes they were diplomats when they met their Scottish colleagues, to exchange complaints or hostages, or to hand over criminals for justice.

They were meant to meet once a month at least and in theory justice should easily have prevailed, but cheating and wrangling were common practice, even amongst men of rank and sometimes of the church as well. In 1542 the English met to discuss some recent killings but the Scots, one of whom was the Bishop of Orkney, tried to pretend that they had no authority to do so. When defeated on that point the discussion turned to hostages, for giving hostages was one of the most successful ways of ensuring that a clan was of good behaviour: hostages had to be persons of consequence, such as bishops or earls. At any rate, the Scots began to haggle; 'and here,' as the English commissioners reported to Henry VIII, 'they began to swear blood, wounds, nails, body and passion of Christ, both the bishop and the others, that they dissimulated not but spake in good faith.'

Clan loyalty was strong on the Border and honesty fairly rare. There was a curious outburst of unrighteous indignation when the Robsons of Tyndale raided the Grahams of Esk and stole sheep. The sheep were suffering from scab and infected the Robsons' flocks, so the Robsons returned, hanged seven of the Grahams and left an angry note to say, 'the neist tyme gentlemen cam to take their schepe, they were no to be scabbit.'

The English and the Scots were really as bad as each other. In Henry VIII's time the English had the stronger forces on the Border, so that the English warden of the West March burnt four villages in one successful raid in 1544. 'There was never within the memory of man,' he boasted, 'so much hurt done with fire in the West Marches of Scotland, as was this day.'

But this was the high water mark of English superiority; soon afterwards, a raid into Scotland ended in disaster. Sir William Eure was killed and many of the Scots, in Liddesdale and nearby, withdrew the allegiance they had sworn to England and were a constant source of trouble thereafter.

The Border was then, as the wardens used to put it, 'very tickle'; the raiders had the time of their lives. Like barristers on the Northern Circuit, they were a half-nomadic tribe, ready to do battle at a moment's notice. On the Border the law operated at three different levels at the same time. There was the law of the jungle, surviving into the age of Shakespeare, and documented in the bulging filing cabinets of Whitehall; there was the law administered by the wardens, who had their own courts, as speedily convenient as a drumhead court-martial; and there was the law of the assize judges who went their well-established rounds for a few months every year or so. But the wardens' duties lasted all year round.

It is easy enough to state that the English wardens carried out simple revenge when they pursued Scottish raiders back across the Border. It proved somewhat tricky in practice, because the raiders had an unpleasant flair for ambush and counter-attack. Sir Robert Carey found it so when he was deputy warden of the English West March. He was pursuing two Scotsmen who had killed a man and when they took refuge in a strong tower belonging to the Grahams of Netherby, he and his men surrounded it. He thought nothing of it when a boy was seen galloping away at top speed but one of his men was Thomas Carleton, an old hand in Border raiding, who knew just how ominous it was, for the Grahams were one of the most notorious of the Border clans.

'Do you see that boy that rideth away so fast?' he warned Carey. 'He will be in Scotland within this half hour; and he is gone to let them know that you are here, and to what end you are come, and how small number you have with you . . .'

Sir Robert sent for reinforcements. When they came it was easy enough to take the roof off the tower and clamber in, and the two fugitives surrendered—but just then a large party of Scotsmen appeared. There was a tense pause while each side stared at the other. They were more or less equally matched, each with some 400 men, and Sir Robert's men needed no encouragement:

'Sir, give us leave to set upon them,' they cried, 'for these are they that have killed our fathers, our brothers, our uncles and our cousins . . . God hath put them into our hands, that we may take revenge on them for much blood that they have spilt of ours!' But he held them back and the Scots withdrew; a very ugly skirmish was averted.

Sir Robert was entitled to pursue criminals fleeing across the Border under a special Border right known as the 'Hot Trod', a hot-foot pursuit. For six days after their crime, raiders could be followed into their own country. When the pursuers crossed the Border they had to sound a horn, carry a lighted turf upon a lance and state their purpose to the first village they came to, so as to show that they were not illegal invaders. The 'Hot Trod' was a legal way of taking immediate revenge, for those caught red-handed could be killed on the spot.

They used some odd phrases on the Border in those days. When a clan offered to protect a village at a price, perhaps of meal or cattle, it was tainted with villainy, and the meal was known as 'black-mail'. Raiders were sometimes caught 'with the bloody hand', or 'red-handed', as it is better known. And there were the 'foul bills'. When the English and Scottish wardens met to exchange information or hostages, their lists of complaints set out the crimes and Border-offences ('attempts' and 'March-treasons' as they were called) which they alleged.

For example, an English complaint was by Sir Simon Musgrave, knight, captain of the Cumbrian village of Bewcastle, upon the Elliots and their accomplices, 100 men and above, for the stealing of '60 old kye (cattle), 20 old oxen and the taking of Thomas Routledge of Todholes, Englishman, prisoner, and his horse.' This was a typical 'bill' or complaint.

If the Scottish warden knew about the matter himself, he could state 'on his honour' that the Elliots were guilty or innocent and that was final. It was considered the most satisfactory method of dealing with such bills, even though a warden's honour was somewhat variable if the guilt of a favourite henchman was involved. But it was the quickest method of pronouncing guilt and although many guilty men were declared innocent, more still were acquitted at the warden's court when witnesses were afraid to come forward, or jurors feared reprisals from the accused's clan if they convicted him—to use the Border phrase, if they declared the bill a 'foul bill'.

Thus, if a man were innocent, the bill would be called a 'clean bill'—the phrase lingers on in 'a clean bill of health'; the bill was declared clean, or it was 'cleaned'—the same thing. Alternatively, a bill was declared foul, or it was 'filed'—the same thing again, 'filed' being a verb as strong and irregular as Border justice in foul cases.

If the bill was not filed or cleaned on the warden's honour, it had to be tried by a jury of twelve, six Scots and six English. They heard the evidence and they delivered a verdict, just as in an ordinary trial, save that they were sworn to their duties in different terms: 'You shall clean no bills worthy to be fouled, you shall foul no bills worthy to be cleaned, but shall do that what appeareth with truth, for the maintenance of the peace, and suppressing of attempts. So help you God.'

The cases were speedily tried. Sir Robert Carey used to send out patrols to catch Border raiders stealing cattle and when successful, 'they were no sooner brought before me,' he wrote, 'but a jury went upon them and, being found guilty, they were promptly hanged.'

But there were difficulties. Under Border law a thief could not be found guilty unless one of his own countrymen gave evidence against him, which could be more than a man's life was worth. In 1597 Sir Robert Carey's brother, John, was Governor of Berwick, where the warden's court was about to hear a Scots complaint that Ralph Selby, an Englishman, had stolen eight score sheep. Another Englishman, servant to Lady Grey, had vouched for the truth of that bill, which was duly filed; it did not make for cordiality between the Selbys and the Greys, 'whereon some hard words grew.' as Sir John Carey noted.

The court was due to sit on Monday. On the Sunday, the rival factions happened to meet in the churchyard. Ralph Selby ran through a servant of the Greys with his rapier, killing him, and a fight broke out.

'The great tumult in town grew very dangerous,' reported Sir John Carey, 'and could hardly be allayed till myself ran into the street, attended by all the gentlemen pensioners, and placed armed soldiers at the corner of every street, ordering the Scots to keep their houses.' The town was at flashpoint and there could easily have been a massacre, or even war; and all for the sake of eight score sheep, valued at £144; but peace was preserved.

A warden's court could be convened almost immediately but if Ralph Selby had been ordered to stand his trial at the assizes, he would have had to wait five months. The stately assizes provided perhaps the best Border justice of all and did not lack authority. Sir Robert Carey said that serious stealing never broke out each year till after Lammas-tide, 1 August, when the Summer Assizes had come and gone.

The Border raiders stood in awe of the assizes, yet the assizes were not proof against them. Some of the jurors were a good deal too sympathetic to the thieves and as one warden complained to London, 'I must with fear and trembling say that direct evidence is not regarded as it ought to be amongst Christians, and oaths but little.'

Assize justice was sometimes defeated by brute force. During Carlisle Summer Assizes 1597, one of the notorious Grahams, 'Jock of the Pear-tree', was kept not in gaol but in the Sheriff's house whilst awaiting trial, so informally that his friends and relatives were allowed to visit him. They came again at dead of night and he simply rode away, with an armed escort of friends to protect him. Another well-known thief, Andrew Rhume, was kept in the prison itself but his friends kidnapped an English merchant and bartered him for Andrew's liberty. Jock of the pear-tree struck again when his brother, Wattie Graham, was awaiting trial at Appleby Assizes. He kidnapped the Sheriff of Westmorland's little son and exchanged him for Wattie.

Not all the captured thieves escaped; some were hanged at each assize but never enough. Some of them, however, were more useful alive than dead because they could be used for bargaining purposes. Sir Robert Carey caught Geordie Burn red-handed in a theft and arrested him. Geordie was a great favourite with the Laird of Cessford, the Scottish warden who was Sir Robert's opposite number. Sir Robert was told that if he spared Geordie's life he could strike almost any bargain he liked with Cessford but that if he had him executed, nobody would be safe from Cessford's wrath. Sir Robert ignored the advice and hanged Geordie Burn. The result was that Cessford plagued the English for many years.

Even when a person was kept safely locked up until the assizes, diplomatic strings were sometimes pulled to ensure that he never came to trial. Thomas Carleton was the experienced Borderer who warned Sir Robert Carey about the boy riding away to Scotland; he was due to be tried at Carlisle but the warden there advised Queen Elizabeth's secretary that Carleton had been indicted on the false information of an 'unfriend', and the case was never heard.

Sometimes persons who had been tried, convicted and actually condemned to death at the assizes were reprieved by order of the Council of the North, without the judges being consulted at all.

It was a time, therefore, when justice was meted out by the assize judges, by the Border commissioners and by the wardens. Although the assizes carried the most authority, the standard did not vary much with the wardens, because they were often the same people. In 1176, the first year of the Northern Circuit, the assize judges included local knights; it still happened in the 16th century, when the wardens were sometimes Commissioners of Assize. The Border commissioners were appointed by the powerful Council of the North, some of whose members were assize judges. There was nothing slipshod about the warden's courts; their procedure was carefully laid down, and was very much like that of the assizes, save that they spoke of foul and clean bills; and it may have been some consolation to those found guilty there that the warden's sentence of death was in the most solemn and religious terms.

Sometimes the assizes and the warden's court were held in the same town at the same time. At Hexham in 1596 there were 59 prisoners for trial at the assizes, of whom only nine were convicted; the warden's court had much the same number to try but only three of them were convicted. So a finding of guilt at a warden's court was by no means a foregone conclusion and there was much to be said for catching a thief redhanded and executing him on the spot.

'Days of truce', when the opposite wardens met, were seldom uneventful, since the wardens had not only to be skilled diplomats but quick on the draw as well. There was a meeting in August 1575 at a place called the Reidswire, an open sloping moorland in a rumpled terrain. Harry Robson of Fawstone (often wrongly referred to as 'Farnstein') was 'fouled by a bill of goods'—found guilty of stealing, that is—and Sir John Carmichael, the Scots warden, asked for him to be handed over to the Scots. The English warden, Sir John Forster, gave some haughty reply, followed at once by a volley of English arrows. A battle ensued in which many people were killed and Forster and others were taken prisoner. Chivalrous treatment followed by ransom was a tradition in those days, and they were allowed to return home. Queen Elizabeth was furious at the incident, and demanded reparation from Scotland. Carmichael was handed over and kept in York prison till inquiry showed that Forster was chiefly to blame.

He was present ten years later, too, when the day of truce was held on a bleak hilltop called Windy Gyle, and was calling over bills with his Scottish colleague when a shot was fired. It killed Lord Francis Russell, one of the English party. A large force of Scotsmen in battle array, waiting out of sight with their flags flying, had given the signal to fire with fife and drums but Lord Francis Russell was the only casualty. The motive is not clear; it may have been private revenge, or part of some spying plot. But it was soon known that William Kerr of Ancrum and others were to blame and King James of Scotland banished them from the realm by public proclamation to the sound of a trumpet, 'putting them to the horn as rebels,' as the practice was called.

Playing a trump made little difference for, at the next shuffle, the knaves were back in the game; six months later, William Kerr was restored to the King's favour and ready for the next foray.

Trying to settle the bills was a frustrating business for an English warden. For years Cessford, the warden of the Scottish Middle March, refused to discuss the killings that had taken place; he had strict orders, he maintained, to leave them for his King to settle with the English Queen. He would, of course, negotiate about thefts and burnings but not on acceptable terms. The English wanted to confine themselves to recent events, when the Scots had caused the more damage; the Scots wanted to go back to the reign of Henry VIII, which tipped the balance of compensation the other way. The English had to make the best of it; few enough crimes were punished, but some of them were and it was better than open war. The affair of Kinmont Willie, however, strained diplomatic relations severely.

Kinmont Willie was one of the Armstrongs of Liddesdale, the most notorious clan in the most lawless of all the Border valleys. A visitor once asked if there were any Christians there: 'Na, we's a' Elliotts and Armstrangs,' came the reply.

Kinmont Willie attended the day of truce in 1596 at Kershopefoot, where the Border runs through a pleasant stream. Under Border law nobody could be captured between sunrise on the day of truce and on the following day. But Kinmont Willie, an experienced robber and murderer, had escaped justice too often and he had not long left the meeting when the

English hunted him down and took him to Carlisle Castle, where he was kept a prisoner.

Not for long, though. Kinmont Willie was one of the Laird of Buccleugh's men, and Sir Walter Scott of Buccleugh was as bold and inventive as his namesake, the famous novelist. Buccleugh was a notorious firebrand in those days, being the Keeper of Liddesdale—its warden, more or less—and having all its lawless inhabitants to draw on. He chose a stormy night to lead 500 men on horseback, equipped with pickaxes, crowbars and ladders. They undermined the postern door of Carlisle Castle and broke in, snatched Kinmont Willie from his cell, left three of the guards for dead and were away before the rest of the garrison realised they had been.

This exploit enraged Lord Scrope, the warden responsible for the security of Carlisle, and soon afterwards he sent a large force into Liddesdale, burning houses, seizing goods and taking prisoners. So much is undoubted fact, though almost everything is questionable in Border history, save the finality of death. He said he only sent 100 men; the Scots claimed it was 2000 but they were drawing up what came to be known as the 'great Bill of Liddesdale'.

The English government believed that such a 'justifiable reprisal ordered by her Majesty in necessary defence of her own border, cannot in equity be called an invasion, but rather honourable and neighbourlike assistance, to maintain the inviolable amity between the princes and the realms,' and they took counsel's opinion to confirm that proposition. But the Scots refused to accept this view and whenever redress for past offences was discussed at wardens' meetings, the Scots presented the great Bill of Liddesdale, valued at an alarming £20,000.

In the following April, the Border commissioners summoned Buccleugh to appear before them, to discuss the complaints which the English and the Scots had against each other and to see how the wardens were carrying out their duties. He chose to enliven his journey from Scotland by entering the Tyne valley in broad daylight with 150 men, burning and killing as he went—on a Sunday too, which made it more outrageous.

It was a matter of grave concern; he had not only burnt the people's houses but forced them from their grazing-grounds, their chief source of income. Buccleugh, on the other hand, claimed that 60 Englishmen had just raided Liddesdale; he had caught them red-handed and was pursuing them under the Border right of the Hot Trod. The Border commissioners could hardly believe this, but when they investigated the matter they were very embarrassed to find that Buccleugh was right. Thus a stalemate was reached, typical in Border affairs; Buccleugh's revenge was rather more drastic than it needed to be and so he owed the English some compensation for it. On the other hand, he had gone back to Scotland and it was no use complaining to anybody but King James which was not much use either.

The monarchs of England and Scotland took a personal interest in their Border affairs. A letter to Lord Scrope in England from 'your loving friend, James R' would cross with a letter to Cessford from Queen Elizabeth, each asking for justice. They were wasted words, for Cessford seemed quite incorrigible.

The first impression Sir Robert Carey formed of him was of a brave and active young man, likely to bring peace to the Border. But fair words had hardly passed Cessford's lips when he rode into England and committed a cruel murder, as if to show what he could do. Sir Robert vowed never to trust him again.

They met at the Border meeting at Norham ford in the autumn of 1597. Buccleugh's honour was impeccable on this occasion; he was due to hand over certain pledges from Liddesdale for their offences but as they were absent he agreed with good grace to become a pledge himself and surrendered to Carey's custody, saying he knew the Queen's majesty to be both gracious and merciful.

Then it was Cessford's turn to deliver up the pledges for East Teviotdale and he had them ready but one of his men fired a pistol and fell off his horse, crying, 'Slain, slain!' 'Treason, treason!' cried another, as planned, whereupon the fray began and shots were exchanged on both sides. By now it was too dark to see properly, so nobody was hurt. Lord Hume, another Scots warden with a sense of honour, caught Sir William Bowes in his arms to protect him and said they should shoot through *him* before they hurt Sir William, who had another lucky escape; someone plucked the dagger from his belt and would have plunged it into his back had not one of the Humes disarmed him. Peace was soon restored and Lord Hume took the English party home with him for a great supper but Cessford and his pledges had slipped silently away. The Borderers were capable of violent treachery and warm hospitality. In Berwick, Sir John Carey was greatly alarmed to have Buccleugh as a pledge with him.

'Let him be removed from hence,' he pleaded, 'to a more secure place. For I protest to the Almighty God, before I will take the charge to keep him here, I will desire to be put in prison myself and to have a keeper of me!'

But Buccleugh behaved admirably and Sir John's kind treatment of him probably persuaded Cessford also to surrender himself as a pledge. He lived, not with Sir John Carey, but with his brother, Sir Robert Carey, Cessford's old enemy, and many heated arguments they had over the rights and wrongs of the past till, in the end, they became firm friends and, on days of truce, did each other as good justice as could be desired.

In the first years of the XVIIth century things were a little quieter. At one day of truce Sir John Carey recognised a man as a Scottish thief and arrested him; the thief was a very popular man amongst his clan and banked on the Scottish deputy warden protecting him. He struck his accuser in the mouth and spoke swaggeringly; he was an astonished man when he was convicted, stripped and hanged in chains: 'Such a piece of justice,' marvelled Sir John, 'has never been done before.' But an even more profound change was about to take place.

In 1603 Sir Robert Carey visited Queen Elizabeth in London and kissed her hand. She was obviously ill.

She took me by the hand [he later recalled], and wrung it hard and said, 'No, Robin, I am not well', and then discoursed with me of her indisposition and that her heart had been sad and heavy for 10 or 12 days; and in her discourse, she fetched not so few as 40 or 50 great sighs. I was grieved at the first to see her in this plight, for in all my lifetime before, I never knew her fetch a sigh but when the Queen of Scots was beheaded.

She was a dying woman. A few days later Carey rode north

49

on an epic journey to Edinburgh, covering 400 miles of Elizabethan roads in 60 hours and weak from loss of blood when his horse kicked him; but he was bringing King James the news of her death.

'The King was newly gone to bed by the time I knocked at the gate,' he recalled.

'I was quickly let in and carried up to the King's chamber. I kneeled by him and saluted him by the title of England, Scotland, France and Ireland.'

It was the end of the Tudor era and of the time when the Border raiders could play one country off against the other, for James united both with a determination not usually ascribed to him. The raiders had one last fling—'Ill week', it was called—as he rode south to London; but they were soon arrested and hanged on a scale James thought, 'savouring altogether of barbarism.' Sleuthhounds were used to track the mosstroopers into their remotest retreats and the Grahams were exported in large numbers to Ireland, though most of them, like the bad pennies they were, turned up again on the Scottish Border. Buccleugh, now wholly devoted to law and order, was as vigorous in hanging or drowning men without trial as any of them and was commended for his services.

By 1612 there was sufficient peace on the Border for customs dues to be levied on horses and cattle crossing it. Times were changing fast but some of the old-fashioned ideas lingered on. More than 50 years later Roger North was present at Newcastle Assizes when Mungo Noble, a well-known thief, was tried and acquitted. Some magistrates were deeply disappointed; one turned to the Judge and said in a thick north-country dialect, 'My Lord, send him to *us* and ye'll ne'er see him more!' He was speaking from more than four centuries of rough Border justice.

So long as England and Scotland remained rival countries, the wardens' courts were the best means of dealing with offenders. But once the two nations shared James as their king, the wardens' courts and the Border commisssioners were abolished and the assizes were able to take over entirely. Thus, in 1649, the Earl of Leicester noted in his Journal:

Letters this day, 6 August, came from Newcastle that there was condemned by the Judges of the Gaol Delivery 29

Mosstroopers, which are Scots that rob upon the borders of this nation and other English felons, and it's concluded that few or none of them will escape the gallows. The like execution hath not been for many hundred of years formerly.

The trouble was now nearly over and the most precarious area in Britain gradually became a charming landscape of peaceful farms. Centuries of cruelty and bloodshed are now virtually forgotten.

FIVE

In Time of Pestilence

'Our best news is that we have good wine abun-
dantly come over; and the worst, that the plague is
in town, and no judges die.'

Chief Justice Hyde,
Letter to Lord Commissioner Whitelocke

It used to be a tradition that, when a judge entered Court, he
carried a little spray of flowers which he laid on the bench
before him. It was a precaution against infection. It has never,
however, been a tradition that members of the Bar should
carry anything of the sort. They are just as prone to mortal ills
as judges are; therefore, when all the nation was scourged by
the plague, was it really to be expected that the law courts
should be immune?

The Black Death occurred in 1348 and the Great Plague in
1665. They are the only figures that matter. Statistics exist for
the Black Death in Preston, Penrith or Pontefract but they
make lifeless reading and are not really reliable, for in towns
the full casualties were seldom disclosed, and in rural areas
only the deaths of the monks and clergy were accurately
recorded. They are less graphic than the Rolls of the Bishop of
Durham: 'No tenants come from West Thickley, because they
are all dead.' Taking the country as a whole, perhaps a quarter
or a third of the population died.

But, devastating though the Black Death was, it has left
behind surprisingly few records of its effects. Many Yorkshire
villages simply ceased to exist, and where the menfolk once
ploughed the fields sheep now crop the grass. The shortage of
labourers in England led to rocketing demands for higher
wages, ending in the Peasants' Revolt of 1381 but, in the
sparsely populated North, the results were less dramatic. In
Cumberland, Durham and Northumberland the lack of
labourers to till manorial lands led to remissions of the King's

taxes and that was all; in Lancashire, complaints were recorded that one William of Everton 'caused one third of the inhabitants to be brought to his house after death.' It sounds macabre but the real grievance was probably that William was charging the parish too much for funerals, or claiming fees due to him as a surgeon for certifying people dead of the plague, when they had not died.

It was not only the bubonic plague that raged in historical times, for there were many other sorts of outbreaks both before and after 1348. There was the 'sweating sickness' (cholera), 'the king's evil' (scrofula, a form of tuberculosis of the skin) and typhus. Sometimes they came singly and sometimes together. Professor Shrewsbury, a distinguished bacteriologist, has recently analysed the different outbreaks. The pestilence in 664 AD, recorded by Bede, may have been smallpox; the 'great pestilence' at Newcastle in 1478 was probably cholera because it came at the wrong season of the year for bubonic plague.

Many of the outbreaks affected only a small part of the country at a time, though this was of course not true of the Black Death. At York, in 1348, the spread of the plague from Southern England was rightly feared and special prayers and litanies were ordered, but to no avail; as an ecclesiastical history of Doncaster poignantly puts it: 'And in these days was burying without sorrow and wedding without friendship and fleeing without refute of succour, for many fled from place to place because of the pestilence; but yet they were affected and might not scape the death.'

Yet there was very little slump in crime. As one writer put it, 'It is a well-ascertained fact, strange though it may seem, that men are not as a rule made better by great and universal visitations of Divine Providence.'

Indeed, the marauding Scots took advantage of it. Hearing of the ravages of the plague in England, they gathered in their thousands near the border to launch a ferocious raid into England and even coined a scornful oath—'By the foul death of England!' The plague and the fire, caused by the Scots within Appleby, changed it from a thriving town into a village. But the Scots did not emerge from the expedition unscathed; they may have taken the plague with them—not bubonic plague, says Professor Shrewsbury, because the flea-ridden

53

rats would not have travelled with them—or they may have caught the plague in Scotland; but their dead were reckoned in thousands.

The Black Death had no striking effect on the law at all but it had far-reaching consequences which were not immediately obvious. It ushered in a plainer style of architecture, because there were not enough stone-masons left for such delicate window traceries as can be seen in the West Front of York Minster, and the Decorated style of architecture which had flourished under Edward II and Edward III came to an abrupt end.

There was a shortage in other skilled professions, including teachers of Latin. Lawyers ceased to conduct their cases entirely in Latin and began to speak English, a process which has almost become complete.

Sometimes the plague led only to some inconvenience. In 1474 the coronation of King Henry VII at York had to be postponed. 1597 was a bad year for the North:

. . . great plague and pestilence in Newcastle, Durham, Darlington, Gateshead . . . and in many towns and villages. It continued all this year at Newcastle and by God's good grace and good management it was not great here but always sparkling by little, still suppressed and extinguished till 27 September 1597. Poor Durham this year was almost undone. Elvet had the plague first, which in John Talentire's house, a walker or lister, and all therein died; it began the 14th May and few or none escaped it that did not fly into other places.

Durham's assizes should have been held on 4 July that year; because of the May outbreak, they were postponed but not long enough for Anthony Arrowsmith, whose trial began there on 26 August. He was charged with murder and the first step in the trial was the 'arraignment', the moment when the clerk of the court asked him if he pleaded 'guilty' or 'not guilty'. To this he stood mute and the jury decided he was holding his tongue deliberately. The consequence was almost more horrible than the bubonic plague, for he was pressed to death in the Market Place.

It was not a death anyone would recommend; he was laid on the ground with wooden shuttering on top of him, and a series of weights laid on top of it, more and more, until he chose to find his tongue, or the life was crushed out of him. Anthony Arrowsmith chose death; it must have been to safeguard the interests of his family. It was still an age when a convicted felon forfeited all his property; if he had pleaded 'not guilty' and been convicted, all his property and money would have been taken from him, leaving his wife and family penniless. He would have been hanged for the murder in any event, if proved guilty, and the only thing that it was within his power to save was his property, for his family's sake. That is why he suffered an agonising public death in the Market Place on 26 August.

Two months later the plague was back in Durham; 400 people died in the Elvet district and as many in the rest of the town; 24 of the prisoners in the gaol died too. In February 1598 the plague had ceased in Durham and on 15 September it broke out again. Between such unpredictable infections, the assizes came and went but other professions had to stand their ground. Thomas Morton, a most saintly man who later became Bishop of Durham and was Chaplain to the Council of the North, which met in York, showed the greatest courage:

In 1602 began the great plague at York, at which time he carried himself with so much heroical charity as will make the reader wonder to hear it. For the poorer sort being removed to the pest-house, he made it his frequent exercise to visit them with food, both for their bodies and souls. His chief errand was to instruct and comfort them and to pray for them and with them; and, to make his going the more acceptable, he usually carried a sack of provisions with him for those that wanted it. And because he would have no man to run any hazard thereby but himself, he seldom suffered any of his servants to come near him but saddled and unsaddled his own horse and had a private door made on purpose into his house and chamber.

The clergy made it their duty to visit victims of the plague and a great many of them died as a result. Lawyers, on the other hand, stayed away from them, whether on assizes or in London, as the historian Dugdale described after the Great Plague of 1665:

If it happen [he wrote], that the plague of pestilence be anything nigh their house, they immediately break up their house and every man goeth home into his country, which is a great loss of learning; for if they had some house nigh London to resort unto, they might as well exercise their learning as in the Temple, until the plague were ceased.

It served their purpose and saved their skins, not to go on assizes into towns where the plague was. But it was not wholly selfish for, if York was infected and Lancaster free of the plague, the Lancastrians would hardly have welcomed the arrival of the barristers, judges and all their attendants, any one of whom could have brought the plague with him and spread it in a town thronged with people. The assizes were a great attraction for, quite apart from the lawyers, there were the jurymen and the witnesses who came to town. It was a great social occasion, and the race meetings were arranged to coincide with the assizes. There was a lot of money to be made in assize week and plenty of farmers coming to town to spend it. Landladies could rent a room for a guinea a week at assize time and be sure of getting it.

It was, therefore, not only prudent for lawyers to avoid towns where the plague was, but in everybody's interest. It was also the law. 'Care to be taken,' ordered the Privy Council in 1636, 'that neither men nor goods come from any suspected place without certificate of health, else to be sent suddenly away or put into the pest house for 40 days till certainty appears.' Lawyers could hardly go round the circuit whilst in *quarantine*, which literally means that period of 40 days.

Furthermore, plague-stricken towns lived under almost siege conditions. In 1630–31, Preston suffered from an outbreak not only of typhus, but of bubonic plague as well; things were as bad there as in London during the Great Plague, which Preston fortunately escaped. Food and fuel had to be brought to a point just outside Preston and left there, so that the inhabitants could collect it without spreading contagion. The harvest rotted for want of reapers. The assize judges therefore ordered that the nearby Lancashire towns should contribute money for the support of the unhappy people of Preston. It was an unusual role for the judges to play and a measure of the size of the crisis, for in times of pestilence it was usually the local magistrates who dealt with the problems, ordering 'watch and ward' to prevent infected people wandering from one town to another. But in the summer of 1631, the magistrates ordered that anybody in breach of the 'watch and ward' orders would answer to the judges for it; so would alehouse keepers who allowed public assemblies, 'to consort together for drinking, dancing, piping, fiddling, bowling, dicing, carding, shooting or any other such exercises in their houses.'

Any such social gathering might have attracted an infected stranger and given the plague a better opportunity of spreading. Most of the burden of responsibility fell on the magistrates. In 1649 (during the Civil War) the Mayor and Corporation of Wigan, a town suffering from, 'a three-corded scourge of sword, pestilence and famine', complained that relief could not be given to the poor, because there were no Justices of the Peace alive to do it. It is rare to find anyone punished at the assizes for an offence arising from the plague, though at York in 1667 a woman appeared before the judges, charged with distributing clothing infected with the plague.

No town on the Northern Circuit escaped its outbreaks of the plague but when the Great Plague began in 1665, Newcastle was particularly at risk. Sailors from London engaged in the huge coal trade put that port into great danger and the keelmen were ordered to *throw* the coal from their keels into the trading ships, so as to reduce the risk of personal contact with the sailors. But the courts were remarkably free from bubonic plague. Indeed, no lawyer or judge is recorded as having suffered from it. It is true that a shivering prisoner at the Guildhall in London was found to be suffering from the plague, but his trial was hastily discontinued and it was the only reported incident of its kind.

Still, some of the London courts moved to Oxford in November 1665, with amusing results, as an Oxford gentleman noted:

The town is so full of lawyers that hardly one can go in the streets. They are the jest of the Court [then in Oxford] and hate of all the people. Their clothes are as much out of date as their speech, which none can understand but when they ask their fees. We do hope in God they shall go out of the town on Tuesday next and all will bless them with the saying of your good wife of Bath. They generally all cursed this town by reason that they cannot get any lodging. They did lay 60 last night in a barn full of hay, not far from my lodging.

On that reckoning, the lawyers emerged from the plague with only a few straws in the hair and some inconvenience. The Earl of Clarendon, the Lord Chancellor, wrote to Sir Harbottle Grimston from Oxford at this time:

> It is indeed a sad season [he wrote], that we are chased from one place to another to save our lives. We have reason to complain of the ill-government of the city of London which, for want of shutting up infected houses, hath scattered the contagion over the kingdom . . . I told you in my last that there is no resolution yet concerning the term; that which is most like to be is that the term will be adjourned . . .

So no judges died of the plague; indeed, the clergy suffered far more, for they visited the poor and sick. It was more dangerous to be a bishop than a judge, in time of pestilence. But lawyers have always been prepared to run some risks. Lord Campbell, the Lord Chief Justice and author of *Lives of the Chancellors,* braved out a cholera epidemic during the Summer Assizes at Gloucester in 1832:

> Tar barrels were burnt all day in the streets [he wrote]. No one entered the county hall except on some sort of compulsion and every one who entered held in his hand some charm against the infection. Yet of a bar above 50 in number, only one man fled the field. There were many deaths daily in Leather Bottle Lane, close by my lodgings but I thought that I, the leader of the circuit, was bound to remain at my post and to give a chance to my juniors.

Was that all? Did the lawyers merely suffer inconvenience from the plague, a few adjournments and nothing more? Yes and very lucky they were, for the plague existed wherever the fleas were infected and there was no shortage of them. There must have been fleas in that Oxford barn but the barristers escaped unharmed. In Dr Johnson's time, the Town Hall at Shrewsbury was stacked with bales of wool, the fleas from which made their presence felt in the lodgings nearby which the barristers had, but none of them caught the plague. As for

Mr Curran, the celebrated Irish barrister and wit, he complained to his landlady that the fleas in his room had made such a determined onslaught upon him that, had they been *unanimous* about which way to pull him, they would have hauled him clean out of bed. It was not bubonic plague which claimed its victims among the legal profession but the law's own special disease—gaol fever.

It is a malady which history has rather overlooked, a virulent form of typhus which brought on a contagious, putrid and very pestilential fever, attended with tremblings, twitchings, restlessness, delirium with, in some instances, early frenzy and lethargy, while the victims break out often into livid pustules and purple spots.'

Its most notorious outbreak was the Black Assize at Oxford in 1577, when a very senior judge—the Chief Baron of the Exchequer—died, together with the High Sheriff, many knights and almost all of the grand jury, some 300 in all. One of the students of Bernard Gilpin, 'the Apostle of the North,' wrote to tell him about it:

This terrible distemper among us, of which you have undoubtedly heard, hath made it indeed a dreadful time to us. During the first six days there died 95; 70 of whom were scholars. This is not conjecture but appears from the mayor's list. The infection does not confine itself to the town but begins to spread in the country where, if our accounts are true, it hath carried off numbers of people, amongst whom poor Mr Roberts. Those who are seized with it are in the utmost torment: their bowels are burnt up, they call earnestly for drink, they cannot bear the touch of clothes, they entreat the standers-by to throw cold water upon them, sometimes they are quite mad, rise upon their keepers, run naked out of their houses and often endeavour to put an end to their lives.

The physicians are confounded, declaring they have met with nothing similar, either in their reading or practice. Yet many of them give this distemper a name, though they have done nothing to show they are at all acquainted with its nature. The greater part of them, I am told, have now left the town, either out of fear for themselves, or conscious that they can do no good.

This dreadful distemper is now generally attributed to some jail infection, brought into court at the assizes; for it is remarkable that the first infected were those only who had been there. Few women or old men have died. God be thanked, the rage of this pestilence is now much abated. It is still among us in some degree, but its effects appear every day weaker.

On the Northern Circuit, 21 years later, gaol fever probably caused the deaths of Mr Justice Beaumont and Serjeant Drew. In 1730, the bringing of infected prisoners to Taunton Assizes caused the death of Lord Chief Baron Pengelley, with perhaps some hundreds more; and in 1750 two judges at the Old Bailey died, with several dozen others.

Well might the Judges wear nosegays, or the courts be sprinkled with herbs and vinegar to lay the infection and cloak the stench from the prisoners; gaol fever was not to be appeased by ritual gestures such as these. It gave the poor debtor more to worry about in his cell than the paltry sum he owed; it gave the hardened felon more to escape from than his shackles. But it gave the general public no cause for concern at all, until John Howard, the penal reformer, awoke them to its horrors.

There is no need to go off-circuit to find gaol fever; so long as there were bad gaols, its risk was always there. All it needed was overcrowding and insanitary conditions. It was almost a miracle that Carlisle escaped it in 1745, when the castle was crammed with prisoners awaiting trial for their part in the rebellion. John Wesley indeed, who was in Newcastle at that time, noted that at least 2000 of the British soldiers there died of the fever and the flux, and they were not kept in crowded cells but in a camp.

In 1775, when John Howard visited the Liverpool Borough Gaol, he learnt that 38 prisoners had been ill of the gaol fever at one time; it was hardly surprising when the prisoners were kept three to an underground cell, some six cubic feet in size. The malady was not always fatal but nobody ran greater risks than he did, entering foul cells while the gaolers stayed outside. When he published his famous book *The State of the Prisons* in 1777, it excited great indignation and compassion; it still does but the affront is to the heart and mind, not to the nose.

It takes a deliberate effort to imagine Howard's physical sensations on entering the felons' cells in York Castle, where they might be kept for 16 hours a day: 'Straw on the stone floors,' he noted, 'no bedsteads. There are four condemned rooms about seven feet square. A sewer in one of the passages often makes these parts of the gaol very offensive—and I cannot say they are clean. Indeed, a clean prison is scarcely ever seen, where the water is to be brought in by the gaoler's servants.'

But in York's City and County Gaol, known as the Kidcots, situated on a bridge over the Ouse, a shortage of water was not always the problem. 'Formerly,' wrote Howard, 'there was no water in this prison but when there was, too much—that is, in a very high flood; then it flows into the room. Now water is laid in.'

There is no need to describe the gaols in all the Northern towns. For each one that was good, another was deplorably bad. In Durham, the debtors were fed on boiled bread and water, their only food. In Hull, seven years sometimes went by without gaol-delivery, a visit from the judges to try all the prisoners awaiting trial; thus the prisoners languished interminably awaiting trial, and all because of the supposed expense of having judges lodged within the town. Yet there were few towns on the Circuit where the judges came more than once a year.

Perhaps the worst prison Howard visited was the debtor's prison at Knaresborough. He described it as: 'Very offensive. A common sewer from the town running through it uncovered. I was informed that an officer, confined here some years since, for only a few days, took in with him a dog to defend him from vermin but the dog was soon destroyed and the prisoner's face much disfigured by them.'

He was not alone in his concern about prison conditions. Dr John Heystrom of Carlisle published a pamphlet on gaol fever in 1781. He found by experience that good results were obtained by treating it with bark (quinine) and port wine: 'we have here prescribed from one bottle to two bottles and a half daily, always with advantage and without any observable incontinence from excess.'

The thought of prisoners enjoying a daily prescription of port may seem amusing but Dr Heystrom was not joking. That year, Carlisle experienced an outbreak of gaol fever which started in a crowded slum outside the prison, the windows of which were boarded up to avoid the window tax. 600 people in the town were infected and 52 died.

As a result of John Howard's efforts prison conditions improved lethargically. In the early XIXth century, Elizabeth Fry and Joseph Gurney carried out their own survey of prisons in the North. The County Gaol at York Castle they considered 'a handsome and extensive building. The debtors are allowed to sell things. Some of the men did not seem to be given enough to eat. They get fire and soap but no clothing, except in emergencies. Felons (tried or untried) are heavily ironed. The women's quarters are good. Water is provided in each yard.'

At York, the male and female prisoners were segregated, which prevented such outrages as were all too common—at Doncaster Gaol, for instance, where during the day male and female prisoners, both criminals and debtors, were mixed together:

> One of the vagrants at this time in the prison [they reported], was a Scotch woman who, having lost her husband and being just recovered from a serious illness, was travelling homewards in company with her little child. She complained bitterly of her situation. 'What could I do?' she said. 'I dare not steal—I liked not to beg—destitute and afflicted—what could I do but apply to the magistrates for a pass? The consequence is, that I am shut up for a week in prison and exposed, perhaps, to the worst and most vicious of men.'
>
> The case speaks for itself [they observed].

They were appalled by the state of Durham Old Gaol, and Carlisle Goal was no better: 'unfit in almost all respects for the purpose to which it is applied,' they decided. Ordinary prisoners had a daily allowance of just under threepence halfpenny for their maintenance. Debtors were much better off, with anything from ninepence to one and threepence; but those who were in prison because they refused to pay under bastardy orders, received no allowance for food at all. There was nothing provided for anybody to do, save indulge their temptations, for the women debtors were not segregated and had either to live with the men, or with the female felons, who slept on straw. Perhaps the felons would find it difficult to carry out much impropriety—they were heavily loaded with chains—but sobriety was hardly the order of the day, as 'the quantity of ale which is said to be introduced into the goal is almost incredible and is of course frequently productive of great disorder.'

It is only fair to show how favourable an impression Lancaster County Gaol made upon them. It was remarkably clean—indeed, 'the prisoners are obliged to wash their faces and hands every morning, at the peril of losing their breakfast.' The prisoners were well fed and clothed and no escape had been known for many years, due to the kindness and vigilance of the governor.

Morpeth too, they found admirable, except that the fourpence daily allowance of food was particularly inadequate when bread was expensive. Still, the benevolent gaoler and his wife produced, 'conspicuously good effects. The prisoners are ruled by the law of kindness; chains are therefore unnecessary for them. They appear to be subdued and softened by the gentleness with which they are treated.'

The Scottish prisons which they visited were on the whole very much worse than the English ones, save that most of them were empty!

As the XIXth century progressed, prison conditions improved and the dreadful dungeons disappeared. Gaol fever became a thing of the past, so that lawyers are likely to catch nothing worse from their clients than a cold. But the battle against poverty and disease was not yet won. The work of Elizabeth Fry and Joseph Gurney was rewarded with the building of fine new prisons, so that the dreadful hell-holes no longer awaited prisoners, whether pending trial or when sentenced.

But the 1840s were the years of the Irish potato famines, when thousands of Irish immigrants sailed across to England and were crammed into dreadful slums: 'The prisons were formerly distinguished for their filth and bad ventilation,' wrote Edwin Chadwick, the Secretary to the Poor Law Commissioners. 'More filth, worse physical suffering and moral disorder than Howard describes are to be found amongst the cellar populations of the working people of

Liverpool, Manchester or Leeds and in large portions of the Metropolis.'

His efforts led to the passing of the Public Health Act in 1848, though it took more than 30 years for many of his desperately-needed reforms to be brought into effect. Poverty is still to be found in England and there is no room for complacency. Nevertheless, the national scene has been changed almost beyond recognition since John Howard's day. Bubonic plague has now long been absent from England and cholera too; it is not likely that, under modern conditions of hygiene, they could ever again have the effects they once did.

In the old days, Newcastle was the largest port on the Northern Circuit and was particularly vulnerable to diseases brought in by sailors. But in 1876, a reorganisation of the circuit system led to the counties of Durham, Northumberland and Yorkshire becoming the North-Eastern Circuit. Since then, the Northern Circuit's chief port has been Liverpool but it has remained immune from plague.

Professor Shrewsbury has explained why: the plague-carrying flea is harboured only by the black rat (Rattus rattus), whereas Liverpool's large rat population is confined to the brown rat (Rattus norvegicus); black rats can therefore never become established there. The large numbers of brown rats present their own health hazards, to be sure; but they are themselves a protection against the black rats and the bubonic plague germs they might harbour. So barristers on circuit can now travel without fear of meeting any pestilence, or of bringing it home with them.

SIX

The Lancashire Witches

'See first whether the evidence be not frivolous, &
whether the proofs brought against them be not
incredible, consisting of guesses, presumptions, &
impossibilities contrary to reason, scripture and
nature. See also what persons complain upon
them, whether they be not of the basest, the
unwisest, and the most faithless kind of people.'
Reginald Scot, *Discovery of Witches*

There is plenty of choice for who is most to blame. When
Henry VIII lusted after Anne Boleyn in 1533, he broke away
from the Church of Rome and dubbed himself Supreme Head
of the Church of England, which made the whole thing respec-
table. Twenty years later, Mary Tudor came to the throne and
restored Catholicism; Elizabeth reversed the process and was
excommunicated in 1570 by a Papal Bull which called her,
'the pretended Queen of England, the servant of wickedness.'
She made Catholics pay crushing fines for not attending
Protestant services and, in return, Jesuit priests were
smuggled into England to spread the word of the old faith.
Everything was ripe for a witch hunt.

'A thousand pulpits are covered in dust,' complained
Bernard Gilpin in the north of Tudor England and Protestant
preachers were sent into its remoter reaches like Victorian
missionaries going into darkest Africa. The old-time Catholic
religion survived strongest here, in an inaccessible terrain
where the sparse population scratched a meagre living. An
American author has likened the people of Lancashire's rural
areas to the Kentucky hill-billies and this is right; most of
Lancashire was on the 'wrong side of the tracks,' and none
further in the wrong than the village of Pendle.

This is how a guide-book described Lancashire in 1673:

The East part is very mountainous, and full of stony and

craggy hills which are barren and bare of wood, being the habitation of Foxes, Coneys and some Otters; amongst which hills these are of chief note, viz. Furness Fells, Riving Pike and Pendle-hill, which are of an exceeding great height, especially Pendle-hill, which seemeth to touch the clouds; and where groweth a Plant which they call Cloudberry.

And on the sterile soil of ignorance the spiky shrub of superstition flourished too.

The authorities believed that Catholic priests were deliberately exploiting witchcraft superstitions in Lancashire. As Sir Richard Molyneux, who styled himself a discoverer of exorcisers, reported to Sir Robert Cecil in 1598:

Some lewd priests in these parts have recently prevailed over certain persons to incline to Papistry. Their practice was in this manner. They had certain women, who pretended to be possessed with unclean spirits, upon whom they practised at some private places, where for the novelty thereof sometimes as many as 500 persons would be drawn together, promising not to betray them. The party possessed would make show to be most horribly tormented and that with very strange illusions; and thus they win daily many unto them.

He gave further details of what they did:

I understand the practice hath been in this sort; two men (to be supposed priests) did carry a woman about with them, and at places where they were entertained did set the woman (whom they alleged to be possessed) in a chair, who would make show to be wonderfully writhen and tormented, in very strange manner, and this they used often, by which they drew many ignorant people to be present at their said exercises as desirous to see the novelty thereof.

If such beliefs were encouraged for subversive ends, it is hardly surprising that they flourished.

The first important English witch trial occurred in Essex, another poor peasant community, where a woman offended narrow minds by saying her prayers *in Latin*. This happened in 1570, seven years after Queen Elizabeth made witchcraft a

66

crime, but James I was obsessed with the subject and it was partly due to his wedding night. His bride-to-be was Princess Anne of Denmark, a high-spirited girl of 16. Twice in November 1589 she set sail from Denmark to join him in Scotland, but November was no month to be making such a voyage and twice contrary winds forced her to turn back. The Danish Admiral in charge of the expedition was quite happy to blame the witches of Denmark for the two unsuccessful voyages because 'he had lately, in the course of his official capacity, presented one of the bailies or burgesses of Copenhagen with a box-on-the-ear, who had as spouse a notable witch-wife.'

James I therefore decided to sail for Denmark instead. Before he left Scotland he appointed several ladies-in-waiting for Princess Anne but one of them was drowned crossing the river Leith and witches were blamed for that too. His voyage to Denmark was difficult and dangerous but he met Princess Anne at Uppsala on the coast of what is now Sweden: 'Immediately at his coming the king passed in quietly with *boots* and all, to her highness. His majesty minded to give the queen a kiss after the Scottish fashion, which the queen refused, as not being the form of her country; but after a few words privily spoken between his majesty and her, familiarity ensued.'

They were married in French, the only language they both understood, and for the next month had each other's company as warmth in the freezing climate.

His views on witchcraft soon became apparent. In the following year, 1590, he and his bride were settled in Scotland and a woman called Agnes Sampson was brought before him charged with witchcraft. After an hour's torture with a rope 'thrawn' (twisted) around her forehead, she was ready to confess to an absurd incident one Allhallows Eve, when she and 200 other witches went to sea in a sieve.

They landed at North Berwick, she said, and they danced. James was shown how they danced, but still was not convinced. More invention was needed if the twisting rope was not to be applied again. At North Berwick Church, she said the Devil made them kiss his buttocks—a standard gesture of infernal allegiance—and made them swear hostility to the King of Scotland, declaring the King to be the greatest enemy he had in the world.

67

So the Devil thought James was his most formidable opponent, did he? *That* should tickle his vanity—but he remained sceptical. She tried a last stratagem:

> Therefore, taking his majesty a little aside, she declared unto him the very words which passed between the King's majesty and his Queen at Uppsala in Norway, the first night of their marriage, with their answer each to other; whereat the King's majesty wondered greatly and swore, by the living God, that he believed that all devils in hell could not have discovered the same, acknowledging her words to be most true, and therefore gave the more credit to the rest that is before declared.

Agnes Sampson was described as, 'No common or sordid hag, but a grave and douce matron, whose serious and discreet answers made a wonderful impression on King James.' But she had confessed to witchcraft and so she was strangled and burnt. James' attitude to witches was no laughing matter.

From this moment on, James can be seen in his more familiar guise; as Sir Walter Scott put it: 'exceedingly like an old gander, running about and cackling all manner of nonsense.' He passed a new Witchcraft Act in 1603, which imposed the death penalty for conjuring up an evil spirit, disinterring a dead body, using part of it for spells, or using spells to harm or kill people. Spells used merely to find buried treasure, or as love-potions, or to harm property, were punished by a year's imprisonment and the pillory; only for a second such offence was the death penalty imposed.

James believed there were three sure tests for a witch: a secret mole, mark or hair would be found in some unexpected part of the body; a fellow witch would denounce her; and the curious ceremony of 'swimming a witch' would show what she was. The unfortunate female had her right thumb tied to her left foot, and vice versa, before being thrown into the water. If she sank, she was innocent; if she floated, she was guilty. It was like the ancient Ordeal of Cold Water and came from the belief that the Devil was composed of more parts of air than water.

The Devil is more usually connected with alcohol; as Daniel Defoe wrote in *Colonel Jack*:

That was a good Story, whether real or invented, of the Devil tempting a young man to murder his Father. No, *he said,* that was unnatural. Why then, *says the Devil,* Go and lie with your Mother; No, *says he,* that is abominable. Well then, *says the Devil,* If you will do nothing to oblige me, go and get drunk; Ay, ay, *says the Fellow,* I'll do that, so he went and made himself drunk as a swine; and when he was drunk, he murdered his Father, and lay with his Mother.

One cynical writer claimed that James I had a further test for witches: he would have them boiled and would taste the broth and say, 'That was a sorceress,' or 'That was not one,' but this is most unlikely, even with James I.

Not everybody shared his beliefs but when Reginald Scot published his *Discovery of Witches* in 1584, ridiculing witches and explaining some of their conjuring tricks, James published a pamphlet in reply. A king who believes in witches does not lack influence and, as the Bible accepts their existence too, it was certainly good enough for most ordinary people. Besides, James I linked a belief in the supernatural with religious intolerance: 'More ghosts and spirits were seen, nor tongue can tell in the time of blind Papistry in these countries, where now by the contrary, a man shall scarcely all his time hear once of such news.' Ignorant fools needed no further encouragement; they could derive much simple pleasure from throwing dead cats at the neighbours they hated, but it was even more satisfying to denounce them as witches; they might be burnt at the stake.

It hardly matters how the Pendle feud began. There may have been a squabble over a right of way, and there was certainly blackmail, seduction and lastly, a burglary. Accusations were made on both sides by and against the two main families and came to the ears of a local Magistrate, Roger Nowell. The Lancashire Witches would never have been tried if it had not been for him. He was a typical local squire, neither a knave nor a fool. Indeed, the most horrifying part of the whole story is the way in which men of the highest intelligence and integrity believed it implicitly. During March 1612 he listened to the witnesses and took down their evidence carefully in depositions, before committing four of the witches for trial at the next Lancaster Assizes.

The most important of them was Elizabeth Southerns, otherwise known as Old Demdike, 'for from this sink of villainy and mischief everything else proceeded.' She was an old woman of 80, who had been a witch for half a century in the Forest of Pendle.

It was a common superstition that every witch had her Familiar, the Devil manifested in the shape of a child or small animal—a hare, a cat, a dog—who would meet and talk with her from time to time and take suck from her at some hidden teat. This was why suspected witches were carefully examined for any unusual moles or marks upon their bodies. So the confession which Old Demdike made to Roger Nowell fitted the usual pattern:

'About 20 years past,' she said, 'as I was coming homeward from begging, I was approaching a stone-pit in Gouldshey in the Forest of Pendle, when a spirit or devil in the shape of a boy met me. Half his coat was black and the other half brown.

' "Stop", he said to me. "If you give me your soul, you shall have anything you ask of me."

' "What is your name?" said I.

' "Tibb," he said. And so, satisfied with his offer, I promised him my soul.

'After this, for some five or six years, he met me from time to time about dawn and always told me to stop, while he asked me what I would have from him, or do? To which I replied, "Nay, nothing; I want nothing yet." And so, after about six years, upon a Sunday moring, when I was sleeping with a little child on my knee, the same spirit appeared to me in the shape of a brown dog, forced his way to my knee, to draw blood under my left arm; and as I had nothing on except for a smock, this devil succeeded in drawing blood from under my left arm. When I woke up, I said, "Jesus save my Child"; but I could not manage to say the words, "Jesus save myself"; and the brown dog immediately vanished from my sight and I was almost stark mad for eight weeks thereafter.'

Her friendship with Tibb obviously brought her no benefit. But she next confessed that she had tried to do one of her neighbours deliberate harm:

'When I got near to his house and met Richard Baldwin, he said to me and my daughter Alison (she led me there, because I was blind), "Get you out of my ground, whores and witches; I will burn the one of you and hang the other." ' "I care not for you—go and hang yourself!" I replied. But almost immediately, when I went through the next hedge, the devil Tibb appeared and said, "Get your revenge on him." So I said to the spirit, "Revenge me either on him or his property." The spirit vanished and I never saw him again.'

Tibb never did Richard Baldwin any harm. Still, Old Demdike at least knew the Black Magic art of sticking pins into little human models:

'The speediest way to take a man's life away by Witchcraft,' [she told Roger Nowell], 'is to make an image of clay, in the shape of the person whom you mean to kill, and dry it thoroughly. When you want them to be ill in any particular part of their body, you take a thorn or pin and prick it in that corresponding part of the body. But if you want part of the body to consume away, you take all the rest of the image, and burn it; and by that means, the body will die.'

There was no evidence that she ever gave anybody even a headache by such magic but other members of her family had tales to tell against her. Alison Device, her grand-daughter, had known her turn a piggin of skimmed milk into butter; try to cure a sick cow and fail; and curse a neighbour's daughter so that she died more than a year later. If this was true, it was an offence punishable by death and women prisoners found guilty of capital offences were burnt to death, not hanged. The stake was not reserved for witches alone.

Her grandson gave evidence too. He had seen the brown dog once; he had heard children crying and cats yowling; and a black cat had once sat on his bed for a whole hour. And Old Demdike's daughter, Elizabeth, confirmed that her mother had had a sore on her left side for the last 40 years. On this overwhelming evidence, she was committed to Lancaster Assizes with three others to await trial.

But the four witches planned revenge. That very week—on Good Friday—many of their friends and relations met at

Malking Tower in the Forest of Pendle and planned to murder the gaoler and blow up Lancaster Castle. At least, Jennet Device said so, and she was all of nine years old. Mr Nowell could hardly contain his triumph: 'All their Murders, Witchcrafts, Enchantments, Charms and Sorceries are discovered; and even in the midst of their consultations they are all confounded and arrested by God's justice.'

Thanks to his discovery Lancaster Castle was mercifully saved from destruction and 20 more witches were committed for trial, but Old Demdike was cunning enough to escape both the majesty of the law and the vigilance of Mr Nowell. She died in prison.

Two judges came for the assizes: one was Mr Justice Altham, whom Sir Francis Bacon called, 'one of the gravest and most reverend judges of this kingdom.' But he only tried the civil cases at these assizes. The Lancashire Witches were tried by the other judge, Baron Bromley, three of whose family were also judges. Nothing further is known of him, save that he clearly believed in witches, but in 1612 he was hardly alone in this. Chief Justice Hale, a senior and most respected judge, certainly believed in them: 'That there are such creatures as witches I make no doubt at all, for the scriptures have affirmed as much.'

With the judges travelled the Clerk of Assize, whose name was Potts. He had a responsible job; a helpful word from a Clerk of Assize could correct a judge before he made some technical error, and he used to assess the size of counsel's fees. He was an important personage in Court and looked it. If, after lunch, his eyelids ever drooped a little, it would only be in the most dignified way. But Mr Potts' eternal claim to fame is that he published: 'THE WONDERFUL DISCOVERY OF WITCHES IN THE COUNTY OF LANCASTER, with the Arraignment and Trial of Nineteen notorious WITCHES, at the Assizes and general Gaol delivery holden at the Castle of LANCASTER, upon Monday, the seventeenth of August last, 1612.'

It could not be more authentic. Potts wrote it with the depositions in front of him and added his recollections of what he saw in court. In an age before shorthand transcripts, this is as much as anyone could hope for. Baron Bromley read the text before it was published and added his approval: 'The whole proceedings and Evidence against them, I find upon examination carefully set forth and truly reported, and judge the work fit and worthy to be published.' So it is the best possible account of the most famous witchcraft trial of all time.

It is necessary [wrote Potts in the introduction], for men to know and understand the means whereby they work their mischief, the hidden mysteries of their devilish and wicked enchantments, charms and sorceries, the better to prevent and avoid the danger that may ensue. And lastly, who were the principal authors and actors in this recent woeful and lamentable tragedy, wherein so much blood was spilt.

One of the most wicked was Old Demdike, who died before the trial; another was Anne Whittle, otherwise known as Chattox; she was 44 years of age. She was:

. . . a very old, withered, worn and decrepit creature, her sight almost gone: a dangerous witch of long standing, always an enemy of Old Demdike. For, anyone who was favoured by one of them, was hated by the other . . . In her witchcraft, she was always more ready to do mischief to men's goods than to they themselves. Her lips always muttered and trembled, but no man ever knew what they said. She lived in the Forest of Pendle, amongst this wicked company of dangerous witches. Yet, in her examination and confession, she was always frank and accurate; for she was often questioned by the court about specific instances but was never found to vary, but always agreed in her evidence about the same things.

She first met the Devil at Old Demdike's house, she said.

'Demdike and I went out of the house to meet him—and he pleaded with me to become his subject and give him my soul. At first I refused, but Demdike argued so much with me, that I consented to be under his orders and instructions. "I must have part of your body to suck at," the Devil said. I would not let him at first, but later asked him what part of my body he wanted. "Part of your right side," he said, "near your ribs," and I agreed.
    At that time there was a spotted bitch there who came with the Devil to meet Demdike, and the dog said to

73

Demdike that she should have gold, silver and worldly wealth at her wish. As soon as the dog spoke, meat, butter, cheese, bread and drink appeared; "Eat your fill," said the dog. We did so. And when we had finished, the Devil, who was called Fancy and Tibb the dog, took away the remnants.'

She was the first of the Lancashire witches to be tried and was charged with causing the death of Robert Nutter by witchcraft. She pleaded 'Not guilty', but she had already admitted it to Roger Nowell in a confession. She certainly had a good motive for wanting him dead.

'Robert Nutter wanted my daughter, Mrs Redfern, to let him have his pleasure of her when he was in Redfern's house; but she would not let him. He was very angry and went off on his horse, saying in a great rage that if ever he inherited the land, she would be turned off the property. I then summoned Fancy, who appeared in the shape of a man in that plot of ground called "The Land."

"What would you have me do?" he asked.

"Go and revenge me on Robert Nutter," I said. He lived about a quarter of a year after that, and then died.'

There were other witnesses against her. Old Demdike had given evidence against her before she died, and her testimony was read out. It was very important, because one of the tests for a witch was that another witch should identify her as such. The murder method was simple and obvious.

'Three yards from the east end of the house,' Old Demdike had testified, 'I saw Anne Whittle, alias Chattox, and Mrs Redfern, her daughter, one on each side of the ditch. And they had two images of clay or marl. Chattox was making a third one, and her daughter was kneading the clay for her to make it with. As I went past, the spirit Tibb, in the shape of a black cat, appeared to me and said, "Turn back again and do as they do."

I asked, "What are they doing?"

"Making three images," the cat said.

"Whose be they?" I asked.

"Christopher Nutter, Robert Nutter, and Marie, his wife," the cat said.

74

I would not go back to help them make images; the spirit seemed to be angry, and pushed or shoved me into the ditch, so that the can of milk I had was spilt. The spirit vanished . . .'

James Robinson gave evidence too. He remembered that after she had had a drink at their house once, several casks had gone sour. Everybody in the neighbourhood believed her to be a witch, and when Robert Nutter fell fatally ill, he believed she had bewitched him. A victim's belief was very important, because it was deemed one of the true tests of a witch.

Potts does not set out the other evidence against her, because her guilt 'is now so obviously proved by what you have already heard, that no impartial man would question it or remain unconvinced.'

But he quotes one of her spells, an ignorant woman's garbled version of a half-remembered prayer. Small wonder that, in the earlier Essex case, a woman was suspect who could say her prayers in Latin.

A CHARM
Three biters hast thou bitten
The heart, ill eye, ill tongue;
Three bitter shall be thy Boot,
Father, Son and Holy Ghost,
a God's name.
Give pater-nosters, five Aves,
and a Creed,
In worship of five wounds
of our Lord.

Another of the witches to be tried was Elizabeth Device, the daughter of Old Demdike. Potts called her a 'barbarous and inhuman monster, beyond parallel.' Her very appearance surely marked her out as evil: 'This odious witch was branded with a preposterous mark by nature at her birth: her left eye, set lower than the other, looked downwards, while the other looked up. The deformity was so strange that the best men present there in that great audience said that they had seldom seen the like.'

He was outraged that she did not meekly admit her guilt. On the contrary, 'she could not contain herself with any self-discipline,' but she exclaimed, crying out in a very outrageous manner against her own children and those who came to prosecute her and bring evidence against her for the death of their children, friends and kin . . .'

When she was first examined [continues Potts], although Master Nowell was very skilful and very careful in dealing with her, yet she would confess nothing until by God's pleasure Jennet Device, her own daughter, nine years old (an unexpected witness), revealed all their practices, meetings, consultations, murders, charms and villainies. Their nature and extent were such as a learned judge described the Gunpowder Plot, the greatest treason that ever was in the kingdom: 'Who could ever tell this to his children, without their thinking he must be making some of it up?' Because when posterity hears of these things, they will think them fiction, not fact.

As Elizabeth Device denied that her confession was true, the main evidence against her was that of her little daughter Jennet Device:

Her mother [says Potts], as she habitually did, cursed outrageously and cried out against the child in such an appalling manner that everyone in court was astonished at her, and the child was so startled that she cried out to the learned judge that she could not speak in the presence of her mother . . . In the end, when nothing else could be done, his Lordship commanded that the prisoner should be removed, and the girl stood upon the table in the presence of the whole court. And she gave evidence to the jury in this trial for life and death.

'My mother is a witch,' she said, 'and this I know to be true, because I often saw her spirit visit my mother in her house, which is called Malking Tower, in the shape of a brown dog, called Ball. On one occasion Ball asked my mother what she wanted him to do. She said, "Help me kill John Robinson of Barley." Ball helped her to kill Robinson, and my mother has been a witch for these past three or four years.'

She gave evidence about the momentous meeting at Malking Tower, where for dinner they had beef, bacon, and roast mutton. She did not mention any wicked plots but named six of the witches present.

Butter would not melt in the mouth of this young lady; she not only gave evidence against her own mother, but also against her brother James Device: 'Although this witness was so young, it was wonderful to the Court that, despite the number of people there, how modestly, calmly and simply she gave this evidence against the prisoner, who was her own natural brother; he could not deny it, but there acknowledged it to be true in every detail.'

But when it came to the trial of some of the other witches, the judge became more wary of the child's evidence. He arranged an identity parade in court, mixing the prisoners with strangers, to see if she could identify the right persons, but she knew them well enough; he asked her if Joan-a-Down was present at the feast at Malking Tower, but it is not a Lancashire name, and sharp little girls of nine are not to be caught out like that.

When the assizes were over, Anne Whittle, or Chattox, had been condemned to death; so had Alison Device and her son James, and seven others. They were executed. These are the witches of Pendle, and it is they who are meant when people talk of the Lancashire Witches. Professor G. B. Harrison has said, 'If, then, the evidence can be taken at its face value, the Lancaster trial reveals the practice of the witch cult in its full horror.'

But there were also tried at these assizes three witches from Samlesbury, a village ten miles nearer Preston. The chief witness against them was a 14 year old girl, Grace Sowerbutts, whose evidence was certainly startling. One of them had stuck a nail into the navel of a sleeping child and sucked its blood; it languished and died. On the night after the burial one of them brought the body home from the churchyard, and cooked it (part boiled, part roast), and they ate it.

'Who would not have condemned these women upon this evidence, and found them guilty of so foul and horrid a murder?' says Potts. But when the judge asked the three accused if they had anything to say, they fell on their knees, weeping and begged him to question the girl more closely to find out who had coached her in her story. At once her face changed, and as the judge questioned her it became clear that

77

she had been given a story to learn by a Jesuit priest. The three accused had incurred his anger because they had once been ardent papists, but had turned to the Church of England. All three were acquitted, and Potts was delighted. So, although the witches of Pendle were convicted on evidence so absurd that it is almost unbearable to read, the judge and jury were not prepared to convict everybody who was accused of witchcraft.

Attitudes began to change in the reign of Charles I, but not in Pendle, which provided more witches for trial in 1633. That odious little girl Jennet Device, a women of 30 now, was convicted with 16 others. The main witness was young Robinson, a lad who was later exposed as a complete liar. He claimed to have been at a witches' coven, when he was in fact stealing wild plums from a nearby orchard.

It was a curious scene he described, quite different from anything in the earlier trials. He visited a house where there was a banquet in progress, with about 60 people present, and he saw them going into a bar where six of them pulled at ropes; down came "flesh smoking, butter in lumps, and milk", all of which fell into basins they were carrying. It resembles no superstition one can think of.

His evidence was untrue, but it is very like another case at York at this time, when a witness claimed that a pull on a rope brought down plum-broth, a bottle of wine, cheese, flour, butter, and so on.

In this Lancashire case of 1633, however, the accused were convicted, and the case caused an immense sensation, as if lightning had struck twice in the same place. Heywood and Broome wrote a bad but successful play on the subject, and young Robinson's father cashed in too. He took the lad from church to church to tell his tale, 'and by that means they got a good living, that in a short space the Father brought a cow or two, when he had none before.'

Seventeen witches were found guilty, but the judge fortunately had misgivings and postponed their execution. They remained in Lancaster Castle Gaol. The Bishop of Chester was ordered to make a report on seven of them, but within a few months three had died—perhaps from gaol fever—and another was incurably ill. He was by no means convinced that they were witches. 'Conceit and malice were so powerful with

78

many in those parts,' he reported, 'that they will easily afford an oath to work revenge upon their neighbour.'

It was a dangerous form of conceit; many an old crone claimed magical powers to boost her standing in the local community. Harvey, the great physician who discovered the circulation of the blood, once visited the house of a woman who claimed to be a witch. She was out, but her toad was in, the creature she claimed to be her 'familiar'. When she returned she found he had dissected the toad, and a very ordinary dead toad it proved to be; whereupon she 'flew at him like a tigress', till he explained that he was the King's physician and that, if she was a real witch, he had come to arrest her. She immediately disclaimed any powers as a witch and her life was spared. But in Lancashire, many of the witches went to the stake without any attempt to withdraw the 'confessions' they had made to Roger Nowell.

Charles I took a personal interest in the proceedings. He had four of the so-called witches brought to London, where Harvey and other notable physicians examined them; Charles did so too and found them free of any sinister symptoms. They were all reprieved from execution. Young Robinson and his father were brought to London too, and questioned separately—something the father had always resisted—and their lies were exposed. They were put in prison, and their final fate is unknown.

But the Lancashire Witches remained in prison too. In 1636, ten of them were still in Lancaster Castle Gaol, one of them, Jennet Device, whose nine year old precocity had sent her mother to the stake. This is the last that is known of them; they were certainly not pardoned as soon as the truth was discovered. Some say that there was too much local feeling for them to be set free. But the darkness of time has closed in on them forever—perhaps they were kept there till they died.

A tide of disbelief was beginning to flow against witches. In only one other county—Essex—was witch-hunting so active, thanks to the Witchfinder-General, Matthew Hopkins, an exceptional figure in Cromwell's exceptional era. But none of these witches attracted anything like as much interest as their Lancashire sisters.

A hundred years after the great Pendle trial, evidence was given that a Hertfordshire witch could fly. 'Well then,' said the genial judge, 'you may—there is no law against flying.' And from 1735, there was no law to send witches to the stake, for the Witchcraft Act was repealed.

Lancashire is still famed for these witches, and their trial, the most famous of them all, is still a source of amazement and fascination. Perhaps it all sprang from a petty feud, and the burglary which Alison Device described in her evidence:

'About 11 years ago my mother and I had our coal shed broken into and all or most of our linen, and half a peck of cut oatmeal, and some meal, worth a total of about 20 shillings or more, was stolen. On the following Sunday, I found a band and a wig on Chattox' daughter, and I claimed them as part of the stolen property.'

They were paid for dearly, in any event.

SEVEN

Judge Jeffreys' Jaunt

'Say that his power lies in words and looks; in
things so slight and insignificant that it is impossible to add and count 'em up; what then?'

Charles Dickens, *A Christmas Carol*

In the whole breadth of history, no figure holds a more universal fascination than Judge Jeffreys. What makes him such a
popular villain is not his debauchery—compared with Nero,
he was a fanatical puritan, the number of his victims, set beside
Hitler's, is almost derisory—but it is the thought of justice,
that thing of spotless virtue, being flung into the mud and
danced upon, that gives Jeffreys a special dimension of
depravity, a wickedness to wallow in.

Lord Chief Justice Campbell described him as entirely free
from hypocrisy, because 'he was not redeemed from his vices
by one single solid virtue.' If he is to be painted in his true
colours, most people would say they were the scarlet of blood
and the blackness of the pit. That view dates from 1685, the
year of the Bloody Assizes. But in 1684 he rode the Northern
Circuit to such a welcome as no judge had ever received
before. He was then at the height of his popularity, which is, to
say the least of it, an unfamiliar idea. But it is worth going back
to the beginning.

George Jeffreys was born in 1648 at Acton in Denbighshire.
One of his grandfathers was a Welsh judge and the other a
distinguished lawyer who edited Coke's famous law reports; it
was no bad pedigree for someone going in for law. At school,
according to Lord Campbell's *Lives of the Chancellors*, he was
known to take undue advantage not only at marbles—most
schoolboys cheat at marbles—but also at *leapfrog,* and a lad
who will stoop to sharp practice at leapfrog is surely marked
out for great things. He was educated at Shrewsbury and later
in London at St Paul's School, where at the beginning of each

law term he watched the procession of the judges and vowed to be one of them some day.

He had to become a barrister first, and on 19 May 1663 he joined the Inner Temple. Two years later was the year of the Great Plague and the story goes that at Kingston Assizes in 1666, when the numbers of the Bar were much depleted by disease, he donned a gown and made his way into court. It is a marvellous legend, that one foul pestilence should spawn another, but the fact is that he was properly called to the Bar two years later, after a full five years study, on 22 November 1668.

He was then a handsome, astute, sociable young man with a proper taste for good literature and a head for drinking. He made good use of it, and built up an extensive practice by clinking tankards with the clerks of important attorneys. Many barristers have started their upward climb via the tavern steps, but few of them had his enormous ability and energy. He was indeed a great advocate, and another great advocate, Lord Birkenhead (F. E. Smith), wrote that 'measured by any standards he was a man of consummate ability.' It was not just that he drank with people who mattered—high society, rich merchants, and not least Will Chiffinch, secretary to Charles II, a master of backstairs intrigue and another great drinker (he never drank Jeffreys under the table, though it was not for want of trying)—Jeffreys also had, in great perfection, the three chief qualifications of a lawyer: 'Boldness, Boldness, Boldness'. He was a marvellous success in criminal cases. Barely five years after his call to the Bar he was the leading practitioner at the Old Bailey and London sessions. Many successful barristers have an inexhaustible gift for tedious and tortuous English; many great advocates had a golden simplicity of style which time and cold print have tarnished into dullness. But, though Jeffreys' towering presence is now gone and his powerful voice silent, his phrases still leap off the page.

A case was heard before the King in Council in which a new translation of the Psalms called itself the 'King's Psalter,' in breach of copyright. It hardly sounds a case suited to Jeffreys' style of advocacy. But he turned directly towards Charles II and said, 'They have teemed, Sir, with a spurious brat, which being clandestinely midwived into the world, the better to cover the imposture they lay it at your Majesty's door.'

Many comely wenches had 'teemed' (given birth to) bastards fathered upon them by Charles II, who was greatly amused. Jeffreys' phrase is not only outrageous, but has tremendous *style*. So has his summing-up when he was judge in the trial of Titus Oates, and reminded the jury that Oates had not long since been treated as a national hero:

Nay [he said], it was come to that degree of folly, to give it no worse name, that in public societies, to the reproach and infamy of them be it spoken, this profligate villain was caressed, was drunk to, and saluted by the name of the 'Saviour of the Nation'. O prodigious madness! That such a title as that was, should ever be given to such a prostitute monster of impiety as this is.

Good God, whither were we running, when many easy people were so strangely wrought upon by this impostor, and when the villainous and black designs of some evil instruments amongst us could prevail so far as to deceive almost a whole nation into the belief of so horrid a false-hood; even at the same time that a hidden treason too deeply contrived, was carried on amongst us but, God be thanked, was not too lately discovered?

. . . and it was therefore fit this cause should be tried in the most solemn and public manner, in order to vindicate the nation from the reproach and calumny of injustice and oppression. And sure I am, if you think these witnesses swear true, as I cannot see any colour of objection, there does not remain the least doubt, but that Oates is the blackest and most perjured villain that ever appeared upon the face of the earth.

No rocket rose as far and fast as Jeffreys. Only three years after his call to the Bar, he became Common Serjeant of the City of London, an astonishing honour for a man of 23. He had come a long way now from the world of petty crime and was doing heavy commercial cases. Rich merchants—the Stationers' Company, for instance, who owned the valuable copyright in the King's Psalter—do not entrust their litigation to stuttering upstarts at the Bar.

Any portrait of Jeffreys which omits his attractive qualities is badly drawn. He was well thought of by the ablest judges.

83

When he appeared before Sir Matthew Hale he was welcomed for his common-sense, a compliment not easily won, though out of court he wheedled his way into the judge's good opinion by fawning upon him.

He was an excellent host and entertained Charles II on several occasions; he had a strong sense of humour which could light up the court like a shaft of sunlight. There was once an excise case about brandy, with samples available for the judge and jury. Jeffreys was appearing against Saunders, a bloated wineskin of a barrister, within whose reach the samples were inadvisedly left:

JEFFREYS: My Lord, we are at a full stop and can go no further.
CHIEF JUSTICE: What is the matter?
JEFFREYS: Mr Saunders has drunk up all our evidence! (Laughter).

But when his jokes were turned against an accused man, and were coupled with a bullying manner, the result was Judge Jeffreys, as he is generally remembered.

In 1678, at the age of 30, he was made Recorder of London, a part-time job he was able to combine with his ordinary practice at the Bar. Thus, he was sometimes a judge and sometimes a prosecutor in cases against those implicated in the Popish Plot, that brain-child of Titus Oates. Some Londoners called Jeffreys 'the foul mouth of the City' and 'our mountebank lawyer'; Charles II, however, was grateful for his services and gave him another part-time job as Chief Justice of Chester, with a salary of £500 a year. He was now entitled to be called Judge Jeffreys, and he continued to add to his notoriety. One of many attacks upon him in Parliament described his behaviour in that office:

His name [said Lord Delamere], is Sir George Jeffreys who, I must say, behaved himself more like a Jack-pudding [a buffoon] than with that gravity which becomes a judge. He was witty upon the prisoners at the Bar. He was very full of his jokes upon people that came to give evidence, not suffering them to declare what they had to say in their own way and method, but would interrupt them because they behaved themselves with more gravity than he . . . In the mornings he appeared with the symptoms of a man that overnight had taken a large cup.

Nevertheless, with the support of Charles II, he survived the mounting hostility towards him and, in September 1683, he became the Lord Chief Justice of England, and in 1685 the Lord Chancellor. He was entitled to be called by these higher titles, and it is only popular usage which has fixed him firmly with the title Judge Jeffreys.

Eighty years after his death a short biography summed him up well enough:

> He was a man of tolerable sense, and had by long practice acquired some tolerable knowledge of the law, tho' as little as 'twas, more than he had occasion to make use of. He had a very large stock of ill nature and wit, in which lay his greatest excellence, that a very unenvied one. But in short his BROW and his TONGUE were the two best accomplishments he was master of.

It is then chiefly a matter of style, that his brow and his tongue should be held against him. His general ability was very considerable. His punishments were probably no harsher than the times demanded, but his ferocity was so great that justice ceased to exist.

During the trial of Titus Oates, the accused objected to a Roman Catholic giving evidence against him. It was an absurd objection, and Jeffreys was right to overrule it. A mild judge would have said, 'I am afraid there is nothing in that point, Mr Oates,' and a testy one might have rebuked him. But Jeffreys' handling of the matter is so instructive that it is worth quoting in full. It even has the undesirable effect of transferring one's sympathies to Titus Oates:

OATES: My Lord, I desire to know what religion that noble lord is of.

JEFFREYS: We all know what religion my lord is of, you need not ask that question.

OATES: That is not the point, my Lord, I must have it declared in evidence.

JEFFREYS: I wonder to see any man that has the face of a man, carry it at this rate, when he hears such an evidence [witness] brought in against him.

OATES: I wonder that Mr Attorney will offer to bring this evidence, men that must hold malice against me—
JEFFREYS: Hold your tongue; you are a shame to mankind.

Thus, Jeffreys overruled an objection of no merit whatever, doing the right thing in a most monstrous manner. That was his besetting sin. During the 'Bloody Assize' that followed the Monmouth rebellion, he tried Dame Alice Lisle, a widow of 70. She may indeed have been guilty of harbouring one of the rebels but the evidence against her was not strong, and Jeffreys' unrelenting pressure on a jury reluctant to convict her assured him eternal infamy. When a witness was giving evidence for her defence and Jeffreys said, 'Hold up the lantern, that we may see his brazen face,' the blood runs cold.

This was in 1685 on the Western Circuit. His three weeks on the Northern Circuit were in 1684, when he received a rapturous welcome. His visit was made for political purposes, and his popularity was part of a carefully laid scheme.

In 1684 many towns and cities ran themselves, appointing their own mayors and aldermen under royal charter. The King had no control over their lawful decisions unless he could persuade the city to surrender its charter; then he could grant it a new charter, which allowed him to overrule them if necessary. Jeffreys was to be the King's agent, resplendent in the King's authority and approval, and irresistibly persuasive when seeking the surrender of the old charters.

In March 1684 Jeffreys went on the Western Circuit, capturing the charter of Plymouth and other cities. According to a newsletter of 30 March, 'some say 500 horse [men] will go out to meet Lord Chief Justice Jeffreys on his return from the circuit, so well is he beloved.'

The lawyer and historian Roger North described the publicity campaign which followed:

After the Lord Chief Justice Jeffreys (of whom I have said somewhat before) was assumed into the King's Privy Council, which was some time before he came into the Cabinet, there went forth a mighty fame of his greatness at court, which was mostly artificial although such incidents commonly blow up reports far beyond truth. When this Chief Justice had chosen the Northern Circuit for his expedition, it was so contrived that, on a Sunday morning when the court was full, the King should take notice of his good services and, in token of his Majesty's gracious acceptance of them, give him a ring from his royal finger. This was certainly so done, by way of engine to rear up a mighty machine of authority; and the printed news informed the whole nation of it. Whereupon the same Lord Chief Justice was commonly reputed a favourite and next door to premier minister, sure enough to eclipse any thing of the law that stood near him.

Before he went on the Northern Circuit, however, there were some charters of the London companies to be obtained. The tactics were exactly the same. On 28 June, the Earl of Sunderland, writing from Windsor to the Attorney-General, made the position clear:

His Majesty, having thought it will be for his service that the officers of the London companies should now on the renewal of their charters be appointed by the Lord Chief Justice, commands me to acquaint you therewith that you may take care that no persons be inserted as officers but such as shall be named by the Lord Chief Justice.

In July, all was ready. The King gave Jeffreys the special ring as a mark of favour, and some advice at the same time: 'My lord,' he said, 'as it is a hot summer, and you are going the circuit, I desire you will not drink too much.'

The advice was ignored. He arrived at York on 14 July with Mr Serjeant Holloway. Sir John Reresby, the Member of Parliament for York, planned to give a hearty welcome to Jeffreys:

This gentleman [he recalled], in whom the King and the Duke both much relied, I resolved to receive with all the respect I could, and the rather because I had been formerly his client, and he had ever been kind to me. The night therefore that he came to York, I caused my officers to receive him with a guard at the town gate, went to wait on him myself so soon as he alighted at his lodging, offered to receive orders from him (but he would not give them), set two sentries at his door, invited him to dinner the next day, which he accepted, with his fellow judge, Mr Serjeant Holloway, and several of the chief gentlemen of the county, to wait upon him. Another night, several men of quality, who took that occasion of coming down with his lordship to see the North, came and took a collation with me; and my lord himself came to me incognito one evening, and being a jolly, merry companion when his business was over, stayed with me over a bottle till one o'clock in the morning.

At York, Jeffreys had no difficulty in obtaining the surrender of the charter. It is not known what cases he tried there, but he had been told in London that there had been civil disorder in Doncaster, which the King felt should never have occurred. Jeffreys' inquiries at York showed that the fault lay equally with the Mayor and Corporation of Doncaster and with some of the soldiers of Sir John Reresby. Jeffreys reprimanded both sides, and the matter was closed.

York's charter gone, and the rest to go. They tumbled down into his outstretched hands, and his welcome never ceased. At Hull he was received with ringing bells and a continuous salute of guns. On 29 July he reached Newcastle, where he not only had to capture the city charter, but also to punish nonconformists, dissenters and the like. It is worth remembering that the reign of Charles II was not just an age of foaming tankards and Nell Gwynn, but also of desperate plots and dangerous malcontents.

The Popish Plot, which came to light in 1679, may have been largely a fraud concocted by Titus Oates, but there were plenty of other authentic plots. There had also been in 1662 the Muggleswick conspiracy in the North of England, planning to seize Durham, to murder all the bishops and senior clergy, and to destroy Parliament; and there was the Ryehouse plot in 1680 to assassinate Charles II. There were many fanatics who sprang from the Roundhead tradition. There were the Fifth Monarchy men whose rising failed in 1661, and there were the Presbyterians of whom Jeffreys had no kind opinion: 'Presbytery has all manner of villainy in it,' he said. 'Show me a Presbyterian and I will engage to show a lying knave.'

There were the Quakers too, not given to friendly persuasion in those days. They fell to the ground foaming at the mouth and quaking in every limb, from which their name derived; they ran about half naked, prophesying doom; and at

Appleby Assizes they even called the judges 'scarlet coloured beasts'.

Jeffreys had no love for the Whigs either, whom he saw as left-wing extremists, nor for any nonconformists. One of their leaders at Newcastle was Alderman Ambrose Barnes, whose biography has a lot to say about Jeffreys' behaviour there: 'His behaviour was alike drinking to filthy excess till two or three a clock in the morning, going to bed as drunk as a beast, and rising again with the symptoms of one who had drank a cup to much.'

One of the clergy in Newcastle had religious views which were fairly moderate but well on the wrong side of Jeffreys' tolerance. He was prudent enough to invite him to a sumptuous dinner where there was enough wine even for his guest's taste. Soon afterwards Jeffreys was told that this clergyman was a subversive influence, but he refused to believe it: 'They tell me,' he said, 'such a man is a Whig, but I find it's no such thing—he is an honest drunken fellow!'

Ambrose Barnes, however, took no such precautions. He belonged to a group of 30 dissenters. One of them, perhaps to gain favour with the authorities, gave them a list of the names of his friends, and it passed into Jeffreys' hands: 'I have here,' announced Jeffreys in open court, 'a black list of damned fanatics, and I am resolved to scour them.'

Severely punished they certainly would have been, for he would have charged them with high treason and done his best to see them convicted and executed. Some of them were in court when he said it; he ordered the doors to be locked for, he reckoned, if he managed to catch the cubs, the old foxes themselves would soon appear. But they had gone to earth, and in the meantime Jeffreys decided to make a fool of Thomas Verney, the one in court who seemed the easiest butt.

'Can you read, sirrah?' he asked.

'Yes, my Lord,' said Mr Verner.

'Reach him the book,' said Jeffreys. Mr Verner was handed a Bible, and read from it at random. It was in Latin. 'Ne judicate, ne judicemini,' he read out.

'Construe it, sirrah,' said Jeffreys, hoping to show up his ignorance.

'Judge not, lest ye be judged,' said Mr Verner, and Jeffreys seemed abashed.

Fortunately for Mr Verner and his friends, Jeffreys had not enough time in Newcastle to try them. Joan Bartram, a gardener's wife, was charged with saying, 'there is none that are honest men will say but the Duke of York is a papist', a scurrilous truth for which she could have lost her life. He sent them to prison to await trial, where they remained seven months, and were finally allowed to go free by a different judge.

Jeffreys was certainly harsh with them, but not absurdly so. Three weeks after he left Newcastle it was found that some Scotsmen had planned to capture Berwick and invade England with 1000 horsemen.

Jeffreys moved on to Durham, but Ambrose Barnes went down to London, where he complained to the King and Council of Jeffreys' behaviour. So he escaped Jeffreys' clutches, but Newcastle's charter did not.

At Durham, Jeffreys gaoled two men who were accused of not having attended church for three years past. They swore they were innocent of this offence, but not until Jeffreys moved on to Bishop Auckland could his colleague, Mr Serjeant Holloway, feel safe to let them out on bail. At Durham, Jeffreys fined the coroner for some breach of duty, and he was dining with the Bishop when the coroner appeared: 'How now, sir?' said Jeffreys, 'I suppose you are come to beg off your fine?' But the Bishop corrected him: at Durham all the fines belonged to the Bishop, and it was for him alone to enforce or remit them. 'Jeffreys,' the account goes, 'was plaguily discomforted.'

On 6 August Jeffreys reached Carlisle and was given a 15-gun salute; the Duke of Norfolk had only been saluted with nine. On the following day he accepted the surrender of the City's charter and addressed the local gentry who made up the Grand Jury. He warned them against dissenters and Justices of the Peace who held Whiggish views. He also attended the assize service in the cathedral, and heard (as the Bishop of Carlisle noted in his diary) a 'sermon preached (length and stuff intolerable) by Mr Nichol', who was a lecturer, and Chancellor of the Diocese of Carlisle. The Bishop's diary is tantalisingly brief. The sermons must have outraged Jeffreys' political views, because on the next day there were the 'trials of the two Smurthwaits, which gave occasion to a severe

90

reprimand to Mr Nichol'—and they must have been guilty of some sort of sedition, because on the following day the two Smurthwaits and a Border thief were sentenced to death. Other persons for trial included the 'Witch of Ainstable', about whom no further details are given; the alleged witch was found 'Not guilty', for Jeffreys, like many other judges at this time, was no believer in witchcraft. Two Williamson brothers were also tried for the now forgotten crime of barratry, an offence committed by scurrilous attorneys in trumping up cases and encouraging hopeless litigation. Jeffreys particularly hated it. As Roger North wrote:

He took a pleasure in mortifying fraudulent attorneys and would deal forth his severities with a sort of majesty . . . He could not reprehend without scolding; and in such Billingsgate language as should not come out of the mouth of any man. He called it 'giving a lick with the rough side of his tongue.' It was ordinary to hear him say, 'Go, you are a filthy, lousy nitty rascal.'

On the following day, according to the diary, 'Junior Williamson found guilty' [of barratry], 'and pilloried with his brother.' The pillory was not always a laughable appointment with bad eggs and tomatoes; if the mob laid hold of stones, men in the pillory sometimes died. All the same, the pillory might seem a pleasanter place than the dock in Jeffreys' court.

Two Scotch pedlars were sent to the pillory for selling clippings, snippets taken from the edge of silver coins. They were lucky—people were still hanged for that offence.

The criminal cases were now at an end. Judges are entitled to rest from their labours; so, 'after dinner,' as the diary tells us, 'my Lord Chief Justice went to Scotland; *desiring to see something as bad as his own country.*'

He went on this little expedition with a considerable retinue; Sir Daniel Fleming, the Sheriff of Cumberland, was one of them, and Sir Christopher Musgrave another. The next day was a Sunday; neither of the judges went to church in the Cathedral, but they may have wished to avoid another vexatious sermon.

On Monday 11 August Jeffreys heard several petitions which had been brought against certain Attorneys, and sent the cases over to the next assizes, because it was time for him

91

and Serjeant Holloway to move on to Appleby. There he heard three arbitration cases between members of the local gentry; it was quite common for senior judges to do such a thing. He had no difficulty in obtaining Appleby's charter, nor Kendal's, where he and Serjeant Holloway were made freemen of the City.

There is something touching in the wistful letter Kendal Corporation wrote him soon after he had left the town: 'Your lordship was pleased to give us not only your word *but your oath* to become a buxom and beneficial member of this corporation.'

But it was too late then—much too late. When Jeffreys reached Lancaster, his reputation had gone before him. Many youths flocked there from Manchester to see him in court, it being a treat to watch him trouncing the nonconformists. One of them was Thomas Jolly of Whalley, a clergyman who had often been arrested for his beliefs and practices in the past, and put in prison too. Jeffreys bound him over, requiring a surety for his good conduct in the sum of £200, which was a difficult sum enough for a clergyman to lay his hands on. Jeffreys would have preferred it to be £2000, but this was more than the law allowed.

Another local troublemaker was a Justice of the Peace named Cole, and a letter from Lancashire explains what happened to him:

Justice Cole is as great a rogue as lives in the King's dominions . . . whilst he is in the commission of peace the rabble will always be factious, for he encourages faction. The Lord Chief Justice had him before him at our last Summer Assizes and, as he was made to appear to be a favourer of conventicles, called him in open court a rogue and 'snivelling canting fanatical rascal' and bound him over in £1000 to appear at the King's Bench.

The letter shows the practical advantages that the surrender of Lancaster's charter brought—it meant that bad justices could be replaced by good ones:

But now the Mayor by the new charter is justice through the whole county, and besides there is a very honest gentleman, Mr Carus . . . If you will not move the King to remove Cole and put in Mr Carus, I will do so myself.

That was precisely what the surrender of charters was designed to achieve.

Judge Jeffreys' jaunt was almost at an end. He was sumptuously entertained by the Preston Corporation, whose charter he was graciously pleased to accept, and then he returned to London. He never returned to the Northern Circuit.

Roger North described what happened next. While Jeffreys had been hearing cases in court, and was being wined and dined out of it, the undersheriffs in each county had been drawing up lists of those recusants who had been committed to prison, and Jeffreys gathered them together to present to Charles II:

> When he returned to London and his great services which argued no less abilities to serve the King were displayed, the next step was his being appointed to attend his Majesty at the Cabinet . . . where, after the King was come, and they were sat, my Lord Chief Justice Jeffreys stood up, and with the rolls of recusants before him.
>
> 'Sir,' said he, 'I have a business to lay before your Majesty, which I took notice of in the North, and which will deserve your Majesty's royal commendation. It is the case of numberless numbers of your good subjects that are imprisoned for recusancy. I have the list of them here to justify what I say. There are so many that the great gaols cannot hold them without their lying one upon another.'

It is not at all clear what game Jeffreys was playing. He showed no sympathy at any other time for the Catholic recusants, and it has been suggested that he was really warning the King in an underhand way how many of them might cause trouble against him if the opportunity arose.

Still, he stood there with his highly-coloured figures of speech about rotting and stinking in prison, and asking Charles to use his royal pardon to discharge all the convictions for recusancy, and thus restore liberty and air to these poor men . . .

'After the Lord Chief Justice had done,' says Roger North, 'and composed his rolls and papers upon the table (*which none there cared to inspect*),' there was quite a long silence, broken at last by Lord Keeper Guilford, who decided to call Jeffreys' bluff.

93

' "Sir," said he, "I humbly entreat your Majesty that my Lord Chief Justice may declare whether all the persons named in these rolls were actually in prison or not." '

Jeffreys hastily interposed, saying he did not surely imagine anyone could suspect he meant that all the names in the rolls were *actual* prisoners, for all the prisons of England could not hold them.

He now wrote similar letters to all the corporations he had visited, thanking them for the great favour and respects he met with when he had the happiness to be among them, and promised that he would do his utmost to prevail upon the King to grant them the most favourable terms in their new charters, 'wherein,' he ended, 'I may manifest myself to be a hearty friend to your corporation.'

They were sadly disappointed with the new corporations when they got them, for they lost many of their existing benefits. Politicians are naturally soapy, but none more saponaceous than Jeffreys. He had served his King well.

Charles II died of an apoplexy in February 1685 and James II came to the throne. The Monmouth rebellion broke out in June, and failed a month later. Jeffreys was sent by a special commission to the West of England to deal with the rebels, and this was his infamous 'Bloody Assize'. Many people hold him entirely to blame for it, but this is quite wrong. James II fully approved of his 'campaign', of which he had daily reports, and when it was over made him Lord Chancellor, the highest office in the law, 'taking into consideration the many eminent and faithful services' he had performed.

His notorious behaviour during Alice Lisle's trial has been described as of 'historic severity', which is something of an understatement. Whenever he chose to debase justice, he was a monster.

It led to his downfall. In 1688, when William of Orange landed in England and James II threw the Great Seal into the Thames, Jeffreys cut off his bushy eyebrows and disguised himself as a sailor. But his luck ran out; he had bullied too many people in court for too long. He had frightened one poor plaintiff out of his wits, who was asked on leaving court how he came off: 'Came off?' he replied. 'I am escaped from the terrors of that man's face, which I would scarce undergo again to save my life, and I shall certainly have the most frightful impression of it as long as I live.'

In Wapping, this same man met the disguised Jeffreys, and raised the alarm. If Jeffreys had been only a moderately bad judge, he might never have been recognised. He was taken to the Tower of London, and died on 19 April 1689 at the age of 41, a prodigy in his own infamous way.

His three weeks upon the Northern Circuit are very little known, and form but a footnote to history. But they help to show him as he really was. Charles II was probably joking when he described him as having 'no knowledge, no sense, no manners and more impudence than ten carted street-walkers.'

Professor Keeton, on the other hand, in his book *Lord Chancellor Jeffreys and the Stuart Cause,* has studied Jeffreys' decisions when he was Lord Chancellor, and found his judgments sound; indeed, Roger North, who was no ready admirer of him, said of him as Chancellor that 'he became the seat of justice better than any other I ever saw in that place.'

Lord Birkenhead's verdict upon him is perhaps the best: 'It is certain that, whoever praises him, and in whatsoever age, he will go down to history as a blustering and bloody-minded rogue, convertible upon a shift of fortune into a fawning coward. And there is much to be said for this view.'

EIGHT

A Coiner's Trial

'*Don Ricardo*:
And what is counterfeiting, tell me that?
Merely to put a craftsman's noble art
Unto ignoble ends.'

Old Play

Some troubles come about quite silently. A wild-fowler on the estuary sands is not aware that the tide has cut him off till he feels it lapping round his ankles; there is no sign that a house has been eaten away by white ants till its timbers collapse in a choking cloud of dust. But the crime which almost ruined the country could be heard as a faint metallic sound: snip, snip.

The snipping comes as each coiner clips a few slivers from the edge of each silver shilling. The slivers mount up, enough to melt into a new coin, and not a word spoken as he puts the clipped coin back into circulation. The coins pass from hand to hand, each man glad to pass it on to his neighbour, and in the end they probably become the wages of a poor man who finds that the few coins in his weekly wage will buy less than half their face value. Indeed, at the end of the XVIIIth century, badly clipped coins were sold to shopkeepers, turnpike men, and waiters at the price of 20 shillings for 5*s.* 6*d.*, a quarter of their supposed value. They usually palmed them off amongst loose change.

So long as coins were crudely stamped by rough tools, the temptation to cut off the edges was always there, and hardly ever resisted. As regular money-lenders, the Jews were frequent offenders, but so were the Anglo-Saxons who worked in the mints, and in 1125 Henry I decreed a drastic punishment: anybody debasing the coinage was to lose his right hand and be castrated. Even so the practice continued; new coins had to be struck five times in the next 150 years.

It was indeed a serious matter. Queen Elizabeth made the offence High Treason, punishable by death, yet still the crime flourished, not least in West Yorkshire. The valleys close to the Pennines were remote enough for officers of the law to be seen coming afar off, and those who brought textiles across from Lancashire brought coins ripe for clipping.

It took so little capital for a coiner to set up in business: a good pair of shears to clip the edges, and a file to restore the milled edge to the coin; a mould of the right size for the melted clippings, and well-made dies to stamp the discs with the proper design. Some coiners made their own shillings, or even halfpennies, but they preferred to counterfeit not only guineas, half guineas and quarter guineas, but even more exotic denominations: pieces of 36s., 27s., 13s. 6d., and 6s. 9d., to say nothing of the Portuguese coins then current in England.

A guinea nowadays is always 21s., but time was when it was worth what you could get for it, and 21s. was the average value. A Quaker who visited Lancaster in the late XVIIth century was astonished at the state of the coins there. He paid 22s. for a guinea, and it fetched 30s. in London; he produced some half-crowns, newly minted and unclipped, and the shopkeepers viewed them with the darkest suspicion, never having seen the like before.

'It may well be doubted,' says the historian Macaulay, 'whether all the misery which had been inflicted on the English nation in a quarter of a century by bad kings, bad ministers, bad parliaments and bad judges was equal to the misery caused in a single year by bad crowns and bad shillings.'

Bad coinage, like rampant inflation, threatened to ruin the country. Daniel Awty, a Yorkshire clipper from Dewsbury, was very active at this time. He used to boast that he could clip three shillings of silver from every pound's worth.

The clippers could make a fortune; one who was caught offered to pay £6000 for a pardon. He was unsuccessful, but he could afford to pay such a sum. Yet, though the offence was extremely serious, it was very difficult to obtain a conviction for it, because juries did not recognise the massive evil it threatened. A few snips here and there seem such a little thing—some of them might even have done a little of it themselves.

What was the answer? A horse-driven mill was installed in 1663 at the London mint, to provide milled edges and better-made coins, intended to discredit the old ones. But the contrary happened, for people still accepted the bad ones, and either hoarded the new ones, or clipped them too.

It made no difference to Arthur Mangey of Leeds; he was hard at work in his goldsmith's shop, chasing the arabesques and fleurs-de-lis on the silver-gilt mace for the Corporation of Leeds. It bears their coat of arms: azure, a fleece suspended, or; on a chief sable, three mullets, argent; supporters, two owls ducally crowned; and on the upper edge of the base is his own proud legend: ARTHUR MANGEY DE LEEDS FECIT, 1694.

He was paid £60 for his fine workmanship, a considerable sum, but worth it. A man of his skill had no need to smear his fingers with crime, but gold and silver have an alluring glitter, even to goldsmiths. He might never have been accused of coining, for clippers could pay their cronies well, but in 1695 Parliament offered substantial rewards for those who gave information against the clippers. Any clipper who informed against two others got a free pardon—an attractive bargain when the law had caught up with him—and anybody who gave information against a coiner received £40.

There is no evidence that the chief witnesses against Arthur Mangey were paid for their help, but it is still a remarkable coincidence that the investigations into his premises should start within a year of the new law coming into effect.

Thus, in August 1696, Arthur Mangey stood his trial at York Assizes. The judge, John Turton, had been on the bench seven years. His most famous trial was to be that of Captain Kidd for piracy, in 1701, but in 1702 he was removed from the Bench for political reasons, and died six years later. Compared with Judge Jeffreys he was a model of judicial behaviour.

It is only right that this history of the Northern Circuit should include one complete trial. This one is short and easy to follow, and the details of the coiner's craft give it an added interest. It does not lack drama, for the shadow of the gallows lay across it. It is a fair sample of British justice in 1696, and is reprinted without any omissions. The most startling thing about it is that so many of the mediaeval procedures which can be seen when the Northern Circuit began in 1176 can still be found more than 500 years later.

YORK ASSIZES, Saturday 1st August 1696
Before the Lord Chief Baron Turton, and a jury.

The Court being sat, proceeded in this manner:

CLERK OF ARRAIGNMENT: Cryer, make proclamation.

CRYER: All manner of persons that have anything more to do at this general Assize of Nisi Prius, Oyer and Terminer and General Gaol Delivery, draw near and give your attendance.

CLERK: Set Mr Arthur Mangey to the Bar (*which was done*). Arthur Mangey, hold up thy hand. Thou stands indicted in the trial of your life and death. If, therefore, you will challenge them or any of them, your time is to challenge them as they come to the book to be sworn.

Every accused person is entitled to challenge jurors, within certain limits, whom he would not expect to try his case fairly. Arthur Mangey would be a very well known figure in Leeds, but not all his acquaintances might have a high regard for him.

Then the Jury was sworn, and the Prisoner challenged some Leeds men. At last those whose names are as follows were sworn:

Henry Bouch, Esquire	Thomas Dickings, Gentleman
Robert Metford, Esquire	James Stansfield, Gentleman
Thomas Ramsden, Esquire	Michael Wilson, Gentleman
Arthur Farrar, Esquire	Giles Dolliff, Gentleman
John Milner, Esquire	William Rousby, Gentleman
Thomas Grimstone, Esquire	John Wood, Gentleman

CLERK: Arthur Mangey, hold up thy hand (*which he did*). You, gentlemen of the Jury, look upon the prisoner and hearken to his cause. He stands indicted in the County of York by the name of Arthur Mangey aforesaid, in the Indictment and against the form of the statutes in that case made and provided. Upon this Indictment he hath been arraigned, and thereunto hath pleaded Not Guilty, and for his trial hath put himself upon God and his Country, which country you are. You are to enquire whether he be Guilty of the high treason whereof he stands indicted (in manner and form as he stands indicted) or Not Guilty. If you find him guilty you are to enquire what goods and chattels, lands and tenements he was possessed of at the time when the high treason was committed or at any time since; if you find him Not Guilty you are to enquire whether he fled for it. If you find he fled for it you are to enquire of his goods and chattels as if you had found him Guilty. If that you find him Not Guilty, nor that he fled for it, you are to say so, and no more, and hearken to the evidence.

When a Defendant put himself upon God and his country, it meant Trial by Jury. Arthur Mangey could have chosen Trial by Battle, even in 1696, for it was not abolished until more than 100 years later. If he was found guilty his goods would have been forfeited, and the jury was under the same duty to assess their value as at the Newcastle Assizes in 1256; and whether he fled from the crime or not had the same relevance as in the days when criminals sought sanctuary.

Counsel for the Prosecution now opens the case, but his name is not recorded. It is a pity that he remains anonymous, because the opening speech for the prosecution gives counsel an opportunity to show that he has mastered the details of a case, and can present it with such clarity that the jury cannot fail to understand it. Here, then, is that speech:

COUNSEL FOR THE KING: My Lord, and gentlemen of the Jury, here is a person indicted for stamping or counterfeiting this King's coin, which any man knows to be high treason. If, my Lord, we prove the fact upon him and that he did actually do the same, we need say no more.

That is the whole of his opening speech! Any counsel who was as brief today would soon find he went *un*briefed. It only shows how fashions change; Arthur Mangey's trial proceeds with great speed, yet seems unhurried; if it lasted a full week in modern times, nobody would think it unduly slow. But it is time for the first witness.

COUNSEL: Cryer, call George Norcross (*Norcross was sworn*).

MANGEY: My Lord, I desire the evidence [witness] may not have the liberty to have any person to stand by him to dictate to him what he should speak.

JUDGE TURTON: He shall not.

COUNSEL: Come, George Norcross, pray acquaint my Lord and gentlemen of the Jury with all the particular concerns you have had with Mr Mangey.

NORCROSS: If it please your Lordship, I was going one day through Mr Wainman's court, and in one of the rooms as I passed by sat Mr Mangey and one Mortimer, another goldsmith. Mr Mangey called of me and desired me to come and take a glass with him, and told me I should be very welcome, so I went into their company. And when we had drunk a glass or two Mortimer left us, so, nobody being near, he told me he wanted a servant, and that he knew none he could have better than myself, for that he looked upon me to be an honest man, and he had some business in haste, and he would give me five shillings a day when he had employment for me. Accordingly, I went the next morning and found my master looking our of a window and ready to let me in, but some scamperers passing by disturbed us, so that I believe it was almost four o'clock before I could get in privately.

JUDGE: Those scamperers you speak of I'm afraid were bad husbands!

NORCROSS: Yes, my Lord. Afterwards I went and my master came himself and let me in, and carried me into a garret chamber and brought me a bag full of money new clipped (I believe it might contain above a hundred pound), and showed me the way how I might both file and rub it, and afterwards sat down and clipped beside me. And I received five shillings that night for my day's work.

JUDGE: This is nothing to the purpose; I do not ask you any questions about clipping, rubbing or filing. Did you ever see Mr Mangey *stamp* or *counterfeit* the King's coin?

NORCROSS: My Lord, after I had been with him some time he told me I was very expert, but (says he) "you have not seen all my art yet." So, bringing up a piece of thin plate as I supposed (but he afterwards told me it was mixed metal and not good plate), so clipping it round into the form of new shillings he began and stamped the one side with exactly the face side of King Charles the Second. Turning the other side with another stamp he made the cross side exactly, and with another instrument at three turns he made nicks upon the edge very dexterously and told me that twenty shillings when finished stood him not above ten shillings, being of mixed metal.

JUDGE: But how did he for spoiling the impression he had made on the face side?

NORCROSS: My Lord, he had a piece of soft wood which he laid upon the main baulk of the house, upon which he laid the piece of money when he stamped the cross side to keep the face side from being harmed; which, when he had placed betwixt the face side and the baulk, he struck upon the second stamp with a forge hammer as he did before, and made the cross side as I told your Lordship before. The place upon the baulk is grown bright with continual use and fair to be seen, and he likewise told me, my Lord, that he paid these shillings by putting four or five in every twenty shillings. And this is the whole truth, my Lord and you gentlemen of the Jury.

Now that the witness had given his evidence, in his own words and without counsel intervening, the accused was entitled to question it. At this time the law did not allow those accused of High Treason to be represented by counsel, but Mangey was entitled to ask questions himself. He was not very lucky in the answers he got.

MANGEY: My Lord, this fellow tells your Lordship they were King Charles the Second shillings. I desire I may show him a piece of money and see if he can tell whose coin it is, for he is an ignorant fellow and cannot read.

JUDGE: Mr Mangey, I believe there is many a person in the nation who cannot read letters upon the book, and yet shall know any piece of money you can show them whose coin it is, by reason of their frequent seeing of it.

MANGEY (*showing him a piece of money*): What coin is this?

NORCROSS (*reading the inscription*): It is a Queen Elizabeth shilling.

MANGEY (*showing him another piece*): What coin is this?

NORCROSS: It is a King William's sixpence.

COUNSEL: Show him one of his own making, and see if he knows that!

JUDGE: Do you see, Mr Mangey? He not only knows the several coins, but likewise can read—which you said he could not. Come, Mr Attorney, what further witnesses have you?

COUNSEL: Call Peter Nicholson, commonly called Peter o'th' Horsemill.

The next two witnesses are both accomplices of the accused, and their evidence ought to be regarded with great suspicion.

PETER NICHOLSON: Here I am (*Who was sworn*).

COUNSEL: Pray inform my Lord and the Jury what you know concerning Mr Mangey endeavouring to corrupt the King's evidence [coinage].

NICHOLSON: My Lord, I was going through a street in Leeds called Bridgegate, and Mr Mangey called me into one Mortimer's house (a goldsmith who keeps a cup of ale, and was formerly Mr Mangey's journeyman, but being accused for clipping is since run away), where Mr Mangey was saying he wanted one to do a little private business he had in hand. And Mortimer answered 'A man fitter for your business, and a faithfuller person you cannot have than Peter here, for he will not fail you in any thing.'

I told him if I could serve him anything I should be very willing, so he bid me be at home and not be absent, for at three o'clock in the afternoon he would come to my house and acquaint me what service I should do him, and drink a cup of ale with me (for my Lord, I keep ale). Accordingly, he came at the time appointed and told me there was one Dorothy Greaves whom he feared would inform against him for buying clippings, and desired me to carry her a guinea, and tell her if she would abscond and go into the country, and not appear against him either at Assizes or Sessions, he would take care to provide horses for both her and me, and I would be the person who should carry her off, and that he would maintain her at his own proper charge.

So, my Lord, I went to Doll and told her what Mr Mangey bid me. So she promised she would go whither I should carry her. So I gave her the guinea, and when the time appointed came Mr Mangey sent me word the horses were ready for us, so I went to Dorothy Greaves to see if she was ready to go. But her answer then was she did not, but the design was to convey her where perhaps she might never come again, so that she would not go with me.

JUDGE: Is this all you can say?

NICHOLSON: Yes, my Lord.

COUNSEL: Call Dorothy Greaves, alias Doll Sim.

DOROTHY GREAVES: Here.

COUNSEL: Dorothy Greaves, pray tell my Lord and the gentlemen of the Jury what you know of the prisoner at the Bar.

DOROTHY: My Lord, I have sold Mr Mangey clippings.

JUDGE: Woman, what quantity?

DOROTHY: At one time, my Lord, three ounces of which I gave information to the Mayor and Aldermen of Leeds. After which this Peter Nicholson came to me as he said, with a message from Mr Mangey that if I would not appear against him neither at Assizes nor Sessions, he had a guinea from him for me. As Peter has told you, I told him I would consider of it, and give him an answer. So, my Lord, I went to the Aldermen I had given my information to and told them what Peter offered me, and they bade me not to refuse the guinea if it was offered me again. So I went to Peter Nicholson and told him if he would give me the guinea, I would convey myself, so he gave it me.

My Lord, a little after this he came to me again and told me the horses were ready; I told him, my Lord, I would not be conveyed by him, for he had cheated me, for I heard Mr Mangey had given him two guineas to give me, and he had but given me one. Another time, my Lord, I received a five shillings piece from Mr Mangey's. On the same account I went to Alderman Massey and made him acquainted with the whole matter. And this is all I can say.

JUDGE: Have you any questions to ask this evidence, Mr Mangey?

MANGEY: My Lord, I can make it appear by my servants in Court, I have turned this woman out of doors several times.

JUDGE: It appears by that, she has been at your house.

The next three witnesses were not accomplices of Arthur Mangey, and their evidence against him would be quite conclusive.

COUNSEL: Pray let Mr Henry Iveson (Mayor of Leeds), Mr William Massey, Mr John Preston, Mr John Dodgson, Aldermen, be sworn (*which was done*). Mr Mayor, pray tell my Lord and the Jury what you know concerning the prisoner at the Bar.

MAYOR: My Lord and gentlemen of the Jury, when George Norcross the King's evidence came to give his information relating to Mr Mangey, he told us in the garret chamber where they wrought was fair to be seen a remarkable place upon the baulk which goes cross the chamber, on which he stamped the shillings he see him coin, which was grown bright and smooth. And a particular place where they used to fix their great shears with which they clipped half crowns, for that they had a lesser pair for clipping shillings and sixpences, and that we might see whether it was as he had sworn.

Alderman Massey, Alderman Preston, Alderman Dodgson, and myself resolved to go and view the room (which we did), and found both the place where the great shears were fixed, and a remarkable place where he used to coin upon the baulk.

JUDGE: Come, Mr Massey, what can you say?

ALDERMAN MASSEY: My Lord, after the King's evidence had given his information against Mr Mangey and mentioned the remarkable places where he clipped and coined, I was desirous to see it, upon which I was one that went to view it. And when I came into one chamber there was in one corner like shelves of a closet, but it proved to be the way that led into the garret where Mr Mangey used to clip and coin; and those boards I took to be shelves proved to be the steps into the garret, and the passage was so straight that I was forced to put off my frock and to creep on my hands and my knees, going in and coming out.

MANGEY: Alderman Massey, you say the passage was so straight—pray, then, how could you get up and down?

JUDGE: Mr Mangey, Alderman Massey tells you he was to strip himself to get up. Alderman Preston, what say *you*?

ALDERMAN PRESTON: My Lord, George Norcross acquainted me that if we would go with him into Mr Mangey's room he would show us something to confirm his evidence. Accordingly, my Lord, we went and found the hole where Norcross had said they fixed their great shears for clipping half crowns, and the bright place upon the baulk where Mr Mangey coined. And when we were in the room

Norcross took up a board and said, 'They used to throw their shears there,' upon which I bid him put in his arm.

And he said he felt nothing, but putting his arm further he pulled out these shears, and observing that betwixt the joints of the boards was so much distance that something might slip betwixt, we resolved to pull up one of the boards just where they clipped, where we found these clippings of half crowns which I put into this purse with the shears, and sealed it up; and it was never opened since.

Here is likewise a pumice stone which George Norcross told us he used in rubbing the money when clipped, and further told us the last time he had use of it he left it betwixt the slates, and looked but found it not. So at our coming out of the house we asked one Mr Benjamin Mangey's wife, who now lives in the house, if she found no such thing wrapped up in a paper and put betwixt the slates. She said, Truly she did find something in a paper, but what use it was for she knew not, and said she had laid it by but would bring it. And upon her bringing it, though at a distance, Norcross seeing the paper said that was it, this being the same.

JUDGE: Alderman Dodgson, what say you?

Alderman Dodgson gave the same evidence touching the chamber as his brethren.

He was the last of the prosecution witnesses. It is now Arthur Mangey's turn to present his case, and although he was not himself allowed to give evidence, he was able to say anything he liked, and to call witnesses.

JUDGE: Mr Mangey, you hear what evidence the King's witnesses have given. What have you to say for yourself, or what witnesses would you have called?

MANGEY: I thank your Lordship, and desire Captain Barton may be called.

CRYER: Captain Barton. *He appeared.*

MANGEY: Captain Barton, pray tell my Lord and the Jury concerning what you saw at my house.

CAPTAIN BARTON: My Lord and you gentlemen of the Jury, I had a curiosity to see the town of Leeds, upon which I got the company of one parson Cowton, a Minister of a church in this City. Having got to Leeds we lighted at Mr Wainman's at the Swan, where when we had been some time Mr Cowton told me the next house to our Landlord's was Mr Mangey's, who was accused for clipping and coining, and if I pleased he would go with me into the house to view the room as it was said he coined in. Which, when I came there, I found it to be a place private enough for such a concern, but they told me he coined upon the main baulk of the house with a stroke of a forge hammer.

MANGEY: Pray, Captain Barton, tell my Lord whether it be possible to do such a thing with a stroke of a forge hammer.

BARTON: My Lord, I must confess (so far as I know what relates to coining) I think it almost impossible to coin after that manner, the baulk not being solid.

JUDGE: Captain Barton, you say you think it almost impossible to coin upon the main baulk of an house because it is not solid. Now, if the main baulk of a house be not solid, then nothing I know is solid; but pray tell me how came you to go to Leeds on this occasion? I am confident you must be employed by Mr Mangey or somebody else.

BARTON: My Lord, I am altogether a stranger to Mr Mangey, and was no ways employed by him.

At this moment there was an unexpected interruption—the informality of this trial is one of its most striking features.

Then one Mr Horsley stood up and desired to be sworn.

HORSLEY: My Lord, I came hither today but as a spectator to hear Mr Mangey's trial, but hearing Captain Barton tell your Lordship that he is a stranger to Mr Mangey, and that he was not sent to Leeds by his order in order to view his room, I thought myself obliged in Conscience to tell your Lordship what I know of the matter. For, my Lord, when Mr Hawley the ordinary at the castle preached his sermon to the prisoners before the Assize, I was one that came out of the city to hear him, and after the sermon I was walking in the castle yard with Mr Mangey, and he told me that he had sent a few to Captain Barton to Leeds to view his room where he was said to coin.

JUDGE: How now, Captain Barton, do you hear what this gentleman swears? Pray, what is your employment?

BARTON: I am made Controller at the Mint for York.

JUDGE: A very pretty man to be employed in the King and Country's service, and comes here in evidence against the

King, and to encourage rogues in that which now the nations groan under! I'll promise you, I'll let you be known in another place. How came you to come hither?

BARTON: I had not comed if one of your Lordship's officers had not comed and told me you sent for me.

JUDGE: But where is that officer? Let him but be found and I'll clap him by the heels, and if the parson was here that went with you, I would do as much for him.

But the officer could not be found, for it was not one of the Judge's officers, but a roguish attorney whom Mangey had employed.

JUDGE: Mr Mangey, if you have any more witnesses, pray call them.

MANGEY: Cryer, call my man Woodhouse.

CRYER: Mr Mangey, it is not my place to call your witnesses.

MANGEY: But pray, Sir, do me that favour, and I shall satisfy you.

It was observed that Mr Mangey gave the Cryer two half-crowns, one of which was rank copper, which the Cryer gave him to change!

CRYER: Woodhouse, Mr Mangey's man.

WOODHOUSE: Here.

MANGEY: Woodhouse, pray tell my Lord what you know of Norcross.

WOODHOUSE: My Lord, this Norcross was one who lived beside my Master's, and kept a cobbler's shop, and has mended my shoes several times, for which I paid him.

JUDGE: But, Woodhouse, have you never known Norcross come to your Master's upon any other account?

WOODHOUSE: No, my Lord.

JUDGE: Nor have you never heard any knocking in a garret chamber?

WOODHOUSE: No, my Lord.

NORCROSS: My Lord, it was agreed betwixt Mr Mangey that to prevent suspicion I was to carry a shoe or two in my hand when I went to work.

JUDGE: How many days might you work in a week?

NORCROSS: Sometimes three or four or five days in a week, sometimes not one day, just as work came in.

JUDGE: You just wrought as work came in?

NORCROSS: Yes, my Lord.

JUDGE: Well, Mr Mangey, have you any more witnesses to call?

MANGEY: Yes, call my servant maid and nurse.

CRYER: Mr Mangey's maid and nurse.

MAID: Here.

JUDGE: Maid, what can you say concerning Norcross?

MAID: He was one who mended shoes belonging to the family, and I never see more of him than carrying and fetching shoes.

JUDGE: Do you know nothing of his going into a garret chamber, and whether you ever heard a knocking there?

MAID: No, my Lord.

JUDGE: But have you no other stairs that lead through this garret but through the kitchen?

MAID: Yes, my Lord, out of the shop.

JUDGE: Then why might he not go that way?

He could, of course, and not be seen. But there was another defence witness to be called.

CRYER: Mr Mangey's nurse.

NURSE: Here.

JUDGE: How long have you lived with Mr Mangey?

NURSE: Twelve months, my Lord.

JUDGE: And do you know George Norcross?

NURSE: Yes, he used to mend our shoes.

JUDGE: Have you never seen him go into a garret chamber where your master and he used to work?

NURSE: No, my Lord.

JUDGE: Call what other witnesses you have, Mr Mangey.

MANGEY: I thank your Lordship. Call Susan the wife of George Norcross.

Mangey wanted to discredit George Norcross by showing that he had been guilty of bigamy, an offence which was then dealt with by the ecclesiastical courts. It was not a time when Roman Catholic priests were in official favour with the Protestant establishment.

JUDGE: What do you call this woman for?

MANGEY: An't please your Lordship, Norcross has two

109

wives of which this is the one; the other lives with him at
Leeds, and I hope your Lordship will consider that such a
person as this ought not to be credited in this case as an
evidence.

JUDGE: Mr Mangey, who ever advised you to bring this
woman has done you no kindness; you ought to have informed the spiritual court of this, and have proceeded
against him according to law, but all that you bring against
the evidence will be insignificant except you can prove him
guilty of perjury or malice. But nothing you yet produce
amounts to that; but let us hear what she says.

Didst thou ever sell Mr Mangey any clippings, or was thou
ever concerned in the clipping trade with him?

SUSAN: No, my Lord, I am George Norcross' wife.

JUDGE: How came you to be his wife? Who married you?

SUSAN: A very honest gentleman, my Lord.

JUDGE: What was he?

SUSAN: A Roman Catholic priest, my Lord.

JUDGE: A very honest gentleman, indeed! Was it in a
church, or a house?

SUSAN: A house, my Lord.

JUDGE: Was you married by the book of Common Prayer?

SUSAN: No, my Lord.

JUDGE: Mr Mangey, whoever it was advised you to bring
this woman missed the matter; she has done you hurt, and
no good.

MANGEY: My Lord, I was not the occasion of fetching her,
she was brought by Esquire Holroyd, Mr Walker, Mr Firth,
Mr Totty, and Mr Lumley. I can prove it by them, she was
not fetched upon my account.

JUDGE: Woman, who hired you to come?

SUSAN: Nobody, my Lord.

JUDGE: Who bears your charges?

SUSAN: The Town, my Lord.

ALDERMAN DODGSON: My Lord, when this woman
came first to Leeds we had her before my Brother Massey
and myself; and examining how she never came to challenge
him for her husband before now, he having lived so long
among us, her answer was, she was hired to it, else had not
comed.

JUDGE: Mr Mangey, have you any more witnesses?

MANGEY: Yes, my Lord. Cryer, call Mr James Blades.

BLADES: Here.

MANGEY: Mr Blades, pray tell my Lord and the Jury if you did not hear that the Aldermen of Leeds promised Esquire Holroyd that if he would go home they would cease his prosecution.

JUDGE: Mr Blades, did you hear these words?

BLADES: No, my Lord.

MANGEY: Call Mr Holroyd.

CRYER: Mr John Holroyd.

HOLROYD: Here.

MANGEY: Mr Holroyd, pray tell my Lord and the Jury what you heard concerning the Aldermen of Leeds promising if you would go home they would cease your prosecution.

HOLROYD: My Lord, I did not say so: I said I met with Mr Lee the Town Clerk of Leeds, and he told me he believed if I would go home, I might, for there would be no prosecution against me. But I told him as I was come to have it tried, I would stay.

JUDGE: Mr Mangey, would you call any more witnesses?

One cannot tell from the transcript of the trial that the Judge was at all exasperated at this point, but none of the witnesses Mr Mangey had called so far had advanced his case in the slightest.

MANGEY: Mr Cryer, call Mr Henry Ellis, Mr John Wray, Mr Joseph Lofthouse, Mr Thomas Pease, Mr George Wainman.

He was now calling evidence to show that he was a highly respected man. Even this was not very successful.

CRYER: Mr Henry Ellis.

ELLIS: Here.

MANGEY: Mr Ellis, pray tell my Lord and the Jury what you know of me.

ELLIS: I have several times had monies of him upon bills, and the money was such as was then current; and what I could not pay he was willing to change.

So answered Wray, Pease and Lofthouse.

CRYER: Mr George Wainman.

WAINMAN: Here.

MANGEY: Pray, Mr Wainman, tell my Lord and the Jury what you know of me.

WAINMAN: My Lord, Mr Mangey was my next door neighbour, and as far as I see of him an honest man. I once bought a parcel of wines of him and paid him for them.

JUDGE: Mr Wainman, did you never hear any knocking in a garret chamber?

WAINMAN: No, my Lord.

MANGEY: Cryer, call Mr Askell, Mr Hassell and Mr Naylor.

But none of them appeared.

MANGEY: Call Robert Colthurst.

COLTHURST: Here, my Lord. This George Norcross was at Rodwell gaol, and I having occasion to go thither I see him there, and he asked me how Mr Mangey did. I told him Mr Mangey would hang him, but his answer was he would hang Mr Mangey. My Lord, Mr Mangey is a man I have several times wrought for, and he always paid me well and honestly; I have addled I believe three score pound of him, and he hath paid me to a penny.

He meant that some of the money Arthur Mangey gave him was bad, but he made up the value with good money.

JUDGE: Then you need not fear to lose anything by him. Have you any more witnesses to call, Mr Mangey?

MANGEY: None, my Lord, but what are called.

JUDGE: Have you any friends in Court that can speak for you?

MANGEY: There's Mr Milner, a Merchant.

MILNER: My Lord, I had never to do with the man in all my life, neither directly nor indirectly but once. When I was newly married I bought some plate of him to the value of forty pound.

JUDGE: Well, but what can you say as to his reputation?

MILNER: He had the same reputation the rest of the goldsmiths in Leeds had.

JUDGE: Mr Mangey, would you ask Norcross any questions?

MANGEY: I hope, my Lord, by what you have heard my

servants speak, your Lordship and the jury will not think that I should ere repose so much confidence in Norcross as to let him see me do such an act as he accuses me for. I must confess I have bought great quantities of clippings of him several times.

JUDGE: The fitter man for you to confide in. Have you anything further to say for yourself?

MANGEY: No, my Lord.

Mangey's final comments upon the evidence were almost as short as the opening speech for the prosecution.

The Judge now sums up. He does not warn the jury about the danger of believing accomplices, but there was plenty of evidence to corroborate what Norcross said. He puts both sides of the case plainly and simply. One has only to look at Judge Jeffrey's style in a case only twelve years earlier to see what an unfair summing-up could be.

JUDGE: Gentlemen of the Jury, you have heard the evidence that hath been given against Mr Arthur Mangey, the prisoner at the Bar, which I shall not be long in repeating of, but give you as short a rehearsal of it as I can.

In the first place you hear George Norcross, the King's evidence, gives you an account of how Mr Mangey and he came acquainted and what agreement they came to, that Mr Mangey was to give him five shillings a day for every day that he wrought with him, which was sometimes three or four or five days in a week but just as work came in; that it was his business to rub and file the money that Mr Mangey clipped; and that he might not be suspected when he went to work, the agreement was betwixt them that he should carry a shoe or two in his hand when he went to work as if he was carrying work home which he had done for the house. But that which is most to the purpose is, he tells you he see Mr Mangey bring a long piece of thin plate which Mr Mangey told him was mixed metal, and out of that he cut a piece as big as a new shilling which, upon a main baulk of a house in a garret chamber, he stamped on one side (with exactly the face side) with an instrument, and then to prevent the impression from being harmed he placed a piece of soft wood betwixt the face side and the baulk, and with a second instrument he made the cross side, then with a third instrument he made nicks upon the edges, and when he had made these 'shillings' as he called them, he told Norcross that twenty of them when finished cost him about ten shillings, and that he paid them by putting four or five in every twenty shillings.

He further tells you the respective places where they performed all their work. One place they had where they placed their great shears to clip half crowns (for they had a lesser pair for clipping shillings and sixpences with), and to give greater credit to what he has sworn you have it confirmed by the Mayor of Leeds and three Aldermen of Leeds, for their own satisfaction went to view the room, and they tell you they found things just as the King's evidence has told you. And for further confirmation you have it proved by these gentlemen that whilst they were in the garret chamber Norcross showed them a private place where they used to lay their shears, and one of them bid him put in his arm and feel if there was anything; whereupon, further putting his arm, they found the shears they used for clipping small money, as also upon taking up a board in the floor they found some clippings of half crowns under the place where the evidence had told them they fixed their shears for that use. You have also a pumice stone shown you with which Norcross tells you he rubbed the money after Mr Mangey had clipped it, all which circumstances confirms Norcross' evidence very much.

It appears further by the other witnesses, Peter Nicholson and Dorothy Greaves, that Mr Mangey did employ Peter Nicholson to bribe Dorothy Greaves with a guinea not to appear against him either at Assizes nor Sessions for buying clippings, which argues much guilt in Mr Mangey. Thus far, gentlemen, you have the King's witnesses, which in my thought is very plain and full.

Now the Defence. Mr Mangey makes it first by showing Norcross a piece of money, saying he could not read, thereby to detect him in his evidence that he could not know King Charles the Second's coin from others (he having sworn it was a shilling in imitation of King Charles the Second that he see him coin). Now it fairly appeared to you that he not only knew the difference of coins, but that he could read the inscription. The second is by bringing his maid and nurse to prove upon what account Norcross used to come to his house, and that they never knew any other business he had but his own calling of mending the family's shoes. He brings likewise Captain Barton (one employed in the mint for York) to tell you he believes it impossible to coin in that room. Now, Captain Barton tells you he went to Leeds out of curiosity to see the town, and not by any entreaty of Mr Mangey, he having no acquaintance with him; but to show you that this was a made journey betwixt them comes Mr Horsley, a citizen, who heard Mr Mangey say he had sent Captain Barton to Leeds to view the chamber.

He brings you likewise a woman who tells you the evidence has two wives of which she is one, and yet by what she says it does not appear it is so, but was hired to come (as you hear Alderman Dodgson tells you she confessed before him), if not by Mr Mangey, yet by some of his accomplices. But, in case she had been lawfully married to him, yet he having never been lawfully convicted of it, this could not lessen or invalidate his evidence against Mr Mangey. Nor do I find that Mr Mangey can charge Norcross with so much as one immoral action, but by making such defence as this he makes himself appear the more guilty.

Gentlemen, if you believe what has been proved against Mr Mangey be true you are to find him guilty, but on the contrary if you believe what Mr Mangey and his servants tell you and discredit the evidence for the King you are to find him not guilty. But, so far as I see, gentlemen, it appears otherwise; but it is not I, but you must be his Judges in this case, so I shall say no more to you.

Then the Jury withdrew and in less than half an hour returned and were called over.

CLERK OF ARRAIGNMENT: Gentlemen, are you agreed of your verdict?
JURY: Yes.
CLERK: Who shall say for you?
JURY: Our Foreman.
CLERK: Arthur Mangey, hold up thy hand. How say you, is Arthur Mangey guilty of High Treason whereof he stands indicted, or Not Guilty?
FOREMAN: Guilty.

CLERK: Lord have mercy upon him. Look to him, Gaoler. What goods or chattels, lands or tenements had he at the time of the High Treason committed, or at any time since?
JURY: None that we know of.

Perhaps the Jury treated the question about the goods which could be forfeited as a pure formality, because the evidence clearly showed that Arthur Mangey was in a thriving way of business as a goldsmith at the time. But it was more likely to be an act of compassion towards his family, for if they had declared he possessed any goods, they would have been forfeited.

CLERK: Then hearken to your verdict as the Court hath recorded it. You say Arthur Mangey is guilty of the High Treason whereof he stands indicted, but that he had not goods or chattels, lands or tenements at the time of the High Treason committed or at any time since, and so say you all?
JURY: Yes.

Then the Gaoler took back his prisoner to the Castle, and the Court went about other business till about ten o'clock at night, when the prisoners who had been found guilty were brought into Court, and Mr Mangey went to the Bar, having his eldest son in one hand and his eldest daughter in the other.

CLERK: Arthur Mangey, hold up thy hand. Thou stands convicted of High Treason for counterfeiting the current coin of this realm. What hast thou to say for thyself why sentence shall not be pronounced against thee, to die according to law?
MANGEY: My Lord, I beg of your Lordship in the midst of judgment to remember mercy, and to have pity on my poor children of which these are eldest of seven; their mother at this time at the point of death in childbed of the seventh.
JUDGE: Mr Mangey, you should have considered the loss your children should have when it was in your power to have prevented it. It is not in mine now to show you any favour, for the sentence which is going to be put on you is not mine, but what the law inflicts, which is:

'That you be carried to the place from whence you came, and from thence be drawn on a hurdle to the place of

Execution, there to be hanged by the neck till you be dead. And the Lord have mercy upon your soul.'

The Execution was deferred till after the time that the ordinary malefactors were executed, and after that he had two several reprieves. At last his death warrant came, in pursuance of which he was executed the second day of October following, in the presence of several thousands of spectators. Before he was put off, he gave out and sang part of the 73rd Psalm, from the 25th verse to the end, and making his Address to the people present he desired them not to throw the ignominious death in the teeth of his wife and children, for they knew not but it might be any of their own cases to die by false accusation, as he declared he did, delivering the Sheriff a paper which he declared as he was a dying man contained nothing but the truth.

After which the Executioner did his office.

And when he was dead and cut down, his body was conveyed in a mourning hearse to York, and the day following was buried at St Mary's Church, Castlegate, York, in great state. Mr Coulton (the Minister mentioned in the trial) preached his funeral sermon, and took his text in the 73rd Psalm, and 25th verse.

So Mangey was hanged. They set up a mint at York that year to circulate good coins in the North; its issue has a 'Y' beneath the King's head. But the days of the Yorkshire coiners were far from over. Seventy years later David Hartley, a Birmingham man, established himself on a lonely spot on the moors near Halifax with his father and brothers. 'King David' they called him, and a golden reign it was indeed. The local people would bring him coins, and he would give them back with half the clippings, keeping the other half for his own profit.

It caused the Customs and Excise much anxiety, and Mr Deighton, one of their officers, pressed too hard on King David's heels for safety. He was lured into an ambush, and brutally murdered in 1759. However, King David's luck ran out 11 years later, when he was hanged at York.

When Arthur Mangey was hanged, some people believed he was innocent—he was, after all, convicted partly on the evidence of an accomplice. In 1832, however, some workmen

117

in Leeds pulled down his old house. In his main room upstairs was a little cupboard, with what seemed like shelves, but in reality narrow stairs up which one might crawl into the secret room in the roof. They found the beam which he had worn smooth with illegal coining, some of his illegal implements, and some clippings from half crowns, which in themselves would have proved his guilt.

Justice had been done to Arthur Mangey.

NINE

A Little Trip Round The Circuit

'How fine it is to enter some old town,walled and
turreted, just at the approach of night-fall, or to
come to some straggling village, with the lights
streaming through the surrounding gloom; and
then after enquiring for the best entertainment
that the place affords, to "take one's ease at one's
inn!"'

William Hazlitt, *On Going a Journey*

The Northern Circuit can mean several things. Until 1876 it
meant not only Lancashire, Westmorland and Cumberland,
but Durham, Northumberland and Yorkshire as well. It also
meant the members of the Bar who travelled from one assize
town to the next with the judges and to them it meant a good
deal of effort and expense.

It was quite a feat to go the Circuit in the days of stage-
coaches. They existed in Stuart times, and in 1685 the roads
were still dreadfully bad. According to the great historian
Macaulay (himself a member of the Circuit), 'It was only in
fine weather that the whole breadth of the road was available
for wheeled vehicles. Often the mud lay deep on the right and
left and only a narrow track of firm ground rose above the
quagmire.'

The journeys could be very dangerous. 'Though my wife
used to fear my passage over Humber,' wrote Thomas
Rokeby, a member of the Circuit in the late XVIIth century,
'yet my coming that way this time was by the providence of
God ordered much for the best, for my fellow travellers which
parted from me to go the usual road rid over the boot tops at
Newark, but I (blessed be God) never rid ankle deep the way I
came; and I never had my health better in all my life than this
journey.'

The danger in crossing an estuary was of being swept away

by the tide. His own nephew was drowned there and the body never found. Similar hazards existed on the western side of the Circuit, at Morecambe Bay; this was the experience of a very famous member of the Circuit, John Scott, later to become Lord Chancellor Eldon.

'In going from Ulverstone to Lancaster,' he wrote, 'you may go by the sea shore, or by a road inland. The former is much the shorter ride, but very dangerous, if the tide comes in. I asked the landlord of the inn at Ulverstone whether any persons were ever lost in going by the sea shore to Lancaster, as our party wished to save time, and go by the nearest way there. No, No, he answered, I think that nobody has ever been lost—they have all been found again at low water.'

John Scott is a most helpful guide around the Circuit. He found it not only risky, but expensive:

One year I did not go the Circuit [he recalled], because I could not afford it. I had borrowed of my brother for several circuits, without getting adequate remuneration.

He first rode the Circuit in 1775, and found it difficult to assemble his equipage.

At last I hired a horse for myself and borrowed another for an inexperienced youth who was to ride behind me with my saddlebags. But I thought my chance was gone for, having been engaged in a discussion with a travelling companion, on approaching the assize town I looked behind, but there was no appearance of my clerk and I was obliged to ride back several miles, till I found him crying by the roadside, his horse at some distance from him, and the saddle-bags still further off; and it was not without great difficulty that I could accomplish the reunion between them, which he had in vain attempted. Had I failed too in this undertaking, I should never have been Lord Chancellor.

Most members of the Circuit lived in London, and only went north for the Spring and Summer Assizes. A placard explains how to start the journey.

YORK FOUR DAYS
STAGE-COACH
Begins on Friday the 12th April 1706.

All that are desirous to pass from *London* to *York,* or from *York* to *London,* or any other place on that road; let them repair to the *Black Swan* in Holborn in *London,* and to the *Black Swan,* in *Coney Street* in *York.*

At both which places they may be received in a *Stage Coach* every *Monday, Wednesday* and *Friday,* which performs the whole journey in four days (if God permits) and sets forth at five in the morning.

And returns from *York* to *Stamford* in two days, and from Stamford, by Huntingdon to London in two days more.

And the like stages on their return.

Allowing each passenger 14 lb. weight; and all above 3d. a pound.

Performed by (Benjamin Kingman
(Henry Harrison
(Walter Baynes

Members of the Bar have keen appetites, and the coaches stopped for refreshments at Ware, in Hertfordshire. William Wordsworth's only comment during a stagecoach breakfast in 1805 was that the buttered toast 'looked for all the world as if it had been soaked in hot water'; it does not do the meal justice. But Master Tom Brown, on the way to Rugby for his first schooldays in about 1830, was a keen trencherman. He (or at least his author, Thomas Hughes) became a barrister, and then a county court judge.

'Twenty minutes here, gentlemen,' says the coachman, as they pull up at half-past seven at the inn door.

Have we not endured nobly this morning, and is not this a worthy reward for much endurance? . . . The table covered with the whitest of cloths and of china, and bearing a pigeon pie, ham, round of cold boiled beef cut from a mammoth ox, and the great loaf of household bread on a wooden trencher. And here comes in the stout head waiter, puffing under a tray of hot viands: kidneys and a steak, transparent rashers and poached eggs, buttered toast and muffins, coffee and tea, all smoking hot. The table can never hold it all; the cold meats are removed to the sideboard—they were only put on for show and to give us an appetite. And now fall on, gentlemen all.

Tom stopped at an inn famous for its breakfasts, and was travelling on one of the fast coaches. This was advisable because the word 'slow coach' passed into the language as a symbol of tedious delay. It used to be said that a man with a wooden leg was offered a lift in a slow coach but preferred to walk, as he was in a hurry.

Tom rode on top of the coach; it was cheaper that way. So did James Losh, the Newcastle barrister, even at the age of 65—all the way from Newcastle to London—and loved it. Anyone may ride on top of a stage coach, provided he knows his place, and does not attempt to mix with the inside passengers. Thomas de Quincey saw an 'outsider' commit this outrage:

> What words, then [he wrote], could express the horror and the sense of treason, in that case, which had happened, where all three outsides (the trinity of pariahs) made a vain attempt to sit down at the same breakfast table or dinner table with the consecrated four? I myself witnessed such an attempt, and on that occasion a benevolent old gentleman endeavoured to soothe his three holy associates by suggesting that, if the outsides were indicted for this criminal attempt at the next assizes, the court would regard it as a case of lunacy or *delirium tremens* rather than that of treason.

When the coach reached Huntingdon it was half way to the Northern Circuit territory. Winter weather presented serious dangers, for passengers had vanished in snow drifts. There was another hazard for stagecoach passengers, amongst whom is the Rev. William Macritchie, a Scottish minister touring the North of England in 1795. He published a most informative Journal: 'At Bawtrey enter Yorkshire,' he noted. 'Pass over a desert common. Dark: converse about robbers: no guard attends us: all of us unarmed. Arrive at Doncaster at eleven p.m., thank god, without any untoward accident having befallen us.'

Clavel, the reformed highwayman, had some useful advice for those who risked being waylaid:

—Never travel with strangers, especially if they seem willing to travel with you.

—Never travel on Sundays; only people with important missions do it, which makes them an obvious target. The roads are quieter, too, and if the worst happens, the judges are not sympathetic to those who travel on the Lord's Day.
—If you must carry large sums of money, travel at night. Highwaymen will not expect it, and cannot aim a pistol accurately in the dark. But beware of inquisitive potboys and postilions. They may be in league with the highwaymen.

There is no record of any member of the Northern Circuit being held up by a highwayman. John Scott carried no pistols, but one of his companions did. One morning Scott awoke in an inn to find a man in his bedroom, dressed in black. 'Please your honour,' said the intruder, 'I am only a poor sweep, and I believe I've come down the wrong chimney.'

'My friend,' said Scott, 'you have come down the right one, for I will give you sixpence to buy a pot of beer. But the gentleman in the next room sleeps with loaded pistols under his pillow, and if you had paid *him* a visit, he would have blown your brains out!'

From Doncaster to York, the road was well repaired and the stagecoach would arrive safely, unless it fell off the side of one of the bridges without rails, as happened occasionally. Members of the Circuit used to travel by stagecoach as far as Yorkshire. George Gray was somewhat incautious about his light refreshments, but he had only just been called to the Bar, and knew no better:

Went into Yorkshire in stagecoach . . . I ate on the road some raisins, which in my pocket happened to mix with a dentifrice made of beaten china, which threw me into so violent vomiting and purging that I had like to have died on the road, and performed my journey with great difficulty.

However, as they approached York, the first assize town on the Circuit, the barristers transferred from a stagecoach into a postchaise. Boswell always did so, and his journal shows why. He was then on the Home Circuit, but the practice seems to have been the same on every circuit:

Hesitated some time whether to take a stagecoach part of the way to Maidstone, as the expense of a postchaise was very heavy; but I considered that the appearance of a lawyer during the circuit is open to observation, and the rule being that it is *infra dignitatem* for counsel to go in public vehicles, I thought it much better to save it any other time. So drove with my servant in a postchaise.

That is why James Parke, a Liverpool barrister, came to be in a postchaise near Grantham. He is the most reliable guide round the Circuit, for John Scott was looking back over many years, and his stories lost nothing in the telling. But James Parke used to write to his wife every day in court while the cases were in progress, and speaks of events which happened only yesterday:

We got here last night at 12 [he wrote from York in 1818], after a tolerable journey, the last stage of which from tired horses, and a crash we got from a drunken driver of another chaise, was somewhat disagreeable, as we had to get out halfway from Tadcaster, and transfer our luggage into another chaise.

Almost everybody is enchanted by the beauty of York. Daniel Defoe, the much-travelled author of *Robinson Crusoe*, certainly was: 'There is abundance of good company here, and abundance of good families live here, for the sake of the good company and cheap living; a man converses here with all the world as effectually as at London.'

James Parke would certainly agree. Here he met his beloved Cecilia, a doctor's daughter, probably at the ball held during assize time, and each time the assizes came round they would be sure to meet again, dance the evening away, and edge their chairs a little closer together during a light supper. Never was there a more devoted couple, as his letters make very clear. When they were engaged he signed them stiffly 'James Parke', and she signed hers 'Cecilia Barlow', but once they were married he became 'her little old man', and she became 'his little old woman in the poke bonnet', otherwise 'Pokey', or even 'Pook'. Such is love.

Although members of the Bar could usually stay at inns, it was a circuit rule that in the assize towns themselves they had to stay in lodgings. It was not a luxurious life. As James Parke wrote to Cecilia, now in London since their marriage:

I have taken my abode upstairs in the back room, where I

breakfasted this morning very sumptuously on some of the potatoes (which are nearly done and what are not eaten are spoiling) and some of the new marmalade.

He was tired when he wrote to her from York:

My darling,
I was yesterday so fully occupied in court, without the interruption of speeches, that I had not a moment to write to you to tell you that I was *quite* well, barring some little wheezing; the day before I was kept in court twelve hours, and too tired when I got home to do anything but dine, play a rubber, and to go to sleep, which I regularly do soon after eleven, and awake quite refreshed at five or soon after.

John Scott had an amusing case there, in which he was led by Edward Law. It arose out of a horse race; some sporting men laid bets on the result, agreeing that the winnings would go to the gentleman who won the race. The plaintiff won, but the defendants refused to pay, claiming that he was no gentleman. If they were right, the plaintiff was not entitled to any money under such an agreement. But how does one define a gentleman? The judge was greatly at a loss:

'Gentlemen of the Jury,' he said, 'when I see you in that box, I call you gentlemen, for I know you are such; custom has authorised me; and, from your office there, you are entitled to be called gentlemen. But out of that box, I do not know what may be deemed the requisites that constitute a gentleman; therefore I can give you no further direction.' (Laughter.)

The jury returned a verdict that the plaintiff was not a gentleman, so he challenged Edward Law to a duel; Law replied that he could not think of fighting someone who was pronounced by a solemn verdict of 12 of his countrymen to be no gentleman. Even so, Edward Law waited for several hours in front of York's coffee house in case his challenger should appear, but he did not.

Another barrister, Roger North, rode through Yorkshire in 1687, visiting a number of inns:

Here if one calls for a tankard of ale, which is always a groat—it's the only dear thing all over Yorkshire, their ale is very strong—but for paying the groat for your ale, you may have a slice of meat either hot or cold according to the time of day you call, or else butter and cheese gratis into the bargain. This was a general custom in most parts of Yorkshire, but now they have changed it, though they still retain the great price for the sale, yet make strangers pay for their meat.

Postchaises had not been introduced in his time, so he rode on horseback, and found that an experienced horse was a great asset on circuit:

It was observable that the horses that had gone once or twice came to understand their trade, and to know the trumpets sounded their ease and accommodation, and at the first clangour of them the horses would always brisk up as at good news. I observed also my horse would not, though a year after, forget a by-lane by which he had passed to a gentleman's house, but would make his proffer to go that way.

Durham is the next circuit town after York, but it was usual to stop overnight at Darlington, even though Daniel Defoe found it had 'nothing remarkable except dirt, and a high stone bridge over little or no water.' At Darlington, James Parke realised he had lost some trousers, and wrote to Cecilia for them:

In the course of my wanderings it occurs to me that I have left behind a part of my court dress, to wit a certain pair of blue trousers. If this be so, which an inspection of any drawers, I mean, *chest* of drawers, will soon ascertain, get William to put them up into a parcel and direct them to me at Mr Hines', Durham.

Most people like Durham, with its climate of 'a sharp and piercing air; but through the plentifulness of coals in these parts, the inhabitants keep such good fires, that the cold is not so offensive to them.' Members of the Bar, however, had cause for complaint: 'On Tuesday I went to the Court,' wrote James Parke, 'of course in the morning, and a place more nearly resembling the black hole of Calcutta I do not know. It seems to have been constructed for the purpose of annoying the profession of the law.'

John Scott defended a highwayman there. The prosecution

case was not strong, and Scott had the sense to leave well alone; he asked as few questions as possible, and the man was acquitted. But clients do not always appreciate such tactics. That evening Scott was sitting in his lodgings when the man burst into the room.

'Lawyer Scott,' he said furiously, 'you owe me two guineas! You were my counsellor today, and you did nothing for me. I am, therefore, come to have my fee back again, and my fee I will have.'

'Sirrah,' said Scott, springing up and seizing the poker, 'although you escaped today, when you deserved to be hanged, you shall be hanged tomorrow for attempting to rob me, unless you instantly depart.'

At that moment his clerk came in, and the highwayman slunk away. Scott had a lucky escape.

Durham, like the other assize towns, had its Assize Ball: 'I went to the ball,' wrote James Parke to Cecilia, 'which was very crowded, and for a Durham ball, good! I did not think of dancing—I thought of *you*, and came home early enough to be in bed by twelve.'

Quite right too—he had only been married three months. But John Scott had been married several years, and had that day won a case brilliantly. 'When I went to the ball that evening,' he recalled, 'I was received with open arms by everyone. Oh! my fame was established; I really think I might have married half the pretty girls in the room that night. Never was a man so courted.'

After leaving Durham for Newcastle the roads become pretty bad; according to Macaulay, no traveller entered that part of the country without making his will. The passengers in a stagecoach certainly had an alarming experience in 1830, a time when the body-snatchers were active:

An artist was travelling by the courier coach from Newcastle to Darlington in company with his rather large and newly made packing case, which carried with it the strong roziny smell of newly-dressed deal; there were also some hampers of 'Newcastle salmon' and sundry old greasy traces on the coach. As evening deepened and all earthly scents grew powerful, the combined savours drew many a mysterious glance from the 'outsiders' who commenced to whisper, then

127

to speak to the guard, who mounting snuffed about with officious activity; the upshot being that horror was depicted on every face.

At last a clergyman stood up, and pointing ominously at the suspected package, asked the artist,

'Is that your box?'

'Yes.'

'There is a very offensive smell *from it,* Sir.' And down he sat.

It was needless to hint at the fish hampers, the dead body was in *that* box, and all shrank from the *Resurrection-man.* When the coach stopped at the Cleaver in Skinnergate the supposed villain ordered great care in lowering his horrid charge, and the clergyman, whose suspicions were confirmed, demanded on behalf of the whole passengers that *the box* should be opened. The apple-faced host laughed outright; 'The luggage of a passenger I have known all my life shan't be touched.'

But the 'whole coach' was peremptory, and the owner, to satisfy the inquisitive multitude, unlocked *the box.* As the lid turned on its hinges, a crack and a screech was heard; all fell back in breathless anticipation of the horrid exhibition, many quitted the room, and a lady fainted away. They looked again, and the most divine face that human genius could portray burst upon them. It was the Madonna from the hand of Raphael! rich in piety, innocence and perfect beauty, which with great care the owner had brought from Italy. The clergyman apologised, the lady knelt (as a good Roman-Catholic should do), and all were enthralled by so wondrous a sight.

Most travellers found Northumberland uncongenial: 'exceeding rough, hilly, and very hard to be manured.' Newcastle itself the Rev. Macritchie thought 'a nasty, sooty, smoky chaos of a town.' James Parke went to the theatre there and heard an actor say:

> *No hand so fair to me*
> *As the hand that grasps a fee*
> *And I don't care a fig for the ladies.*

'I thought before I went to bed,' James assured Cecilia, 'to tell you that it is not true as applied to lawyers, and that I do care much more for one than for all fees in the world.'

Barristers are incurably romantic. At an Assize Ball in Newcastle, John Scott saw the young Miss Elizabeth Surtees. It was love at first sight—they eloped the next year in the classic manner with a ladder to her bedroom window, a hasty gallop over the Border, and married the next day in Scotland.

From Newcastle, the assizes wheeled westwards towards Carlisle. William Cobbett, on one of his Rural Rides, was not poetically stirred:

Found everywhere such abundance of fine turnips, and in some cases of mangel wurzel, you scarcely see any *potatoes*, a certain sign that the working people do not live like hogs.

But James Parke was enchanted by the landscape:

I set off from Newcastle at half past two, and rode leisurely by by-ways along the bank of the Tyne to Hexham which I have often told you is the prettiest ride in England, save the lakes, and not even saving them, in some respects. I found now and then the shade of trees, which was much required, but as the ride was almost always close to the river it was less oppressive than otherwise I should have felt it. At Hexham I found Ley, Cross and Coltman at dinner, which we made agreeable enough, and in the evening I rode six miles to a quiet little inn on the river side, at Haydon Bridge where I slept.

Westward from Hexham the road becomes wild and desolate; the places of entertainment are scarce indeed, with almost nothing for the traveller to drink unless it rains. James Parke spent the next night at Gilsland, a twopenny-halfpenny spa, although a senior member of the Circuit warned him against it.

But the accounts of the novelty of the thing induced us to disregard this good advice, and we went to the watering place where we found about 20 or 30 people—tea ready, fiddles playing—the doctor philandering a crummy damsel from Annan and the place nearing such an appearance of gaiety that we were fain to feed all our horses for the night, and to take the best accommodation that offered. I accordingly slept in a parlour, where I was bit to death by fleas, dreamt I was going to fight Ley Halcock, and awoke in the morning after a very short sleep to witness the filth of the apartment, which rivalled any that I had seen in an Irish Inn, and left the worst English Inn at an incredible distance. I got a sick stomach with this, and I have not recovered from Gilsland yet.

He reached Carlisle on the following day, and several members of the Circuit went with him to the fairground. They saw a giantess six feet four inches tall, and 'the Emperor of the Conjurors', who joined them in a putting game:

I was however heartily tired and went to bed with great delight at an early hour. I regret leaving Carlisle, on account of the air and bathing principally, and the comfort of the court, where one has room to sit at ease.

At Carlisle Assizes, John Scott encountered Bearcroft, a very successful barrister who practised mainly in London. It was his first visit to Cumberland, and he was paid an enormous fee of 300 guineas to prosecute a salmon poacher. He was not the only London barrister to assume that he knew everything, and that members of the Northern Circuit knew nothing. John Scott decided that his best tactics were to conduct the case entirely in the Cumberland dialect, which is Greek to most Southerners. So he asked the first witness if he had made 'ould soldiers' of any of the salmon.

John Scott knew, and the witness knew, that salmon caught out of season had white flesh, instead of red, and so salmon poachers used to hang the fish in a chimney to smoke them until they turned the colour of a soldier's red coat: hence 'old soldiers'.

Bearcroft was completely baffled, and asked Scott to explain. But he retorted that surely a London counsel marked 300 guineas on his brief could understand a simple thing like that. Furthermore, it was not for him, with a fee of only five guineas, to help a London counsel whose value was evidently 60 times as great as his own.

The Cumberland jury could, of course, understand every word of the case, and thought that Bearcroft and the Judge must be fools if they could not, so John Scott's client was acquitted. Bearcroft was not amused. He swore that no fee should ever tempt him to come among such a set of barbarians again, and departed.

From Carlisle, James Parke rode south by night, and rhapsodised on the silver mantle which the moon threw over Windermere. When he came to Appleby, the next circuit town, he found that 'the little inn was full of poachers, gentlemen poachers I mean, and I was obliged to sleep out at a small bench at the bottom of the garden.'

John Scott had something of a close shave at the assizes. 'I cross-examined a barber rather too severely,' he recalled. 'He got into a great passion. I desired him to moderate his anger, and said that I should employ him to shave me as I passed through Kendal to the Lancaster Assizes. He said with great indignation, "I would not advise you, lawyer, to think of that, or to risk it." '

There were never many cases at Appleby. James Parke paused at Milnethorpe to write to Cecilia:

The little old man, whilst his mare is eating corn, thinks he cannot spend his time better than by writing a few lines to his dearest Pook, more especially as he thinks there will be no time to write before the post leaves, and his arrival at Lancaster; and perhaps the little old woman might suppose her husband lost in the mountains, or drowned in the Lakes if she did not hear from him very often.

The roads in Lancashire were as bad as anywhere on the Circuit, but there were consolations, as the Rev. Macritchie noted:

In passing along the public roads in this country, one cannot help remarking the good breeding of the people, displayed even in their children. You never meet a country person here, young or old, but salutes you with a bow or a curtsey, and a 'good-morrow', if it be in the forenoon, and a 'good-night', if it be late in the afternoon or towards evening.

He warmed to his subject a little more than a clergyman should:

The women of Lancashire seem to be in general of an agreeable person, a remarkably good look, and a sound,

131

healthy constitution. They have something *bewitching* about them, indeed; but many of the first-looking country girls wear black stockings during the week-days, which is by no means an improvement to their charms.

After three weeks on the Circuit the barristers approached Lancaster, the last assize town. There is a great demand for transport during assize time; according to Thomas de Quincey, 'the consequence of this was that every horse available for such a service, along the whole line of the road, was exhausted in carrying down the multitudes of people who were parties to the different suits. By sunset, therefore, it usually happened that, through utter exhaustion among men and horses, the road sank into profound silence.'

He managed to find a seat on the mail coach, however, and the coachman was most informative:

The Summer Assizes, he reminded me, were now going on at Lancaster; in consequence of which for three nights and three days he [the coachman] had not lain down in a bed. During the day he was waiting for his own summons as a witness on the trial in which he was interested, or else, lest he should be missing at the critical moment, was drinking with the other witnesses under the pastoral surveillance of the attorneys.

There is a limit to human stamina. De Quincey suddenly realised that the coachman had fallen fast asleep, and that the coach was thundering along the highway at 13 miles an hour on the wrong side of the road. It collided with a light carriage, whose occupants were killed.

Charles Dickens found Lancaster to be 'a pleasant place. A place dropped in the midst of a charming landscape, a place with a fine ancient fragment of castle, a place of lovely walks, a place possessing staid old houses richly fitted with old Honduras mahogany,' though he felt that 'if a visitor on his arrival at Lancaster could be accommodated with a pole which would push the opposite side of the street some yards further off, it would be better for all parties.'

James Parke had no idea before he got to Lancaster how many briefs would be waiting for him. Senior members of the Circuit could count on being in almost every case; fledglings at the Bar would hope against hope, and be disappointed. James did quite well:

> We got here to dinner at six, and I found a tolerable number of Briefs today, and I dare say I shall make a decent assizes, though I have a notion the business is not good. The Breach of Promise of Marriage, into which you wished to peep, is to be tried, and heaps of very amusing love letters read.

Cecilia did her best to see he was properly fed at his lodgings, for he wrote:

> The rhubarb is not arrived yet: perhaps it may today.

James had gone this assize on horseback, for although a postchaise was more comfortable in winter months, a horse gave him more freedom to enjoy the countryside during the summer. It might have proved his last ride on that animal:

> I have had, I find, a very narrow escape of the loss of my mare. The stable in which she has always stood at the assizes, till now, was last night on fire, and 14 horses destroyed. Amongst others Law has lost a white mare, and both his dogs are missing, whether suffocated, or whether they have escaped is not yet known. Fortunately I had put my mare in the same stable with my brother, at another place, otherwise I might have suffered. How the accident arose is not known. It is a sad thing that so many poor animals should die without the possibility of any escape. I suppose it was the fault of the ostler, leaving some candle in the stable which fell among the straw . . .
> Everybody is open mouthed at the Master of the Inn, who, it is said, would not let the stable door be opened, as he was afraid the air would excite the smoke into a flame, and that the stable would be burned down, and that it was half an hour before the door was broken down, during which the poor horses were smothered. None of the stalls was burned and it was only the straw and hay, and the smoke completely smothered them.

John Scott seemed to find amusing cases wherever he went, and Lancaster Assizes was no exception. His client was a farmer whose daughter had run off with a young man; the farmer sued him because he had lost her useful services around

133

the farm. ' "Mind, Lawyer Scott," said the farmer, "you are to say that the man who runs away with another man's daughter is a rascal and a villain, and deserves to be hanged."

"No, no," said Scott, "I can't say that."

"And why not?" demanded the farmer.

"Because I did it myself," Scott replied, having eloped with Miss Elizabeth Surtees and married her. "But," he added, "I will say—and will say it from my heart—I will say, that the man who begins domestic life by a breach of domestic duty, is doubly bound to do everything in his power to render both the lady and her family happy in future life; *that* I will say, for I feel it." '

Scott won the case, and obtained £800 damages for his client, and was walking away from the court feeling pretty pleased with himself when a juryman disillusioned him.

It was an age when, once juries retired to consider their verdict, in civil or in criminal cases, they had to stay together without food or rest, no matter how long it took them to reach their verdict.

The assizes were almost over, and this juryman had been released from further duties, but he went into court to say goodbye to the other jurors, and found himself sworn in on the jury in the farmer's case. When they retired to consider their verdict 11 of them were against the farmer, and only he was for him; but he had a bottle of rum in his pocket. He sipped it from time to time, and the more they argued with him, the more he said that he was keeping the rum to himself, and would see which of them would last out longest. Finally, after several hours, they gave in; and that is how Scott won the case.

Lancaster Assizes were now at an end, and the members of the Circuit dispersed. John Scott and a colleague headed north for Northumberland. They stopped for dinner at Kirkby Lonsdale, where two other travellers were dining. They thought of sending their servants on to bespeak beds for them at the next town, but it seemed selfish to reserve rooms when accommodation was hard to come by.

They were once again on the road when, galloping up behind them, came the servant of the two men they had left in the dining-room. He wanted to know where he should book rooms for his masters. Scott took it ill that they should steal a march on him when he had held back, but gave the servant the name of a hostelry. The result was that on the following morning Scott strolled out of the best hotel in town, and the two men emerged haggard from a dreadful night in a wretched alehouse. And Scott went home.

James Parke, however, was still not free; he had to go to Chester for an election. Election candidates used to brief barristers to watch their interests because there was so much bribery and cheating; it was well-paid work, but very tedious:

The Counsel do what is called their duty [wrote James to Cecilia], that is they fight every question, so poor I am doomed to sit in a high box in the midst of the mob for at least three days more, that is the very least. I have not found my writing case. Why did you not write to me, my love. I have never been so long without hearing from my love. Give a portion of my love to Sarah, but take what you please yourself.

He expected to be there 'at least three days more' . . . Every barrister's wife knows that short cases can become long cases without warning; on the other hand, long cases can become longer still. And with each successive letter, the day of their reunion seemed more remote. Thus:

I trust you will keep all your good looks for me, which I *hope* to see the day but two after the day after tomorrow, that is Saturday,

was followed by:

My dearest old *heart,*
You will be nearly as vexed as myself to hear that it is a matter of *hope* merely that I shall quit this on Saturday. The probability is that it will be Monday . . .

Then it became:

Tomorrow at three it will certainly end.

and the last letter says:

It is doubtful whether even Monday will conclude.

But, at long last, James Parke's little trip round the Circuit came to an end. For some members of the Bar it had been profitable, and for all it had been arduous. As he left the circuit territory the Rev. William Macritchie cast a keen naturalist's eye upon the passing scene:

> Observe the *Sagittaria sagittifolia,* and in one place the *Jasione,* which I had not seen a plant of for several hundreds of miles; but these stagecoaches are a bad business for botanists.

James Parke used to spend three days riding from Newcastle to Carlisle; now it takes less than three hours. Barristers dart up and down the motorways, and circuit life is very different.

Yet something of the old spirit lingers on. Only a few years ago at Lancaster Assizes the Judge came into Court to find one of the Counsel missing:

MR JUSTICE HINCHCLIFFE: Mr Bell, I have been waiting to try this case since 10.30. It is now 11.0 a.m. Where is Mr Lord?

ALISTAIR BELL: My Lord, I very much regret that my learned friend must have been delayed by the inclement weather.

JUDGE: That is no excuse. When I was a young man at the Bar I was invariably at court one full hour before my case was due to be heard.

MR BELL: Perhaps the weather has worsened since your Lordship was a young man.

JUDGE: Where precisely is Mr Lord coming from?

MR BELL: My Lord, the BBC newscasters announced this morning that blizzards have cut off all roads leading from both sides of the Pennines. My learned friend is struggling from some obscure place in the middle.

JUDGE: It is sheer nonsense to try to motor in this weather.

MR BELL: My Lord, determination sometimes overcomes even madness. My learned friend is a very determined motorist. I feel sure that at this very moment he is bowling along the motorway to this court.

JUDGE: You're doing very well, Mr Bell. You have been talking for a quarter of an hour, and he still has not come.

MR BELL: May I respectfully suggest that your Lordship retire for a short time?

JUDGE: I don't want to retire. This is the warmest room in the building.

136

MR BELL: My Lord, the jury would be more comfortable.

JUDGE: Very well, I shall retire, but when he does come you can tell your learned friend that I am very cross.

His Lordship then rose, the score being one up to the Northern Circuit.

TEN

The Gallows on Harraby Hill

'When I came next to merrie Carlisle,
Oh, sad, sad seemed the town eerie;
The auld, auld men came out and wept,
"Oh maiden, come ye to seek your dearie?" '
A Jacobite ballad

Of all the historical events which belong to the Northern Circuit, the '45 Rebellion must be the most remarkable. It was the last foreign invasion of England, lasted only two months, and was almost entirely confined to circuit territory: nobody south of Derby even set eyes on the rebel forces. It was somewhat remarkable that the rebellion ever started at all. On 23 June 1745 Prince Charles Edward, the Young Pretender, landed on the little island of Eriskay in the Outer Hebrides. London, the Prince's ultimate goal, was 500 miles away. Donald McDonald and the other Highlanders who met the Prince that day thought it an impossible adventure, and advised him at once to return home—meaning France, which he had just left.

'I am come home,' replied the Prince, simply.

One man was ready to support him, young Ranald McDonald. 'I will follow you to the death,' he said, 'were there no other to draw a sword in your cause.'

Others followed his lead. A month later the Prince had 600 men, and could easily have been stopped by the 3000 English troops under Sir John Cope. But Sir John turned aside to Inverness, leaving open the road south, and set sail for Edinburgh, hoping to reach it before the Prince. His calculations were wrong; the Prince got there first, and the city fell into his hands. This news reached Newcastle on 18 September, and caused great alarm. John Wesley, who was there, preached a sermon on an appropriate text from Jonah:

'Who can tell if God will return, and repent, and turn away from his fierce anger, that we perish not?'

On the following day, Sir John Cope occupied a strong position at Prestonpans, just outside Edinburgh. But when the Prince routed him in a brilliant victory, and the English survivors fled for their lives back to England, the alarm in Newcastle became a panic. As Wesley observed:

The walls were mounted with cannon, and all things prepared for containing an assault. Meantime our poor neighbours, on either hand, were busy in removing their goods. And most of the best houses in our street were left without either furniture or inhabitants. Those within the walls were almost equally busy in carrying away their money and goods; and more and more of the gentry every hour rode southward as fast as they could.

The rich could afford to flee; the poor were obliged to stay; Wesley chose to remain.

Although General Wade and his garrison were at Newcastle—Wesley visited the troops and preached to them—the town was dangerously insecure. A captured spy revealed that the Prince planned to capture Tynemouth Castle with its cannon and ammunition, and afterwards march to a hill commanding the town. 'And if he had done this,' wrote Wesley, 'he would have carried his point, and gained the town without a blow.'

Few worthwhile precautions were taken. Wesley's house happened to be graced with battlements. 'A surly man,' as Wesley described him, came from the army and ordered him to pull his battlements down, in case they might be of use to the enemy. Wesley wrote to the man's commanding officer, assuring him that he was perfectly prepared to pull them down, provided he was asked nicely. The battlements stayed up.

Nevertheless, the rebels ventured no nearer than 17 miles to Newcastle; they made for Carlisle instead. It was a much easier prize.

Nobody could accuse the English of brilliant strategy. General Wade's forces included artillery, to be sure, but as there was no good road to Carlisle it had to stay in Newcastle. Instead, Carlisle's military strength was reinforced by one man—a Colonel Durand—sent to command the King's forces there. Even 'forces' is a laughable word for a garrison manned by 80 ancient invalids and four gunners, one of whom was a decrepit old man, and two of whom were half-trained civilians. He asked for 500 reinforcements, and was refused them; he sought the help of the local citizens, and was denied it. As for the city walls, they were encrusted with domestic dwellings, which made defence more difficult, but he was not allowed to clear them away.

So the people of Carlisle did nothing to help him, and when the enemy cavalry first appeared he could not even open fire because the citizens were flocking to market outside the town, and he might have injured them.

On 12 November the rebels entered Carlisle and would have captured the castle guarded by Colonel Durand had they not received news that General Wade was marching towards them. They left the city immediately and moved eastwards to Brampton, a better battle-ground. The news was false; the English were nowhere to be seen. So the Scots returned to Carlisle where, despite Colonel Durand's entreaties, the citizens surrendered without a fight. England now lay open to the invaders.

The rebels marched on towards London, 8000 of them at first. But the further south they went, the less enthusiastic they became. Their numbers trickled away, so that only 4500 of them reached Preston. Manchester made no resistance to their entry—it was 'captured by a drummer and a whore', as it was said—and the pealing of bells welcomed them. Here they hoped to recruit another 1500 men, and Francis Towneley, a gallant Lancashire gentleman, raised the Manchester Regiment to join them. It only contained 200 men, hardly ideal recruits, but they would have fought anybody for the sake of fighting.

By the time they reached Derby the rebels had lost heart, and retreated north, with the Duke of Cumberland in pursuit. When the Prince next passed through Carlisle he left it defended by Colonel John Hamilton and 100 men. The Duke began to bombard the city on 27 December 1745, and three days later the garrison surrendered on no terms save that the men were not to be put to the sword forthwith. The Duke was sorry to make even this small concession: 'I wish I could have blooded [my] soldiers with these villains,' he wrote, 'but it would have cost us many a brave fellow, and it comes to the same end, as they have no sort of claim to the King's mercy, and I sincerely hope will meet with none.'

One of the Carlisle garrison who surrendered was Private James Miller of the Manchester Regiment.' 'We were barbarously treated,' he recalled, 'the soldiers rifling us and taking everything of value from us, both money and clothes. They did not offer us any provisions for three days, and on the fourth, but one small biscuit a man.'

He and many others were taken to Lancaster, kept in irons, and fed upon offal and hides. Eighty of his companions died there of disease; he and the rest were taken back to Carlisle, where they awaited trial on a diet of a pound of bread a day, and beef twice a week. It was not much, but few prisoners in those days got more, and many much less. There were almost 400 prisoners now at Carlisle, to be tried for treason in due course, but where could they be housed? For a while they were kept in the cathedral, much to the clergy's disgust; it took six weeks' cleaning, and much fumigation after they had gone, to make the place fit again for public worship.

On 16 April 1746 the rebels were finally defeated at Culloden, the massacre which earned the Duke the name of 'Butcher' Cumberland. A few of the prisoners—the most important of them—were tried at London; Colonel Hamilton, for instance, and Colonel Towneley. Both were tried on 15 July, were convicted, and sentenced to death. But the usual death on the gallows—'to be hanged by the neck until you are dead'—was too good a death for traitors. Women were burnt alive for high treason, and men heard the judge say, 'You are to be hanged by the neck, but not till you are dead, for you are to be cut down alive, your bowels to be taken out and burned before your face, your head severed from your body, your body to be divided into four parts; and those are to be at the King's disposal. And the Lord have mercy on your soul." '

This dreadful fate Colonel Towneley met with great bravery; his last wish was to hope that he would be happy in the next world. The other prisoners could hardly be happy in this world, whilst expecting the same fate. To arrange their trials, Philip Carteret Webb, the prosecuting solicitor, travelled north from London with his staff on 18 July. It was not going to be easy for him to prove the prisoners' guilt. During a battle the King's forces did not record the details of

141

their prisoners upon official forms in triplicate. Who then could claim to have captured Jock and Tom, and swear what part they played in the campaign? Mr Webb could hardly hold a mammoth identity parade in which the victors filed past the vanquished, to see whom they recognised. Besides, some of the prisoners were now at Lancaster and York. As Mr Webb recognised: 'The sending of witnesses from Penrith to York will be endless, there being perhaps 100 different persons engaged in taking the rebels.' It would be easier if the citizens of Carlisle could identify them. So they were taken to the castle 15 at a time to look the prisoners over, 'though,' as was noted, 'they having coats and breeches instead of plaids and none, were not so easily known to those who saw them in nothing but dirty plaids.'

Each prisoner had acted separately in the rebellion, so the evidence against him was separate and his trial had to be separate too. Trials in the XVIIIth century were far quicker than today—six were often heard in one day—but there were several hundred trials to be heard, and the courts could never have coped with them all. The problem was solved by a device used after the 1715 rebellion for the less important rebels. Those who were prepared to plead guilty and to throw themselves upon the King's mercy, were assembled in groups of 20, and lots drawn among them. The one in each 20 on whom the lot fell would be tried, and could be executed; the other 19 would be sure of saving their skins, but would be transported for life.

Justice by drawing lots sounds rough justice indeed; yet justice it still was. Would not many of the prisoners, if there was a 19 to 1 chance of escaping execution, prefer transportation? Was not the luck of the draw worth having? Of course, no man was obliged to submit to this legal lottery; he could stand trial in the ordinary way. But the odds in favour of an acquittal were hardly as high as 19 to 1.

This method, having been used successfully in 1715, was now used again. This was what happened to Alexander Stewart, the Prince's footman, who was taken prisoner after Culloden, and found himself in Carlisle Castle on 17 August 1746:

About two o'clock in the afternoon [he recalled], a rascal of the name of Gray, Solicitor Hume's man from Edinburgh, with his hatful of tickets, presented the hat to me, being the first man on the right of all the 20 that was to draw together. I asked Gray what I was going to do with that, and he told me that it was to draw for our lives, which accordingly I did and got number 14. So he desired me to look and be sure. I told him it was no great matter whether I was sure or not.

He was lucky; the lot fell on Alexander Hutchinson, the Prince's groom. Stewart soon learnt what his own fate was to be.

They came all out to the yard where we was sitting on the grass, with a very large paper like a charter, and read so much of it to us as they thought proper, and told us that it was to petition their king for mercy to us, and that it was to go off that night for London, and as soon as it came back we probably might get home or else transportation; for such mercy that was but to hang only one of 20 and let 19 go for transportation, pointing to me in particular with his finger and told me if that Popish spark [Prince Charles Edward] had carried the day he would have hanged 19 and let only the twentieth go free.

This process solved the problem of too many trials. But another unexpected problem faced Mr Webb—that of accommodation. He must surely have assumed, when he left London, that Carlisle would readily furnish lodgings for himself and his staff. But he was wrong: 'There was an absolute refusal to furnish any of us or our servants with bed,' he wrote. He applied to the local dignitaries for help, but the Deputy Mayor was 'a cunning and designing fellow', clearly in sympathy with the rebels, so that Mr Webb and his staff 'soon began to experience what it was to be in a rebel town.' It was bad enough for him, but worse for prosecution witnesses who hoped to find beds in Carlisle: 'I foresee that they will have none, or will be reduced to lie on straw,' he wrote.

As to the members of the Bar, they presumably managed to stay in their usual lodgings; there is no record of them having to sleep together in a barn, as they did at Oxford during the Great Plague.

It must have been a busy assizes for them but nothing is known of their experiences. No doubt the wealthier prisoners could afford counsel and solicitors to defend them, and the poorer of them—of which there were many—would have to do without. However, it is clear that the prosecution were quick enough to offer no evidence against them in deserving cases, and the judges were careful to note any grounds which would justify a reprieve from the gallows for those found guilty. Four judges were needed to deal with all the trials: Mr Justice Burnet and Mr Justice Dennison, Baron Clarke and Lord Chief Baron Parker. (The last two judges were from the Exchequer Division of the High Court, where commercial cases were tried; it was part of an old historical tradition that they were called Barons, otherwise they would have been Mr Justice Clarke and Lord Chief Justice Parker.)

The prisoners' hardships were very severe. There was no room for them indoors at Carlisle Castle, so they had to be housed in tents and wooden huts within its surrounding walls. It was something of a miracle that typhus did not break out. The Judges were so concerned that they recommended that many of them should be removed to Whitehaven or other towns, though it made it very difficult for counsel and solicitors to visit them there for conferences.

At this difficult time, the French prisoners were the last straw. Many had been captured at Culloden beside their Scottish allies but, being foreigners, there was no question of them being tried for treason. Whereupon—since they had the run of the town—they had the effrontery *to enjoy themselves,* giving balls and plays to the townspeople. So the judges, fearing that it might have a bad influence upon the jurymen and witnesses in Carlisle, ordered them to be taken elsewhere. The judges then moved on to York, where 75 prisoners awaited trial. The judges attended an assize service where the text of the sermon was: 'And Moses said unto the judges of Israel, slay ye every one of the men that were joined unto Baalpeor.'

It needs a little explanation. Some of the Israelites were fraternising with the Moabite women and worshipping their heathen god; Moses ordered them to be killed because they had abandoned their own customs and laws. It was thus an ominous text for traitors.

A month later the judges returned to Carlisle in their

coaches and six, to try the prisoners there. The fullest account of any trial is contained in one of those sensational pamphlets which described the careers of popular criminals. It may well not be wholly true, but it describes the case of Thomas Cappoch, whose history was certainly colourful.

After leaving school in Manchester he went to Oxford as a student, where 'he made up a great many veneral medicines for young rakes; for by such he was respected, because his low jests and buffoonery afforded mirth and pastime to such gentry only.' The university authorities were not amused and expelled him, so he travelled the country selling medicines until, putting his huckster's talent to a different trade, he turned Methodist preacher. He stole £200 from the Methodists in Newcastle; he tried to obtain a curacy in Kent by forging a letter from the Bishop, and was clapped into prison. But the rebellion offered him his golden opportunity. Amongst an unthinking rabble his talent could shine, 'but'—as one opinion ran—'he much oftener got drunk than prayed, or did his duty as an officer.'

The charge against him was high treason, and the words of the indictment orchestrated it with a thunderous resonance typical of the XVIIIth century law. The first charge against him alleged:

That, with several other traitors (to the jurors unknown) not having the fear of God in his heart, nor regarding his duty and allegiance, but being moved and seduced by the instigation of the Devil, as a false traitor . . . to put and bring these kingdoms into intolerable and miserable slavery . . .

The second charge was more specific:

That he, on the 10th day of November last . . . did appear, arrayed in a hostile manner, at the City of Carlisle aforesaid, with 3000 persons and upwards, in a tumultuous and rebellious Manner, and Guns, Pistols, Swords, Clubs, Staves, and other weapons, offensive as well as defensive, with drums beating, colours flying, pipes playing, and there being so arrayed, did in a warlike and hostile manner levy a cruel war . . .

145

It makes him sound like an epic hero; he was really a blustering knave.

He first joined the rebels at Manchester, where he was seen throwing seditious leaflets from the windows of the Bull's Head; it was a convenient way of combining treason and tippling. He swaggered through the streets with the rebels' white cockade in his hat and a sword at his side. When the troops moved north again he acted both as chaplain and quartermaster, and had to find billets or quarters for the troops, but he was happiest when he reached Carlisle. He foisted himself on Dr Waugh, the Chancellor of the Diocese, who was accustomed to dealing with proper clergymen, and not someone who would come in drunk and swear at the curate. When the Young Pretender granted Thomas Cappoch his wish and promised to make him a Bishop, he preached sermons in the Cathedral to earn his title.

At his trial, the prosecution was represented by no less than five members of the Bar—Sir Thomas Bootle, Mr Noel, Mr Williams (Attorney-General for North Wales), Christopher Fawcett (Recorder of Newcastle), Owen Brereton Esq. (Recorder of Liverpool) and Swaynton Jarvis Esq. Cappoch's counsel should have been a Mr Clayton, but he failed to attend and David Graham, a Scots advocate, volunteered to take his place. There was ample evidence of Cappoch's brazen behaviour, and he was happy to enhance it—he cross-examined all the prosecution witnesses himself, 'to whom he behaved very insolent,' as the pamphlet says. 'His counsel said very little in regard to his defence, for the prisoner's behaviour before the court was rude and insolent and impudent beyond imagination.'

It was a valid defence for a man to prove that he acted wholly under duress, the rebels making it impossible for him to avoid doing what he did. Some of the prisoners at Carlisle were successful in this line of defence, but Cappoch's difficulty was that nobody forced him to preach treason from the cathedral pulpit. Mary Humphries, his mistress, gave evidence that at Manchester the rebels dragged him into the Bull's Head against his will, but nobody believed a word of it. The pamphlet called her 'a very wicked hussey, for she had the impudence to say in court if he was hanged, she would be hanged with him. She called him "dear Tommy", and really behaved in such a manner that if she had not privately departed the City of Carlisle, the mob were determined to make her undergo the discipline of the horse pond.'

The pamphlet certainly makes lively reading. However much it may exaggerate the events of the trial, there is no doubt but that Cappoch once forged a Bishop's testimonial. Fraud and impudence was nothing new to him.

The jury convicted Cappoch after less than a minute's consideration, at which he laughed in their faces, and told his colleagues, still awaiting trial, that if Our Saviour was here, these fellows would condemn even Him.

But would the jury have convicted anybody in the dock? The figures do not suggest so. 34 of the 125 men who were tried were acquitted—more than one quarter—and were the jury fair because of the judges, or in spite of them? Baron Clarke's notebook helps to answer that question. It came to light only a few years ago and is now preserved in Carlisle's public library.

According to a Jacobite marching song, the rebels were:

> *Ragged and treacherous,*
> *Lousy and lecherous,*
> *Objects O' misery, scorning and laughter.*

But one can see them through the Baron's eyes. His notes were intended to help the judges decide which of the guilty should be reprieved, and his gaze was surely compassionate.

Thomas Hayes, a Manchester labourer, was found guilty of taking part in the rebellion. 'NB a poor miserable fellow,' wrote the Baron, since he was not one of the ring-leaders. Somewhat surprisingly, he was hanged; the judges' opinions were usually followed, but they did not have the final say in the matter.

John Henderson, an officer of the guard, had drunk treasonable toasts at Carlisle; the rebels made him their gaoler. 'NB this man a better sort of them. Jury did not stay a minute to debate—never went from the Bar—and he appeared throughout the trial to have been a very actively busy man.' He was later executed at Carlisle, because he had played no minor role.

John Coppock, on the other hand (no relation of Thomas Cappoch), a young Manchester sailor who served as a drummer, was caught hiding in a garret. 'Guilty, but the jury desired he may be recommended to the court to save his life, and we have promised it.'

Richard Morrison, valet-de-chambre to the Pretender's son ('Q. A compassionate case?') was needed to give evidence for the prosecution in an important trial; he was sent to London and pardoned two months later.

Andrew Johnston, 'a fine young fellow of 18—a gentleman's son in Annandale', was pardoned on condition he enlisted in the army, which he did. But no such mercy could be extended to Major James Brand, a quartermaster; 'NB a bold daring fellow.'

He wept when he was sentenced to death, thus earning the scorn of Thomas Cappoch: 'You puppy!' he said, 'What the devil are you afraid of? We shan't be tried by a Cumberland jury in the other world!'

Francis Buchanan was 'a laird of good estate . . . his trial lasted eight hours, and all the four judges present.' No other trial lasted so long; the judges clearly thought him very important. He was connected with a mysterious death in Scotland, and a significant letter in his handwriting had been intercepted. The Lord Justice Clerk wrote from Scotland to Mr Webb, the prosecuting solicitor, saying that 'it would be of more consequence to His Majesty's service . . . to get rid of such a person than to convict 99 of the lowest rank.' So he was executed, regretting to the last that he had not drawn his sword in the Prince's name.

Donald McDonald, the laird of Kinloch-Moidart, had been a rebel since the very day when the Prince landed at Eriskay, and was his aide-de-camp. He was 'a principal man in the Pretender's Army . . . Guilty after a very long trial of six hours.'

He deserved to be remembered not only in his own right, but as the original of Sir Walter Scott's Fergus McIvor, the Scottish chief whose appearance in court is the climax of *Waverley*. Baron Clarke has not recorded what Major McDonald said before sentence of death was passed upon him. But these are the words Scott gave Fergus McIvor, as he addressed a crowded courtroom:

I cannot let this numerous audience suppose that to such an appeal I have no answer to make. But what I have to say, you would not bear to hear, for my defence would be your condemnation. Proceed, then, in the name of God, to do what is permitted to you. Yesterday, and the day before, you have condemned loyal and honourable blood to be poured forth like water. Spare not mine. Were that of all my ancestors in my veins, I would have peril'd it in this quarrel.

In the book, Fergus McIvor's faithful follower would have been spared if he had petitioned the King for mercy, but he chose to die with his master. No such incident is recorded in Baron Clarke's notebook, though some of the rebels must have preferred to die for their cause.

Some of the defendants were acquitted with the consent of the prosecution, such as John Thoris, a little crippled boy. The Pretender once met him, and asked what use he could be among the rebels. 'Sir,' replied the little boy, 'though my body is small, my heart is as big as any man's you have.'

John McQuin, however, 'a rough, strong Highlander', admitted his guilt; 'no recommendation for mercy was made, but he is not shown to have been a man of no importance.' The double negative is a little puzzling. If he had been shown to have been a man of *no* importance, he would have been reprieved. He was *not* shown to be so, and might well have been executed. However, he was pardoned upon enlisting in the army.

James Reid, the piper of Lord Ogilvy's Regiment, was recommended for mercy by the jury. 'He bore arms sometimes,' which was important, and even if he had not touched any weapon, Lord Chief Baron Parker ruled that it made no difference:

No regiment ever marched without musical instruments such as drums, trumpets and the like he said, and a Highland regiment never marched without a piper, and therefore his bagpipe, in the eyes of the law, is an instrument of war.

Captain George Hamilton was tried for three separate incidents in England, and must have been very active. 'Full proof against him but no circumstances of cruelty or ill usage' by the rebels against him was shown. When he was executed, the hangman held up the remnants of his body, shouting, 'Good people, behold the four quarters of a traitor! God save King George!'

It was the traditional phrase, and was not barbarous simply for barbarity's sake. The four quarters were displayed in four different towns, and the head in a fifth; his fate was thus more widely displayed, and it was difficult for his friends to build up a martyr's fame on one fifth of his carcass.

The most appealing entry in the notebook concerned John Ballantine of the Atholl Brigade. His witnesses proved that 'he was forced into the service by a party of rebels who took him by violence out of his bed, threatened to stab him if he did not go with them, and did not allow him time even to put on his clothes, and that afterwards they placed a guard on him to prevent him making his escape.'

Baron Clarke has recorded the result of the trial:

Not guilty. On his acquittal this poor piper blessed King George and showed such unaffected signs of joy on his delivery as I never saw—he jumped and danced in the Bar with his irons and could not be contained by any means from expressing his joy and gratitude.

The trials were now over. Thomas Cappoch had not been idle in the meantime; he tried to saw through the bars of his cell with a knife, but was discovered. He tried to bribe the sentry, too. It is surprising that none of the prisoners escaped for, as Mr Webb the prosecuting solicitor reported, the gaoler at Carlisle Castle was 'a very bad man of whom anything ill may be expected.' It is surprising also that none of the prisoners died of disease at Carlisle.

Before the judges left the city, they recommended that some of the prisoners should be reprieved. Cappoch was not one of them, and on 18 October 1746 he was drawn on a black hurdle from the castle to the gallows on Harraby Hill which overlooks the town. Prisoners used once to be dragged along the ground unprotected, but hurdles were later employed so that they suffered much the same indignity, but reached the gallows in full possession of their faculties.

Cappoch, incorrigible to the last, then preached a seven minute treasonable sermon and asked God to bless all his enemies, 'especially that corrupted Baron Clarke.' He was hanged, drawn and quartered.

Eight other prisoners suffered the same fate that day, and another 22 were executed at Brampton, Penrith and Carlisle during the following month. It was not unduly harsh, seeing that the rebels aimed to overturn the throne, and treason is not to be tackled with a feather duster. The drawing of lots among the prisoners was novel, but 60 years earlier the Monmouth rebels would have been glad of it; 250 of them were executed, but only 120 of the rebels of the '45 suffered death.

The judges come out of this unhappy story well and were highly thought of in their day. Lord Chief Baron Parker held his office for 30 years, and when he retired some wished that his successor could have retired in favour of him. Mr Justice Burnet was the son of the historian Bishop Burnet; after a misspent youth, he too became highly respected.

Mr Justice Denison was a King's Bench judge for 23 years, and on his death received an epitaph from Lord Mansfield which every judge would be proud to share: 'A thorough knowledge of the legal art and form is not litigious or an instrument of chicane, but the plainest, easiest and shortest way to the end of strife.'

Little is remembered of Baron Clarke. He had been on the Bench but seven years when he died of goal fever at the 'Black Sessions' of the Old Bailey in 1750. His notebook is his best memorial.

Of all the rebels active in Carlisle, Colonel Towneley was the bravest. He was game to go on fighting when the King's forces were closing in and, when the castle surrendered, complained angrily that it was better to die by the sword than to fall into the hands of those damned Hanoverians. But when the executions were over, and the heads set on pikes over the gates of Carlisle, for all to see, his too was set there. So it remained as the seasons turned, and as memories faded of the hopes and wrath which the rebellion had aroused. As time went by, his skull lost all horror or interest for the people of Carlisle. When it was last seen, a wren had made her nest in it.

ELEVEN

Poor Bozzy

'Dr Johnson was very kind this evening, and said
to me, "You have now lived five-and-twenty
years, and you have employed them well."
"Alas, Sir," said I, "I fear not. Do I know
history? Do I know Mathematics? Do I know
law?" '

Boswell's *Life of Johnson*

Some lawyers, so they say, are born; some made. I think it
must be best to have been bred to the law, to have a father who
can not only read the Riot Act, but construe its every clause; to
see him pass the marmalade each morning with the air of
understanding its possessory title. That is to live the law, and
breathe it. Now, the grandfather of James Boswell was a
lawyer, and his father was an eminent Scottish judge; much
good it did him, though.

He was highly strung as a child, and needed a private tutor.
At the age of 13 he went to Edinburgh University, the usual
age to do so in those days, and studied classics and Hebrew.
He made two lifelong friends: John Johnston and William
Johnson Temple. Many of his letters to them survive and
provide almost as good a picture of him as his *Life of Samuel*,
the most famous Johnson of them all. He had a great talent for
companionship, and a keen eye for the foibles of his friends.
Yet, if the proper study of mankind is man, its improper study
is woman. In both fields, Boswell was an outstanding student.
He was less successful, however, at university; after four years
his health broke down. From then onwards serious study
never came easily to him.

Perhaps he lived too long under the shadow of his stern
father, whom he accompanied upon the Scottish Northern
Circuit (since Scotland had circuits too) for three weeks when
he was 18. His father's legal aptitude certainly did not rub off

on him. He studied law at Glasgow for only a year or two and then, like a hunting hound unleashed, sped to London. He became a Roman Catholic, though not for long; plunged into the world of wine and women; and if he had no special talent for song, began at least to take up his pen. He fell into the dangerous company of the three founders of the Hell-Fire Club, and might have vanished in the quicksands of debauchery had Dr Johnson not met him.

The affinity between that ill-matched pair makes them the most interesting partnership in literary history. They were separated by 31 years in age; Boswell was elegant and Johnson uncouth; Johnson deep and Boswell shallow; but both of them had a genius for making friends; Boswell was, in Johnson's phrase, 'a most *clubbable* man.'

Of that friendship, the outward visible sign was sparkling conversation. Johnson's pearls of wit have not lost their lustre after two centuries but, without Boswell's care, they would have vanished for ever. His was a somewhat specialised gift of selection, not unlike John Aubrey's description of the preaching of Bishop Launcelot Andrewes, as a monkey tossing playthings into the air: 'Here's a pretty thing, and there's a pretty thing.' Still, they are pretty even today. Boswell's quicksilver mind was his greatest asset, but he should have settled down to steady work. Johnson told him so.

Boswell would have loved to be a Guards officer, all strut and style, and irresistible to women. But his influential friends knew him too well to trust him on that path. So at the age of 21 he went to Utrecht to resume his studies. Dr Johnson accompanied him as far as Harwich, and teased him during the journey:

That gentleman there [he told the coach passengers], has been idle. He was idle at Edinburgh; his father sent him to Glasgow, where he continued to be idle, he then came to London, where he has been very idle; and now he is going to Utrecht, where he will be as idle as ever.

Boswell was furious at being teased in public—in front of a lady too! But the Doctor was right. He did his best to settle down to work. He learnt something of modern languages, but more about women. So he was little better off, and two years later Johnson prescribed a cure.

I shall therefore [he wrote], consider only such studies as we are at liberty to pursue or to neglect; and of those I know not how you will make a better choice, than by studying the civil law, as your father advises, and the ancient languages, as you had determined for yourself; at least resolving, while you remain in any settled residence, to spend a certain number of hours every day amongst your books.

Boswell followed that advice. Three years later, in 1766, he joined the Faculty of Advocates, ready to practise at the Scottish Bar. Johnson wrote to congratulate him:

The study of the law is what you very justly term it, copious and generous; and in adding your name to its professors, you have done exactly what I always wished, when I wished you best. You gain, at least, what is no small advantage, security from those troublesome and wearisome discontents which are always obtruding themselves upon a mind vacant, unemployed and undetermined.

Thus discontent was banished, for a time.

To his new career he brought that unrestrained zeal essential to beginners at the Bar, and disastrous to middle-aged practitioners, who have learned no better. His vigorous defence of a sheep stealer in court was only matched by his unwise attempts to gain public sympathy for him out of court; the man was later hanged for another offence, in any event.

Early the next year he was telling Temple: 'I am now advancing fast in the law. I am coming into great employment. I have this winter made 65 guineas, which is a considerable sum for a young man. I expect that this first year I shall clear, in all, above a hundred pieces.'

This was good progress indeed. And to Lord Chatham he declared: 'I begin to like it. I can labour hard; I feel myself coming forward, and I hope to be useful to my country.'

So, at the age of 26, he applied himself earnestly enough. As he wrote to Temple: 'I am kept very throng [busy]. My clerk comes to me every morning at six, and I have dictated to him 40 folio pages in one day. It is impossible to give you an idea of my present life . . . I am doing nobly. But I have not leisure for learning . . . It is very odd that I can labour so hard at law when I am so indolent in other things.'

He might well have lacked leisure; one Scottish trial in the late XVIIIth century lasted for 43 consecutive hours. Not all his skill as a pleader was reserved for his clients, however. Once, having arranged to meet a young lady, he was honest enough to tell her that he had contracted an ailment during one of his grosser encounters.

'How like you the eloquence of a young barrister?' he asked Temple, describing the scene. 'It was truly the eloquence of love. She bad me rise; she took me by the hand, she said she forgave me.' And she had sense enough to take her affections elsewhere.

Two years later, in 1769, he married. His enthusiasm for the Scottish Bar gradually drained away, partly from indolence, partly from boredom, and partly from the crushing melancholy that used to wear him down. It was not that he lacked ability.

During the next four years he did little enough in his profession. Even so, in 1773, by way of diversion, he took Johnson on the celebrated Scottish tour. But he had not yet tried the English Bar, whose pastures seemed greener on the other side of the border. In May he wrote to Temple: 'I have now ate a term's commons in the Inner Temple. You cannot imagine what satisfaction I had in the form and ceremony of *The Hall*. I *must* try to prevail with my father to consent to my trying my fortune at the English Bar.'

That meant asking further funds from his father, who was noticeably cool; he had thrown good money away often enough upon his wayward son's sudden enthusiasm for any new project. Thus he was at the same time keen on joining the English Bar, which he had never tried, and weary of the Scottish Bar, even in a simple appeal case.

Do you know [he wrote], it requires more than ordinary spirit to do what I am to do this very morning? I am to go to the General Assembly and arraign a judgment pronounced last year by Dr Robertson, John Home, and a good many more of them; and they are to appear on the other side. To speak well, when I despise both the cause and the judges, is difficult. But I believe I shall do wonderfully. I look forward with aversion to the dull labour of the Court of Session.

He thought the Scottish Bar was beneath him, and wrote to

155

Temple describing himself as a 'coarse labourer in an obscure corner.'

No doubt [he continued in the same letter], the practice of the law here is sometimes irksome to me. But it is often a kind of amusement. I have to consider and illustrate *quicquid agunt homines* [the ways and conditions of men]. I have to treat of characters, of the history of families, of trade and manufactures, as contracts concerning them are the foundations of many lawsuits; in short, the variety of subjects of which fragments pass through my mind, as a pleader, engages my attention and, as upon most occasions, I become warmly desirous of my client's success, there is the agitation of context, and sometimes in a certain degree the triumph of victory.

For Boswell the law was good or bad according to his seesaw mood. 'I have been remarkably busy this summer,' he said. 'I wrote about threescore law-papers, and got £234 in fees during last sessions of two months. The court rose yesterday, and this day the clouds have begun to recede from my mind . . .'

During the summer vacation he rode south into Cumberland, and reflected on his career. 'It pleased me to think, as I rode to Penrith, how different a man I now was from what I was 17 years ago, when I first rode along this road, running off from Glasgow to London. I was now a settled advocate with a wife and children.' At the age of 36 he was certainly an advocate with a wife and children, but he never settled. That was his greatest tragedy.

What confidence could he have had in a profession he called 'law-drudgery', or in his own ability when he sought Dr Johnson's help in the simplest possible case?

'I am engaged,' he wrote, 'in a criminal prosecution against a country schoolmaster, for indecent behaviour to his female scholars. There is no statute against such abominable conduct, but it is punishable at common law. I shall be obliged to you for your assistance in this extraordinary trial.'

He sought assistance more and more from the bottle. Yet still the prospects of the English Bar lured him on. Although he was the most congenial companion, he could not dine with anyone in those days without button-holing him and asking whether he ought not to come to the English Bar. No answer would be wrong; he would enter it in his journal, mull it over and adopt it at least till the following day. But no answer would be right, either; sooner or later he would reject it and resent it. It used to take a man five years in London from being admitted to an Inn of Court until he became a qualified barrister. It took Boswell eleven years, and in 1781 he was still hovering on the brink, afraid to take the plunge.

'I languished for London,' he wrote in his journal; 'yet feared I should not be able to rise to any eminence there. Sir John Pringle said to me one day this summer, "I know not if you will be at rest in London; but you will never be at rest out of it." I felt a kind of weak fallacious attachment to Edinburgh. But, I considered, "I hope to be in Heaven, which is quitting Edinburgh. Why then should I not quit it to get to London, which is a high step on the scale of felicity?" I thought I might try the English bar and be sent down a Baron of Exchequer. In short I was very wavering.'

Dr Johnson died in December 1784, and perhaps this irreplaceable loss made him turn to the English Bar more determinedly. Six months later, at any rate, he wrote to his old friend Sir Joshua Reynolds to commission a portrait.

London, 7 June 1785
My dear Sir,
    The debts which I contracted in my father's lifetime will not be cleared off by me for some years. I therefore think it unconscientious to indulge myself in any expensive article of elegant luxury. But in the meantime you may die, or I may die; and I should regret very much that there should not be at Auchinleck, my portrait painted by Sir Joshua Reynolds, with whom I have the felicity of living in social intimacy.
    I have a proposal to make to you. I am for certain to be called to the English Bar next February. Will you now do my picture, and the price shall be paid out of the first fees which I receive as a barrister in Westminster Hall. Or if that fund should fail, it shall be paid at any rate five years hence by myself or my representatives.

Sir Joshua accepted. The portrait is pleasing enough, and anyone who met Boswell when he sat for it, on the threshold of his career at the English Bar, would surely have been conquered by his charm, and would have backed him as a winner.

In January 1786 he made what he expected to be his final appearance at the Scottish Bar.

Tuesday 17th January: Went to the Court of Session, and first walked in with my hat and stick as a gentleman. My spirits were good, so that though I felt awkwardly, I was not uneasy. My brethren stared at me a good deal in the Inner house. Upon which I said, 'I must go and put on my wig and gown, not to be particular.' Having done so, I walked about and shook hands with numbers, and talked quite easily of having two strings to my bow, and not ceasing to be an *advocate* by taking my degree as a *barrister*; and I was most agreeably surprised to find that I might go and come as I found most agreeable.

He appeared there again the following day. 'I was listened to with attention, and my petition had the effect of showing the judges that their former interlocutor, which had been pronounced in my absence, nem. con, was not just.' He was complimented on his performance, which he said had on him 'a wonderful effect'.

Yet, such was his change of mood that the next day, 'I felt with disgust the vulgar familiarity of some of my brethren, and contrasted it with the manners of my London friends,' and on the day after he was heartily displeased with the servility of the judges of the Court of Session.

In the following week he set out for London, and on the journey a London solicitor gave him much advice which would have been salutary for a day-dreamer like Boswell: 'The truth is,' he noted in his journal, 'that *imaginary* London, gilded with all the brilliancy of warm fancy as I have viewed it, and London as a scene of real business, are quite different.'

On 9th February 1786, the great day came for him to be called to the English Bar. He went to the Inner Temple, settled his outstanding bills and dined at the students' table for the last time.

Some time after dinner [he wrote in his journal], the head porter announced a *call*. Then I, the Hon. John Elliott and Mr William Dowdeshall (nephew of the Chancellor of the

Exchequer) were introduced (with each a band, and holding a *pileus* or black cap) into the chamber where the benchers were sitting at table, and were told of our being called to the rank of barristers at law. I said, 'We return you 10,000 thanks for the honour that has been done to us,' and then retreated. I *added* this ceremony to the Laird of Auchinleck, on my own conscience. Mr Salte, the Treasurer, followed me to the door, took me by the hand, and said, 'I wish you all the honours of your profession.'

He had often been advised to join the Northern Circuit, and so on the following Monday he went to see Judge Willes' son, who was then the Junior of the Northern Circuit; Boswell, as the newest member of the Circuit, would be the Junior now. But it was time to hurry along to court and be sworn in as a member of the Bar. His immense success at the Bar was guaranteed—in his own mind, that is.

Young Strange then came and accompanied me to a barber's shop in one of the passages from the hall where he and I put on our gowns, wigs, and bands, and then he showed me all the way into the Court of King's Bench where I took oaths, along with a number of other people. It was remarkable to experience that no notice was taken of it. I then took my seat at the bar, and felt myself a member of the ancient Court of King's Bench, and did not despair of yet being a judge in it. My mind was firm and serene and my imagination proud.

One of his greatest talents was for spending money. That night he and two young colleagues held a banquet at the Inner Temple, the splendour of which was marked by the lighting of the great chandelier, for candles could be a most expensive item.

I had fixed the dinner by myself. My two brethren joined me. I ordered everything. We had a course of fish, a course of ham, fowls, and greens, a course of roast beef and apple pies, a dessert of cheese and fruit, Madeira, port, and as good a claret as ever was drunk . . . The lustre was lighted, which had not been the case for 30 years, as I was told. The company dropped off gradually. Malone and Courtenay and I walked home, in excellent spirits and not drunk, towards eleven. It shall ever be in my mind *dies memorabilis.*

He was now, at the age of 45, a member of the English Bar, and only nine days later—most young barristers would have thought it a miracle—he received his first brief, in a perjury case. He owed this stroke of fortune to the fact that the solicitor had known him when he was at the Scottish Bar. But he recorded nothing about the brief save that the fee was two guineas. 'I had a boyish fondness for my first brief and fee, and put up the guineas as medals.'

The case was heard two days later. It would have been an exciting event enough without his first having to go to Clerkenwell Green to give evidence against two pick-pockets he had helped to catch, there being a risk of his getting back to Westminster too late. However, he got back just in time, and an experienced member of the Bar told him what he had to do—rise to his feet, tell the court that the charge was one of perjury to which the defendants pleaded 'not guilty', and sit down again. But he was led by Erskine, one of the greatest advocates England has ever seen, who told him he must explain the case in greater detail, and wrote down for him what he had to say.

'I felt a *little* trepidation when I first heard my voice *in Banco* [in Court], but I was not uneasy and did very properly what I had to do and no more.' They lost the case because they had not been provided with a sufficient record of the trial at which the accused had given perjured evidence, but Boswell was still grateful to Erskine for the trouble he had taken to help him.

Two days later Boswell was invited to a levee given by the Lord Chancellor, and arrived too late because he had been drinking. But the Lord Chancellor had read and admired Boswell's book on Dr Johnson's Scottish tour, and asked how the *Life of Johnson* was progressing; it was not finished for another five years, because he could seldom apply himself to hard work.

He was too idle to go to court regularly, and missed the chance of another brief because the attorney did not know where to find him.

But the Northern Circuit was about to begin, and before Boswell left London he called on Jack Lee, a great member of the Circuit in his day, who was now getting too infirm to ride the Circuit. 'Attend regularly the courts,' Lee advised him, 'take notes, think nothing beneath you, and have as much conference with your brethren upon law as you can.'

With these wise words in his ears Boswell went to the Blue Boar Inn at Holborn for the coach which would take him north, and on 16 March 1786 he proudly wrote to a friend, 'My address is Barrister-at-law, York.' He had no work there, and could hardly expect it; still, it was early days yet. 'How long I shall continue,' he wrote, 'will depend on the circumstances.'

It is a great pity that Boswell's journal for these York Assizes has been lost; but he was Junior of the Northern Circuit, a sort of treasurer-cum-secretary, and the Circuit records he kept still survive. His duties began on 18 March 1786, when £19 6s. 4d., the balance of the Circuit funds, was handed over to him. It was Grand Night at York, when each member of the Circuit was expected to attend; five were fined for being absent, five for arriving late, and three were excused because they were ill. These details were recorded, together with the 'congratulations' of one member of the Circuit by another; it was a Circuit custom that anyone congratulated should provide wine for the mess.

On Boswell's first evening, 'Mr Chambre was congratulated on his travelling the Circuit in his carriage decorated with a large cock'—ribald laughter, no doubt—and duly required to provide of wine 'one gallon, paid'.

'Mr Sergeant Bolton was congratulated on his great accession of business—one gallon paid.'

It was all harmless fun, but the same could not be said of a mysterious orgy at Newcastle just before Boswell joined the Circuit. His records simply state, 'It was resolved that an entry made of a special court held at Newcastle last summer should be expunged, and that all the members who composed that court should be fined one bottle each except the Junior at the time, who was excused on account of duress.'

Another of his duties was to answer a letter from a Mr Burke, who had left the Northern Circuit, and had written the customary letter of light-hearted farewell to his colleagues. Part of Boswell's reply is enough to show the style of the thing.

York, 18 March 1786

My Dear Sir,

Your farewell letter addressed to John Wilson Esquire, Northern Circuit, was read by me to the Grand Court with an audible but faltering voice, as indeed from the tenderness of your own feelings you may conceive how we were affected upon being informed that we had lost you . . .

Our withers were not unwrung with grief; dejection was visible even in the bluff countenance of Sir John Cockell, and a general cloud hung over the whole legal hemisphere.

But you know my dear Sir (and happy it is that we can with truth say so) that melancholy cannot last long with *us* and I am sure your benevolence will be pleased when you are informed that we soon resumed that merriment which is the genius of the Northern Circuit and joined heartily in those excellent songs that I doubt not will for ever vibrate in your ears.

Mr Burke had evidently decided to practise in the Midlands and West of England, for Boswell continues:

As we fear you are too delicate a plant for our northern blasts, we unite in wishing that more gentle breezes may blow propitious to your fortunes. May your fate at Monmouth be very different from that of its Duke. May you be as successful with the ladies at Shrewsbury as Captain Plume was. May you be a pretty fellow at Abingdon. May your Alma Mater Oxford deliberate the triumphs of your eloquence and may Stafford, Hereford, Gloucester and Worcester join in the chorus not without libations of ale, cyder and perry.

After warning him that he could not return to the Circuit without a formal charade of contrition: 'riding upon a black ram', Boswell signed the letter as Junior 'by authority of the Grand Court of the Northern Circuit.'

From York, the Circuit moved on to Lancaster. Boswell's journal begins again during the journey westwards over the moors:

Tuesday 28th March: Bolton and I set out in a postchaise, and were rationally hearty. Came to Skipton to dinner,

162

found six of the Circuit sitting. Let them go on, and was resolved to stay that night. Walked out after dinner and saw vast lime rock. Tea, after which came another division of our brethren, and we supped together. I had quite English Circuit ideas realised. Heard of Norton's death [a member of the Circuit]. Was like one in a regiment.

Wednesday 29th March: I had been much pleased with the wild moors. Dined at Hornby. A number of us there . . . Bolton had given me much instruction upon the road, and had recommended me to go as a special pleader both to learn the necessary legal forms and to hang out a sign of being in earnest to take business.

Thursday 30th March: Went to Court [at Lancaster] a little to show myself. Dined at our mess. Having got into small lodgings, was quiet.

Friday 31st March: Had a *motion* handed to me in Court with half a guinea by Mr Cross of Preston, Pronothary of the Court of Lancaster. Bolton had made me acquainted with him, and I suppose I owed my being thus launched on the Circuit to him. Attended forenoon and afternoon. Dined at our mess. Quiet at night.

1 April was Grand Night at Lancaster. This is what Boswell noted in the Circuit records: 'Sir Thomas Davenport having died at York, and Mr Norton's corpse being still lying in the town, the Circuit had resolved to have no Grand Night, but it was afterwards settled that we should meet in a quiet manner.'

But the wine flowed, and 'animal spirits broke loose,' as the journal puts it. Whereupon three members of the mess were congratulated for having resisted 'the temptation of the Devil, and Mr Serjeant Bolton moved that the Circuit should have a devil of its own. Four candidates were promptly nominated though the election was deferred until their full merits could be considered.' The shadow of the grave did not lie very heavily upon that night's assembly.

A debate then arose on an issue now covered with moss and ivy, whether the clerks or servants of members of the Bar should bring down records to the assizes. 'The question,' recorded Boswell, 'was agitated with very great warmth . . . the Junior gave his casting vote against the question so that it was lost at this time—but the Junior *afterwards* upon *more cool* information declared that he ought not to use his casting vote, and wished that the question might be renewed at a later time.'

So it was adjourned until the next York Assizes. But the phrase 'more cool' is significant. Boswell was obviously heated with wine. Grand Court was never sober to a fault in those days, and Boswell needed little encouragement to drink too much.

The next day was a Sunday, and Boswell went to church, but in the evening, 'I drank rather too liberally. In the evening went to our inn, and (what was not decent) played at whist. I supped at the mess, and was in too high spirits.'

On the next evening there was an Assize Ball, as occurred at each assize town.

Monday 3rd April: At court forenoon and afternoon. This is to be understood constantly unless I mention *not*. Dined with the judge—a private party—Dr and Mrs Martin etc. Ate and drank rather too well. After court returned to duty and played whist. Then assembly. Danced a minuet with Miss Nelly Walsh, an elegant pleasing girl very like Mrs Rudd. She and I also *took* to one another . . . I danced three country dances with Mrs Martin—foolishly, for it heated too much. I liked the ease of the Lancaster Assembly much, and was pleased with the sweet *tone* of the Ladies.

Tuesday 4th April: A little feverish; dined very moderately at the mess—drank teas at Dr Martin's with young Willes and Chambre, etc, and played at vingt et un.

Wednesday 5th April: Dined at the mess moderately. Evening went to the assembly, but wisely did not dance. Played at whist and drank tea with the Ladies, and was quite gay. Here now did I *perfectly* and *clearly* realise my ideas of being a Counsel on the Northern Circuit, and being an easy gentleman with Lancashire Ladies, with no gloom, no embarrassment. *How* I was so well I know not.

Boswell, it seems, had at last found a life which appealed to him.

Thursday 6th April: Last night a feigned brief had been left at my lodgings.

That is all it says. Up till that point the members of the Northern Circuit had been very kind to him. Serjeant Bolton, a senior man, had gone to a lot of trouble to help him, and had introduced him to attorney who sent him a brief. His colleagues had also arranged for him to defend a female housebreaker called Margaret Hamilton, alias Montgomery; she was convicted.

But they also had a fondness for practical joking. Lord Eldon in his Anecdote Book tells the story of an application for an iron cylinder to be brought into court; it was not until the judge granted the application that he was told it was far too large to get through the door. They briefed another member of the Circuit to appear in a case for the inhabitants of Humtown, a non-existent place; so there was nothing new in them arranging a fake brief for Boswell.

They prepared it with a fee of one guinea—no unwelcome sum—and crammed it with so much legal jargon that his poor head, spinning still from the previous night's carousal, could make nothing of it. Law books might have helped him, but they had been cunningly hidden away.

It is the nightmare of every beginner at the Bar not to know what he is talking about, and to be known not to know. Boswell rose trembling to his feet before an astonished judge, and applied for a writ 'quare adhesit pavimento', which only sounds genuine if one's knowledge of law is poor, and of Latin worse. When the Judge asked what it was he blushed and admitted that he did not know; he turned more scarlet still when another member of the Bar announced, amidst general laughter, that on the previous night Boswell 'adhesit pavimento'—had been stuck to the pavement, dead drunk. 'There was no moving him for some time,' it was explained. 'At last he was carried to bed, and has been dreaming about himself and the pavement ever since.'

Poor Bozzy. His drunkenness was disclosed in a public court. So, after only one month on the Northern Circuit, he went straight back to London and soon resumed his dissipated life; restless as ever, he considered becoming a Judge in Scotland. Thus, only three months after joining the Northern

Circuit, he wrote his letter of farewell; he joined the Home Circuit instead, which visited the Home Counties.

Chelmsford, 28 July 1786

My Dear Bolton,

To a man of less firm nerves than you I should not apply to announce my having quitted the Northern Circuit, because I consider it as an event of such sadness, that only you can receive and communicate the shock without sinking under it. You, my jovial companion from York to Lancaster, you who can without a sigh behold Senior Serjeants fall around you and seem more valiant in fight than before.

When I was employed last Lent Assizes at York to answer in suitable terms of condolence our Brother Burke's valedictory epistle, little was it thought that I should so soon be in his situation. Even he whose voice now melts in mournful lays will shortly want the generous tear he pays.

I am now a *Home* Circuit man or, if you please, a *Homer*. I am very happy in my present state which I am sure you will be glad to hear. This also is a pleasant circuit. We are too apt to suppose that other planets are less agreeable than that which we inhabit.

Your purse I left better than I found it, your records I brought up to the last syllable of my time with exact fidelity. I taught you to sing the Erse song 'Hatyin foam eri'. More I cannot say for myself. Less I was unwilling to say.

I beg to have my very cordial compliments presented to the Northern Circuit and, as in my way to Auchinleck every Autumn I may have occasion to be where you are, I should reckon myself very fortunate if you would be pleased to grant me the privilege of making one of a society for which I shall ever retain an affectionate regard.

I am
My Dear Serjeant
Your faithful humble servant
James Boswell.

So he went the Home Circuit. Like so many of his enterprises, it started well. The first assize town he came to was Chelsmford, which he liked. On the first day he wrote in his journal:

I knew by this time most of the Counsel upon this circuit, and soon acquainted with more. I found myself the *Junior* here as upon the Northern, but the office was not so burthensome, there being no *Courts* and no *Records*. I had only to take care of dinner and supper in the Bills. Indeed, I was considered as the chair, and every speech made in the way of general communications were addressed to me. I resolved to be upon my guard, and to establish a character for sobriety and prudence.

On the second day, 'Attended the court; dined and supped at the mess. I was much upon my guard to acquire a character of prudent resolve, though pleasant. The counsel upon this circuit were very moderate in drinking.' So far, so good. He went back to London for the weekend, and on the Monday rejoined the Circuit at Maidstone.

I got small quiet lodgings at Mr —————the organist's, who had a noble harpsichord which cost him £70, the last which Kircher made with his own hands. He told me he *allowed his housekeeper* to let a part of his house at the assize times. I then drank tea at the coffee house, and spent the evening at Parkington's lodgings, playing whist with some more of the Counsel.

He attended court on the next two days, as a young barrister should, to watch and learn, but although his journal for 2 August 1786 says 'I was so much pleased today, feeling myself quite at home in *Kent* . . .' (he breaks off in the middle of a sentence), he went back to London without having a single brief at those assizes, though he could hardly have expected one.

During the autumn he attended the courts at Westminster and, now that he was in town, wished he was back home in the country. 'I *thought* to myself, "Now here I am in London, living in the best society, and not at an improper expense, so that supposing I should not get practice at the English Bar, I am enriching my mind, and can retire to my estate when I please." My debts however disconcerted me . . .'

In the spring of 1787 he went to the Surrey Assizes, where he had a general retainer of five guineas for Lord Portmore and Mr Langton, but his journal gives no further details. In May, however, he was given a brief in a case of Trover (a claim for goods found in the possession of someone they do not belong to). The attorney did not tell Boswell when the case was to be heard, and neither Boswell nor his clerk took the trouble to inquire, with disastrous results:

> I this morning thought I would call at his house [noted Boswell], and inquire. I found it was to come on today. I went down, but found that it was over. This vexed me, though I affected not to mind it. Bearcroft was the leading counsel, and had non-suited the Plaintiff [had the case struck out in his absence]. Some of the counsel told me I had been called for, and Bearcroft turned round and said, 'I was obliged to you for your assistance this morning.' I followed him into Alice's Coffee House and asked an account of the case. He looked gruff and said he had forgot. I marked him for a *Bear*. It occurred to me that this visible neglect might hurt me much in my chance of getting practice.

There is little more to be said about his law practice in 1787, for he tells us little. He had a client in July, and he went the Home Circuit again, and was mortified to find that one of his friends repeated 'only one disagreeable thing he had heard of me at Chelmsford: *that I had been very drunk*. Not true.'

But it is all too probable.

So he hardly got a single brief that year. At least, he does not say so; and there was never yet a hen that cackled more proudly over its daily egg than a fledgling barrister over a new brief. Of course the novelty wears thin after a while, and to an overworked barrister, each new set of papers feels like another nail in the coffin. But Boswell never reached that state of things. He had begun to be taken up by Lord Lonsdale now, a new prospect for him with a rosy glow, as the fire may seem to someone poised on the edge of the frying-pan.

Sir James Lowther, the First Earl of Lonsdale, was the largest landowner in the North of England, controlled nine seats in Parliament, known as his 'nine-pins', and 'was more detested than any man alive.' He fought duels, as Boswell nearly found out to his cost, and kept company with the notorious Lord George Gordon, whose riots made an ugly page in English history. Such was 'the bad Earl', whom Boswell would have done well to avoid. But he hoped to obtain a seat in Parliament from him, and fawned on him disgracefully.

Friday 21st July (1786): I found to my no small spirits a card from Lord Lonsdale asking me to dinner next Monday to a turtle. This was truly a stirring of the blood. I considered and said to myself, 'Well, it is right to be in this metropolis. Things at least come forward unexpectedly. The Great Lowther himself has now taken me up. I may be raised to eminence in the City.'

The Earl must have enjoyed his company, as who did not— and may have been amused to have him in his entourage; but all Boswell got from him was the Recordership of Carlisle, which carried as much prestige as any job could which required its holder to turn up once a year, granting or refusing licences for public houses, for a salary of £20 a year. He can hardly have looked on it as profitable, though it must have been worth more than the occasional brief at Chelmsford. But he hoped that better things would flow from his powerful patron. 'The more strings with which I am connected with Lowther,' he thought, 'the better.'

He went to Carlisle early in 1788, and was accepted by the Mayor and Corporation as their new Recorder, though with Lowther's approval the matter was a foregone conclusion. These formalities over, he returned to London, where he had a divorce case in the House of Lords.

When Counsel were called in, I had no uneasy apprehension and stated the case to my satisfaction. I soon was satisfied that the Lord Chancellor saw through my reasoning; and it is very unpleasant to talk what one is conscious is mere plausibility when it is addressed to a man of sense. His Lordship said, 'Mr Boswell, you state your cause very ingeniously. But—' and then he put a question which showed he knew the fallacy, and smiled. However, it was my business to do justice to my client, and I spoke about an hour.

He lost the case, but it was no shameful defeat. That summer he joined the Northern Circuit again; he could hardly be Recorder of Carlisle without doing so, but he was not enthusiastic about it.

York, 12th July 1788

. . . You knew what a circuit is [he wrote to his friend
Malone], by supposing something rather better than what
you have seen; and you may guess how I contrast my situation with yours. I am, however, animated with the
consciousness of acting with a very manly spirit, and though
a dreary remonstrance from my Spanish brother, that I am
lessening myself when there is not the least probability of
my getting business, I attend diligently, I take good notes, I
feel a gradual accession of knowledge, and I look forward
with hope. Indeed, I was assured of three briefs at Newcastle before I left London.

But they never came.

He wrote to Lowther again, hoping to get a seat in Parliament, and was refused. Thus 1788 went by. Boswell had
nothing to show for it, save £20 for sitting once as Recorder of
Carlisle. It was almost nothing, and it seemed almost nothing.
Indeed, the records of Carlisle's Michaelmas Sessions that
year make the same point. They give the names of the Mayor
and the Magistrates, and Boswell's name is written in almost
as an afterthought.

1789 set in with no better auguries. On 10 January he wrote
to his old friend Temple:

I am in a most *illegal* situation; and for appearance should
have cheap chambers in the Temple, as to which I am still
inquiring; but in truth I am sadly discouraged by having no
practice, nor probable prospect of it. And to confess fairly
to you, my friend, I am afraid that were I to be tried, I
should be found so deficient in the *forms,* the *quirks* and the
quiddities which early habit acquires, that I should expose
myself. Yet the delusion of Westminster Hall, of brilliant
reputation and splendid fortune as a barrister, still weighs
upon my imagination.

It is true that his rough draft of the *Life of Johnson* was
almost complete, but it was not enough to console him. 'I
hesitate,' he wrote, 'as to going the spring Northern Circuit,
which costs £50 and obliges me to be in rough, unpleasant
company four weeks. I wish to keep *hovering* as an English

170

lawyer, for I much fear that *now* I should be more unhappy than ever in Scotland.'

His criticism of the Circuit may have been accurate, because whatever Boswell's failings were, he certainly knew a gentleman when he saw one. It was not long since he had dined with the Archbishop of York, the judges of assize, and the rest of the Circuit; when the guests came to go, there were only two people whom the Archbishop asked to stay the night, and Boswell was one of them.

He was, so to speak, a polygon of virtue; irregular, with no telling how far the different sides of his character would go, if produced. Whilst staying with Lord Lonsdale in May that year he fell dead drunk from his horse, and injured his shoulder, thus missing a case in London. In July he suffered the tragic loss of his wife, to whom he was devoted, and soon afterwards went to stay with Lord Lonsdale again, uncongenial though it was. 'My mind was so sore from my late severe loss that I shrunk from the rough scene of the roaring, bantering society of lawyers . . . Such is my melancholy frame at present, that I waver as to all my plans. I have an *avidity* for death. I *eagerly* wish to be laid by my dear dear wife. Years of life seem insupportable.'

He managed wonderfully well to hide his grief, even though Lord Lonsdale was holding a *dance*! But that evening he lost his wig—his ordinary, day-to-day wig. It sounds a very minor misfortune, yet it was nowhere to be found, and he looked a fool without it. He spent the day in his nightcap, and suspected that Lord Lonsdale had played a cruel prank on him. But lost it was, and he had to travel 25 miles to Carlisle, wigless and grotesque, to buy another. On his next visit to Lord Lonsdale, however, it was found. He did not even confide to his journal where it had been.

By November 1789 he had reached the depths of despair:

I have given up my house and taken good chambers in the Inner Temple to have the *appearance* of a lawyer. O! Temple, Temple, is this realising any of the towering hopes which have so often been the subject of our conversations and letters? Yet I live much with a great man [Lonsdale] who, upon any day that his fancy shall be so inclined, may obtain for me an office which would make me independent.

In short I cast about everywhere. I do not see the smallest opening in Westminster Hall . . . And the delusion that practice *may* come at any time (which is certainly true) still possesses me.

A man cannot live on delusions; nor can he live on good terms with the likes of Lord Lonsdale, unless he bow and scrape, and be all smiles. Boswell could not do it; Lord Lonsdale, seeing him somewhat out of humour, accosted him with brutal frankness: 'I suppose you thought I was to bring you into Parliament;' he said, 'I never had any such intentions.'

He accused him of touting for the office of Recorder, which was unforgivably true, and Boswell snapped back. There could be no more favours after that. He would not even accept his resignation as Recorder on the spot; Boswell had to travel on to Carlisle, to perform his duties for the last time, simply signing orders as to poors rates. Any fool of a magistrate could have done as little.

That night he wrote to Temple once again: 'I am alone at an inn, in wretched spirits, and ashamed and sunk on account of the disappointment of hopes which have led me to endure such grievances. I deserve all that I suffer.'

Nine days later he was still there, more wretched than ever:

I remained a few days at an inn [he wrote to Malone], and then went to lodge and board at the Mayor's, an old grocer, now the postmaster, with one daughter such as might make a man forget the difference of sex; but they are both very civil, and I have an excellent room. Except one evening when I drank tea with a clergyman and one morning that Sir James Johnston and I breakfasted together, I have had no other company at any meal till today, when I made one with a few of the corporation at my inn. I, who was lately in London, with all its variety and animation!

Mercifully, his resignation as Recorder was soon accepted. Thus, by midsummer 1790, Boswell had lost his Recordership and was parted for ever from the 'Northern Tyrant', as he called Lonsdale. In the following year his *Life of Johnson* was published and was an immediate success, except with those of his friends who suffered from Johnson's comments on them now public in print. He returned to the Home Circuit, where

172

fortune never smiled on him, and died in 1795, a disappointed man.

There are many books about successful men at the Bar; none have been written about the failures. Boswell's story may be the only one worth telling.

TWELVE

A Modest Success

'Not having read Mr Hamilton's work, it is not fair
to condemn it as a whole, but I think upon consideration he must be ashamed of many of his
abusive expressions.'

James Losh, *Diary,* 21 April 1832
(discussing a religious tract)

Generally speaking, the more distinguished a lawyer is, the
more easy it is to write his biography. Cicero's greatness is
preserved because he wrote down his speeches; he used to
regale his friends with them, a habit to which Queen's Counsel
are mercifully not prone. When a striking advocate appears in
a sensational case, the newspapers print his every word. But
most members of the Bar are quiet, unassuming men who
enjoy a steady reputation in their lives, and leave nothing to
posterity. James Losh, the Newcastle barrister, would have
shared this fate had he not kept a diary which was not so much
meticulous as obsessive, taking himself greatly to task for
careless omissions: 'Having regulated my journal several times
lately the weather etc. has occasionally been omitted.'

It is his diary which makes it possible to obtain a detailed
portrait of a man who was a dull plodder at his work, and yet
had vision; a man who could be surprisingly mean and petty,
yet one whose generosity and compassion towards others
made him nearly a very great man.

He was born in Cumberland at Woodside near Carlisle on 10
June 1768, and from an early age possessed a strong imagination:

At a very early period (I distinctly recollect it before I was
seven years old) I formed a habit of castle-building; and
whatever I read, or heard in conversation, which interested
me, operated so strongly on my imagination, that my whole

mind was occupied by it, until some new and more vivid idea—some more 'attractive metal'—usurped its place.

When very young, Robinson Crusoe, buccaneers, giants, mosstroopers, dragons etc. operated strongly on my fancy. From 12 to 18 I was a lover and a hero of romance. During this period sometimes my heated imagination found vent in poetical effusions, principally dramatic. I seldom, however, pursued any one subject until it was reduced into a complete drama, or regular poem; but I have frequently in an evening whilst wandering in the fields, composed several acts of a tragedy—and from the new passages which I occasionally though very rarely, reduced to writing, I am inclined to think that my verses were not deficient either in smoothness or vigour.

He did well at school and was passionately fond of reading, but inclined to be indolent, at least by his own compulsive standards. When he went up to Cambridge to read classics his knowledge of history, philosophy and politics was far beyond that of most of his colleagues. He dreamed of great things, and his dreaming kept him from the academic distinction he might have reached. He went to London and was admitted to Lincoln's Inn at the age of 21. Soon after being called to the Bar he joined the Northern Circuit, at a time when he had hopes of making a name for himself as a political firebrand.

T Vaughan, C Ward and I went the summer circuit together in 1794, and were then constant companions—we excited great dread among the creatures of administration and were, I believe, generally considered as three men likely to make a noise in the political world, and to be as successful in our profession as any of our contemporaries.

But a natural diffidence kept him from the life of politics which so much interested him:

Whilst I lived in London, the dread of failure, the knowledge that much was expected from me, and a certain nervous shrinking from *shame,* prevented my ever speaking in public. When I settled in the country (after a long illness) these feelings became blunted and I spoke as a barrister, clearly and without difficulty. When *strongly excited,* I have now and then spoken eloquently.

175

His health dictated his future career. He might have stayed in London indefinitely—he published a little edition there of *Areopagitica*, Milton being his favourite poet—but he developed tuberculosis. At about this time he first met William Wordsworth, who often visited him when he was living between Bristol and Bath, as his health required; he began his married life there in 1798 with the daughter of a Cumberland doctor, Cecilia Baldwin, whom Wordsworth regarded as having great activity of spirit. But when his diary begins, on 1 January 1799, he was convalescing in Cumberland at her father's house, with plenty of skating and walking to build up his strength, and a little gentle study of the law—*Blackstone,* and the Term Reports.

In the spring they moved to a house near Newcastle, Jesmond Dene, which he rented for £23 a year, including the garden and a small field; his household consisted of two women and one manservant, a horse and a low gig. He took chambers in Newcastle, too, 'and began the business of a provincial barrister—with weak health, little knowledge of my profession, and less love for it. God will protect me.'

At first he had little business at law and could expect none but, unlike modern barristers, he was also a business man, with a share in an alkali works, a brewery and a coal mine. The law did not then occupy much of his time: 'My usual mode of living now is to go to Newcastle between ten and eleven, to remain in my chambers etc. till about three, and then return to dinner.'

With plenty of leisure for reading, he joined the Newcastle Literary Society. For years he dreamed of becoming an author, but somehow he could never bring pen to paper, save in his diary. He never hit on a striking phrase, but his judgment was sound enough. Here, for his diary's benefit, he reviews the *Book of Genesis* from a general point of view:

A most interesting and valuable work. The account of the manners of early times is most natural and excellent, and many passages exhibit fine specimens of the true pathetic, of simple and elegant narration and of accurate delineation of character. I ardently wish my health and habits would allow me to acquire the Hebrew language, and enable me to peruse the scriptures in the original.

His first brief was in the summer of 1799, when he was led by

176

Jonathan Raine in a prosecution for forgery; Losh himself did not have to open his mouth. He also dined at Bar Mess.

Dinner with the Circuit. The party much what I remember it five years ago—noisy and disagreeable—much familiarity, and little friendly ease. Perpetual attempts at wit and repartee with nearly perpetual failures. Great affected spirit of independence but much envy and servility in reality. I speak however only of the general spirit, as there are many valuable exceptions.

In 1800, his second year on the Circuit, he had a little more work at the assizes, and dined at Bar Mess, where he was 'disgusted as usual with the noise etc. of *my brethren.*' Still, he went on holiday immediately afterwards with Cecilia, and what a holiday it was, enjoying the Lakes with his friends the Lake Poets! They went boating on Derwentwater with Coleridge:

4th September 1800: We passed all the morning on the lake in Calvert's boat. The day was fine, and I was never more delighted by the glorious scenery of what I consider as the finest of the Lakes. Dinner, tea and supper (Coleridge and Calvert). I never saw Coleridge to more advantage. He perhaps always talks rather too much, but so well that one readily forgives him. His manners are gentlemanlike—he shows great knowledge upon all subjects, and is certainly very eloquent, but he is too enthusiastic, and there is rather an appearance of affectation and pedantry in his choice of subjects and manner of conversation . . .
Wordsworth (whom Coleridge considers as the first Poet now living) is about to publish another vol. of his Lyrical Ballads, which have had great success—he is also engaged in a great moral work in verse.
5th September: Breakfast with Coleridge. Call with Cecilia at Armathwaite. Sailed on the lake and visiting Barrow which is a beautiful place and not much spoiled by its owner. Called at Wordsworth's cottage in our way. Miss Wordsworth only was at home; she showed us the inside of their house which is remarkably neat, the very place as far as I could judge it, being dark. The garden and orchard are well made and very pleasant. The situation is delightful in the

vale of Grasmere. They pay only £5 a year rent and 6d. for tares. They seem happy and cheerful.

6th September: Breakfast Miss Wordsworth, William Wordsworth and his brother John. After breakfast we proceeded to Aldingham by the edge of Coniston Lake—a very fine ride (in Dr Baldwin's chaise). Perhaps the head of Coniston is little if at all inferior to anything amongst the Lakes. Dinner at Lowick Bridge. (Present were) Carlyle, Lubbern, and Mr Wordsworth.

When he returned to work he decided to specialise mostly in Chancery law, such as bankruptcy cases, where his business knowledge came in useful, and in property disputes, where he was sometimes an advocate, and sometimes an arbitrator. He was a little shocked to find in one case 'several instances of what is called *hard swearing* occurred, and one where there must have been deliberate perjury on one side or the other.' His more down-to-earth colleagues at the Bar would only have been surprised he was surprised. He had a lot to learn, and he knew it, too. So he went on steadily studying law, and his confidence improved.

'I conducted a prosecution against two women for highway robbery,' he wrote in 1801, 'by no means well, but better than I expected, and with less uneasy feelings than I ever endured before on similar occasions. The women were sentenced to die. Serjeant Cockell, however, who tried them, assured me that they should not suffer.' They were presumably reprieved.

The following night was Grand Night, that special Bar Mess when members of the Circuit take particular pleasure in making fun of each other. James Losh thought it 'a scene of folly, a mixture of coarse humour, envy and insolence, which though it may amuse some minds, appears to be only fit to excite disgust. Perhaps however a man leading a life of retirement is scarcely a fair judge upon subjects of this nature.'

Quite so. James Losh found the Circuit noisy and disgusting, but 34 years of his spidery diaries certainly show up some of his own limitations. A modest diffidence was to his credit in his early days, but had become a wearisome bleat at the age of 69. He was cool about many of his betters when he was young, but when he was old he looked anxiously at newcomers to the Circuit, in case they took any of his practice away from him.

178

He was also a prude: he read Lord Nelson's letters to Lady Hamilton, 'and then gave up reading this wretched and disgraceful publication in disgust,' but not until he had been perusing it for four hours!

When he records that he went to the Literary Society and heard 'a very sensible well-written paper on Taste by Mr Clark, from whose appearance and manners I should not have expected anything good on that subject,' there is something oddly familiar about his style, which combines an air of superiority with such plodding prose. It is amazingly like *The Diary of a Nobody,* whose author invented Charles Pooter as the embodiment of querulous mediocrity. He could never have heard of James Losh, but he and Charles Pooter are clearly one in spirit:

POOTER: I should very much like to know who has wilfully torn the last five or six weeks out of my diary. It is perfectly montrous! Mine is a large scribbling diary, with plenty of space for the record of my everyday events, and in keeping up that record I take (with much pride) a great deal of pains.

LOSH: I wrote and received 16 letters, inclusive of those on professional subjects. I observe that I generally write more letters than I receive, and this I do not well know how to account for.

POOTER: We all then ate our breakfast in dead silence. In fact, I could eat nothing. I was not only too worried, but I cannot and will not eat cushion of bacon. If I cannot get streaky bacon, I will do without anything.

LOSH: My own health upon the whole has been good, but the changing flannel for cotton waistcoat drawers etc. seems to have had some little effect, in making me susceptible of colds and slight rheumatic complaints. I have also had for some time a slight pain and disagreeable feeling in the Tendo Achillis of my left leg, which sometimes gives me a little uneasiness.

The great difference between them is that Losh had a passion for general knowledge, and noted: 'During this last journey I acquired much information as to the nature and use of turnips,' whereas Charles Pooter had a sense of humour, of a sort: 'My entry yesterday about "retired tired", which I did

179

not notice at the time, is rather funny. If I were not so worried just now, I might have had a little joke about it.'

The only smile provoked by the whole of the Losh diaries is when he took his children to see *Much Ado about Nothing*: 'William being only five years old fell asleep, as might have been expected.'

With no sense of humour, and a prudishness which made him think of expurgating Fielding's *Tom Jones* for the general public, no wonder Losh hated Bar Mess. Yet Losh was a man of considerable stature, and kept all his doubts and waverings to his diaries. Robert Southey knew him well enough, and thought of him as 'coming nearer the ideal of a perfect man than any other person whom it has ever been my good fortune to know; so gentle, so pious, so zealous in all good things, so equally minded, so manly, so without speck or stain in his whole habits of life.' Southey, be it remembered, was not only a poet, but wrote biographies of John Wesley and Lord Nelson.

Nobody was more ardent than Losh for reform; at elections, when there was so much bribery and cheating that each candidate was represented by counsel, he made handsome fees but still prayed for the whole rotten system to be swept away. Even before Dickens was born he was working to improve the lot of the poor with soup kitchens, hospitals, and schools for ragged boys and girls. It is easy to forget how important this was. Northumberland, especially in the industrial areas like Newcastle, was one of the worst areas in the country for illiteracy among children. This is perfectly illustrated by the career of George Stephenson, the genius who founded the railway system. Although his father was a mechanic in a Newcastle coal mine, George never had a proper schooling, and could neither read nor write. But a keen interest in the progress of the Napoleonic wars drove him to night school; he learnt to read and write there.

His son Robert was much more fortunate; George sent him to school to learn mathematics, and also enrolled him at the Literary and Philosophic Society in Newcastle, an organisation in which James Losh took an active part. Robert used to bring back books from the Society's library or, if he was not allowed to remove them from the premises, would copy their plans and drawings, and go over them with his father when he got home. Thus George Stephenson himself benefitted from the charitable efforts of James Losh or people like him.

James Losh was deeply devout, and reviewed each Sunday's sermon in his diary; he saw all the great actors when they came to Newcastle—Kean's Hamlet was the finest acting he ever saw—but he had no great ear for music: Paganini's efforts seemed to him 'much more wonderful than pleasing.'

Literature was his greatest love. He read as much as he could; his bankruptcy work often required him to wait up until midnight for a debtor to put in a belated appearance, and he could spend seven hours then finishing Sir Walter Scott's latest novel. He helped organise the Literary and Philosophic Society, where they met every month for earnest papers such as 'some account of the source of the Ganges etc.' It is hard to imagine grown men wanting to go out to hear dreary lectures, but it was an age when public lectures were a great means of spreading knowledge amongst people thirsty for it. So he went regularly to the Society, where once 'we had a translation from Schleger's account of the Elephant read by Mr Salvin.'

It was odd that he, who so aspired to literary success, could not even write a paper for that Society; but one does not have to be a sheep to appreciate mutton. In his diary in 1824 he discusses Wordsworth's style:

He has a vigorous mind, considerable learning, and (in my opinion) true poetical genius. But he has taken it into his head that he is a great metaphysician, and delivers with an air of dignity, and clothed in oracular language truths or errors (sometimes one and sometimes the other) which, when understood, prove not to have been worth inquiring about, and quite on the surface. In my long intimacy and correspondence with Wordsworth, I often endeavoured to cure him of this; and until he was spoiled by *overpraise*, and irritated by *overcensure* and ridicule, I flattered myself that my endeavours were not in vain.

The thought of Losh coaching Wordsworth in poetry is a fascinating one; no doubt he would have left his 'Daffodils' undisturbed, but would certainly have taken away from him the absurd 'Spade! with which Wilkinson hath tilled his lands.' For Losh was quite right.

But he was first and foremost a barrister, and here his diary

181

is puzzling indeed. He was defending a man at Durham Assizes for stealing a £100 Bank of England note, which had been found upon the accused. The jury found him guilty, not of stealing, but of endeavouring to appropriate the money for his own use. Mr Justice Bayley told them they must either find him guilty as charged, or acquit him altogether; so the jury retired again, and soon returned with a verdict of 'not guilty'.

The judge told the accused that he had had a narrow escape, and warned him to beware of his conduct in future; the accused bowed gratefully to the judge and jury and was about to leave the dock when one of the jurors said, 'My Lord, I think the prisoner guilty.' The judge turned to them, and said a few words which nobody else could hear; they retired again, and after two hours returned with a verdict of 'guilty'. The accused was almost overcome, and was taken speechless from the court. The judge told James Losh that his client would be entitled to the benefit of any point which might arise from the jury having retired a second time.

It is one of the most extraordinary things that could happen in a barrister's career, but it comes from the *Carlisle Journal* in August 1824; all that James Losh's diary says about it is, 'Business in and out of Court 10 (hours).' It is one of his standard phrases.

His heart was not altogether in his work; he felt that 'the business of a provincial barrister on the circuit was irksome, and in some degree degrading'—perhaps because it depended on the whim of the attorneys who briefed him. Yet he kept doggedly at it, and could get up at dawn with the best of them to catch the early mail-coach. He endured the long sessions at the assizes: 'In court 15 hours. No dinner; sandwiches in court.' And he made a living from his profession.

Two years after starting in chambers in Newcastle he earned £300 a year at the Bar, and was making steady progress when a calamity befell him: the Bank of Carlisle stopped payments, and his two brothers became bankrupt. He feared that ruin would overtake him at any time, and it was too much for his highly-strung nerves. A doctor advised him not to go into court, and this is why he came to miss an incident at Carlisle Assizes in 1803.

A case was being tried which caught the imagination of the whole country, because it arose from the seduction of a beautiful rustic girl by a heartless bigamist or, as Wordsworth put it in Book VII of the *Prelude,*

> *. . . a Story drawn*
> *From our own ground, the Maid of Buttermere,*
> *And how the Spoiler came, a bold bad Man.*

Mary of Buttermere worked at the Fish Inn, then a very remote place indeed where, as De Quincey described it, 'stands a cluster of cottages, so small and few that in the richer tracts of England they would scarcely be complimented with the name of hamlet.' John Hatfield was a cheap confidence trickster, so compulsive a liar that he had forgotten what truth was. He had already married and left two women when he met Mary, whom he married and left in due course for another girl, all of which was very wicked, but would not have been fatal. However, during his stay in Cumberland he called himself 'The Hon. Augustus Hope', and not only received letters in that name, but *franked* letters in that forged name too, which was then a capital offence; indeed, he was convicted of it and hanged.

Wordsworth and Coleridge took a keen interest in the case and Wordsworth visited him in custody before the case came on, but Coleridge was not allowed to, which may have piqued that wayward man of genius because, according to Coleridge's own recollection: 'At Carlisle I alarmed the whole court, judges, counsellors, tipstaves, jurymen, witnesses, and spectators by hallooing to Wordsworth who was in a window on the other side of the hall—dinner!' But Coleridge's sense of humour was quite irrepressible; James Losh quotes one of his riddles:

> *Why is a murderer like an unborn Ass?*
> *Because they are both Assassins.*

1803 was James Losh's worst year. An infant son died; he and his wife bore it with great stoicism and he continued working steadily, though the effort was considerable. Gradually the clouds passed away. The Bank of Carlisle started paying out again; his brothers got back on their feet, and his work became more and more profitable. He took new chambers in Dean Street; his income rose soon to £2000 a year, and he could give more of his time and money to charity.

183

He was prosperous and contented, though he viewed most things dispassionately—even Acts of God:

About two o'clock a most tremendous storm of thunder, lightning and rain took place. Our house at Jesmond was struck by the lightning in a very extraordinary manner. The chimney most to the East was struck and the funnel at the top split, and the soot forced into the dining room below as completely as if it had been regularly swept . . . A barometer hanging in the passage above stairs was broken and the woodwork much torn. Two large holes were made in the wall in the kitchen and the lock of a clout found open. Two servants who were in the kitchen declare that they saw two *balls of fire* roll along the kitchen door and pass out at the door.

I have not been able to ascertain the course of the electric matter, nor to trace the cause of the different effects which it had produced. Thank God no human being was hurt.

It is at points like this in the Losh diaries that one wishes he had managed to write a book; and it is while wading through page after page where he has nothing interesting to say whatever, that one realises why he never did. James Losh certainly had plenty of *information*—it was the quality he most admired in others—and he and Henry Brougham were keenly interested in an earnest enterprise called the Society for the Diffusing of useful Knowledge. Losh was asked to write a pamphlet for it about the learned Dr Paley, but the popular thirst for that information remained unslaked; he never wrote it. He was, however, capable of great perception. He visited the haven of Boulmer, near Alnwick, where smuggling was carried on.

10th April 1821: my business was attending the county magistrates on the behalf of the Crown respecting some smuggling transactions. Mr Cockerill and I went to Boulmer to examine witnesses, and I never saw anything more striking than the state of that village as showing the miserable effects of over-taxation and excessive duties. Geneva (gin) may be bought in Holland for 1s. 8d. per gallon and the selling price in England is 19s. 6d. This enormous difference resulting from the duty upon the importation of foreign spirituous liquors. The consequence is that smuggling holds out such temptations that the greatest exertions are made to carry it on . . . The worst consequences of all are, however, the profligate habits and utter disregard of morality of most of those concerned in the traffic. Boulmer is a small fishing village, well situated both for catching and selling fish . . . but with the true spirit of gamblers or desperate speculators, they neglect their ordinary affairs, seduced by the hope of immense profits from smuggling, and hence the men are lazy drunkards, the women profligate and dirty, and the children ragged and without education.

The greatest passion in James Losh's life was the quest for knowledge, and so he was always particularly drawn to those who had *much information,* as he put it; many of his colleagues failed this requirement dismally. But the quality was often to be found in unexpected places—the little village of Seaham, for instance, near Sunderland:

> *11th June 1829*: We dined upon bacon and eggs at a small public house kept by one Chilton, an ingenious man who has himself constructed a very fine electrical apparatus, and who appears to repair with great neatness musical instruments, barometers, thermometers, etc. He is a miller by trade, and only attends to the other matters at his leisure hours.

James Losh was no fool when it came to science, as his diary for 1802 shows. During a stay in London he attended one of Humphrey Davy's famous lectures at the Royal Institution; Davy had yet to prove wrong the current theory that all acids contained oxygen, so that 'oxymuriatic acid' (as it was sometimes called) was wrongly named:

> *25th February 1802*: Business and Lincoln's Inn Hall two and a half hours. Davy's lecture at the Royal Institution two. Afterwards dined at the Prince of Wales' Coffee House with Coleridge and Davy . . . Davy's lecture on the oxygenated mercuriate acid was by very far the best lecture I ever heard—clear, simple, well-arranged, and the experiments all successful. I had much pleasant and interesting conversation at and after dinner with Davy and Coleridge on metaphysics chiefly. Davy believes that *time* is perceived

by the mind independent of any external objects—that is, when any *idea* presents itself to the mind it necessarily conveys along with it some tolerably distinct notion of the time when it was first received. Davy appears to me the ablest and clearest headed man I have met with in London. . . . Davy gave me an invitation to attend his lectures as long as I stayed in town. I had some conversation with Davy also about *dreaming,* curious rather than satisfactory.

He and Davy had a very high regard for each other. But he was forced to take sides against him over the invention of the miners' safety lamp. George Stephenson, before turning to railways, developed the 'Geordie' safety lamp at about the same time that Davy developed another on similar principles. It was not the first time that two men of genius reached the same conclusions independently, but too much of the credit went to Davy—people in Northumberland thought so, anyway. One can quite understand Davy's point of view; he was a national figure of great eminence, and nobody had heard of this upstart Northumberland miner who claimed to have discovered the lamp first. James Losh found himself in the middle of this controversy:

13th November 1818: I had a letter from my old acquaintance Sir H Davy, written with much ill-humour and little discretion, as a rebuke to me for taking part with Geo. Stephenson in the dispute as to the Safety Lamp. In my answer I endeavoured to treat Sir Humphrey with civility, and even respect, as a man of science and a benefactor to mankind, at the same time that I vindicated my right of judgment.

James Losh never lost his wide range of interests. Ten years later—he was then 59—he chose to travel all the way to London on the outside of the stagecoach; it offered so much more to his inquiring mind.

14th April 1828: I set out upon my journey to Britton Hall and London taking my servant Noel with me. We left Newcastle at three-quarters before six in the Leeds coach and reached Leeds soon after seven at night. I went on the outside the whole way, and we travelled safely and by no

186

means unpleasantly. As I sat on the box with the coachman, I was not much annoyed by the dust; I saw the country to advantage, and had the means of inquiring as to the names of places etc. One man drove the coach four or five stages who had been a driver of coaches for above 50 years. Another (from Ware to London), a well-informed man, a reader (and not in vain) of our best English poets, and a great advocate for the March of Intellect, expressing doubts however of the wisdom of over-educating the lower *orders of the community*!

Education for the poor was one of the great causes James Losh supported; but the coachman had more surprises in store for him:

I met with a coachman who talked of 'the powerful genius and transcendant imagination' of Milton—of the March of Intellect, and of the best mode of educating the *lower orders* of the people! Notwithstanding *all this learning,* my friend the coachman was a shrewd and intelligent man, and well acquainted with places, the state of cultivation, etc. I have since heard that many coachmen clear from £200 to £300 a year, so they may well talk of the 'lower orders' of the people.

When one remembers that Wordsworth rented his cottage at Grasmere for £5 a year, and James Losh rented his much more sizeable establishment at Jesmond Dene for £29 a year, it is clear that the coachman had a very well-paid job.

The years passed by rapidly for James Losh, not uneventfully, for he saw Napoleon change from the hope of the reformers to a despotic tyrant, and then a defeated emperor; England grew more desperate for political change. But through this time, he rode about from sessions to sessions, and from one bankrupt estate to another, and he cultivated his garden for three hours a day. He was no mean expert in plantation, and when Wordsworth wrote slightingly of larches, Losh knew better:

Great masses of the larch alone are certainly formal; and when planted in low grounds it is by no means beautiful; but the vivid green of the larch in the spring with its bright flowers, and its pale yellow leaves in the autumn, are not only pleasing in themselves, but also harmonise well with other trees. And when planted in high and rocky situations, it accords well with the scenery, and even adds to its wildness and alpine character.

He brought up eight children with his own mixture of fondness and earnestness. Every father is proud of his son's latest utterance, but not quite in James Losh's terms:

John (four years old) made a complete syllogism which however is not I believe uncommon to young children. He observed some heaps of lime in a field, I told him they were for manure. Some time afterwards he said, 'Lime builds houses, lime is manure, therefore manure builds houses.'

He was forever fussing about his health; at the age of 45 he was tormented by 'circumstances to which I cannot give a name even to myself,' and vowed in his diary (discreetly couched in Latin) 'to avoid illicit love and consequently escape disease.' It seems to have been an isolated indiscretion, and he was deeply ashamed of it, for he was a devoted husband. But one aspect of his character was profoundly ugly, and he never even recognised it—avarice.

His rich uncle would not alter his will in favour of James Losh and his family, despite all efforts, and when at the age of 76 he married a servant woman, Losh feared that the bulk of the old man's fortune would become 'her prey'.

At last he lay dying, and Losh hastened to his bedside; after a 'long and interesting conversation' he persuaded him to leave the management of his affairs to him. No sooner said than done; his will was made in a way Losh trusted 'to be satisfactory to all parties concerned.' He died the next morning, giving Losh that *moderate independence* he had often wished and prayed for.' The widow was allowed to stay on at the house—a condition in the will, presumably—but Losh managed the property, and was better off by £15,000.

Five years later his cousin was gravely ill. He hastened to her house, hoping for £12,000 under her will, but she died before he could speak to her, and he found she had left him nothing; he was quite rich enough from his uncle's will and his coal mine, she thought, and she was right. He was outraged by her

188

dishonourable conduct: 'I went to look at her in her coffin,' he noted, 'and it is a comfort to say that I looked at her remains with sorrow rather than anger.'

His avarice must certainly be held against him. It was the only ungenerous side of his character; although it must be set against his better qualities, it does not outweigh them. It is easier to understand his actions and forgive them if one shares his horror when failure of the Bank of Carlisle caused the bankruptcy of two of his brothers, and almost brought him down as well:

20th July 1803: This has been a wretched day. The Carlisle Bank must stop and the most grievous consequences will follow. God grant us all resignation, and wisdom to make the best use of his chastisements. I have drunk deep of the misery arising from pecuniary embarrassments today, the disgusting labour of talking to men who urge their demands unlike gentleman of Christians, and the humiliating feelings attendant upon such business. May it be my uniform care to avoid all similar circumstances.'

He avoided it partly by persuading his uncle to alter his will, but mostly by his own considerable efforts. He continued to live a hard-working, philanthropic life. He could have retired now, past the age of 60, but easy indolence was not for him. He might have aged into a crusty complainer, for he was often the senior at Bar Mess, but no man alive was more go-ahead than he. He had the vision to see the benefits to the country of a railway between Carlisle and Newcastle and, at the first meeting to consider the project, plunged in while others stood hesitant. It is hardly surprising—he had not only a considerable interest in modern science, but also a brother, William Losh, who owned an iron foundry in Newcastle; William Losh and George Stephenson patented an iron rail and chair to seat it on in 1816, and they worked together closely in the first critical years of the Railway Age. At any rate, when the Carlisle to Newcastle railway was first discussed in 1825, James Losh was made the Chairman of the Board of Directors; he was the ideal choice. A Mr Giles was appointed the railroad engineer, to survey the route and draw up the plans, but it was Losh who recognised the substantial merits of the other candidate, Mr Isambard Kingdom Brunel.

His health broke down again at this time, but after a holiday he was back at work as before. He was never a great advocate, but was sound enough; he sometimes prosecuted murder cases when the great Scarlett was defending. He was the chief speaker at public meetings to abolish the slave trade, and to reform Parliament.

In 1832 he visited London, and called on two of his old friends: Henry Brougham, now Lord Chancellor, and Lord Grey, the Prime Minister. Both were glad to spend some hours alone with him, for they valued his opinion; though he was only a provincial barrister, he came close to being a great man. Lord Grey was in the middle of the battle to get the Reform Bill through Parliament, and abolish rotten boroughs. 'Losh, I am too old for my work!' he said.

But James Losh was not. He was now 69, and 1833 was the last year of his life; he was as active as ever as a barrister and spoke out against the employment of children in factories, till an ignorant mob broke up the meeting. He obtained the necessary government loan for the railway, and had a superb crop of alpine strawberries in his garden; and he sat as the Recorder of Newcastle, an office which had been denied him so long as Catholics and Nonconformists were barred from public office.

10th April 1833: Business out and in the court as Recorder ten hours. Several prisoners, mostly women, were there for offences not very serious in themselves, but there were circumstances—such as former guilt, connection with a bad gang, etc., which induced me to transport four or five of them.

People wonder today what sort of person could send any-body for transportation. James Losh could. He was a careful lawyer, and a liberal reformer in the forefront of those who campaigned against the cruelties of the slave trade, chimney sweeping by little boys, and children working in factories; he did all he could to support hospitals and schools for the poor. Once again he imposed the same punishment:

3rd July 1833: I feel confident that I did right in sending a profligate woman to Botany Bay, for an offence, pilfering from a drunken man, not normally punished so severely.

190

She was not merely a common woman herself, but had at the least another and also a Bully upon her establishment. As she was young and healthy looking, she may do better in New South Wales. Here she must have been a pest to society.

In August 1833 he went to the Cumberland Assizes, not as a barrister, but as a Grand Juryman: his uncle's estate within the county entitled him to do so. Here he met the Lord Chief Justice; he found an amiable and able man who failed Losh's great test: 'I should not expect to find him possessed of much *abstruse learning.*'

Losh never changed. But Wordsworth did:

7th August 1833: My old friend Wordsworth, the poet, dined with us at Woodside. He is now an old and somewhat infirm man, but he retains all his activity and energy of mind: having at the same time *got quit of* much of his pompous and declamatory manner of conversing. I avoided politics and all subjects likely to cause irritation on either side, and we passed a very pleasant and tranquil evening. His wife and son accompanied the Bard.

It was their last meeting. A month later Losh took up a new appointment as Revising Barrister for North Yorkshire, passing through the lovely country around Barnard Castle on a fine autumn day.

19th September 1833: We went in our carriage to Romald-kirk where our revising duties did not detain us above two hours.

The drive to Barnard Castle and from Barnard Castle to Romaldkirk on the Yorkshire side of the river is very fine. The day was beautiful and scenery very picturesque. Many of the trees were beautiful of their kinds—particularly the ash and the holly.

On our return to Greta Bridge we crossed the river.

Here the diary ends, after 34 years of recording great events and tedious trifles, for at Greta Bridge, after four days' illness, James Losh died. His statue is still to be seen in Newcastle at the premises of the Literary and Philosophic Society; his name is now quite naturally forgotten on the Northern Circuit. But after his death Wordsworth noted it as a year which had robbed him of Coleridge, of Charles Lamb, James Losh, and two others. To be reckoned in that company must, at least, be considered a modest success.

THIRTEEN

The Truth About Dagger Money

> 'Witness our frequent terms, sessions and assizes;
> and in what pomp and state the judges in their
> circuits, by the sheriffs, knights, and justices, and
> all the country, are attended,—ofttimes for the
> hanging of a poor thief for the stealing of a hog or a
> sheep—nay, in some cases, for the stealing of a
> penny.'
>
> Alexander Rigby, MP for Wigan, in 1640

A little wickedness can be quite fun. A very small skeleton in the cupboard—a slightly misspent youth—gives solid citizens something to look back on with pleasure. Many people in Newcastle still believe that the judges had to be paid 'dagger money' to buy their own protection when they rode that part of the Circuit, because it was so plagued with cut-throats. Local barristers may yet nudge themselves at the thought, and deem themselves gay dogs. But dagger money has not quite so sensational a history.

Perhaps from the first the practice was the same. The judges gathered in London to choose the Circuits they wished to ride, the most senior having first choice. In the early days of the circuit system judges, and sheriffs appointed to act as judges, were allowed to sit in justice in the counties where they lived, but this led to corruption and abuse, so a law was passed that judges should not without special permission go the Circuits within which they lived. The practice is still followed today.

Who, then, chose to go the Northern Circuit? Not the judges who lived there, nor any others if they could help it, because the Northern Circuit, to an extent equalled only by the Oxford Circuit, was considered the 'longest and most painful'. Just how unpopular it was is shown by a remarkable letter written in Latin in about 1262 to Walter of Merton, the Chancellor, by one of the itinerant justices whose name is not

given, but who was connected with Knaresborough Castle and
Scarborough:

> Greetings to his Lordship, and my faithful and proper
> service to him in all things.
>
> I entreat your Lordship, with all the persuasion I can
> muster, that you can see your way to arranging that I do not
> have to go on circuit into Cumberland. I should hate to have
> to toil up there; it is such a long way, and the unpleasant
> climate is extremely bad for my constitution. I should tell
> you that I was informed I had to do it by the Earl of Carlisle,
> and I told him I would never have wanted to go there
> without your express command, even if I was ordered to by
> his Majesty the King. If the justices really have to go out on
> circuit and you want me to go somewhere at any time, could
> you please arrange for me to do the counties of Cambridge
> and Huntingdon, with the King's blessing and expenses
> paid? I could get my provisions there for a long time—
> bread, beer, meat, hay, wood, and oats, and other trifling
> necessities.
>
> If anything new turns up after I have gone, some bother
> that needs sorting out, by all means turn to me first, and let
> me know by letter if you want me to come back to court and
> stay there, or go back to my own part of the world and wait
> at Scarborough or Knaresborough Castle or at any of my
> other estates for better times. I am ready and willing to
> perform your wishes in every possible way.
>
> For God's sake do not forget to let me know how things
> are with you and the court, and also your instructions in
> what I have mentioned. Long may your Lordship flourish. If
> you have to stay in London and war breaks out, the three
> jars of wine I have in my chambers near to your own are for
> you to take and drink. My good wishes once again.

When the judges' choice of circuit was approved, they
named the towns at which they proposed to hold the assizes—
usually where the gaols were, to avoid unnecessary movement
of prisoners—and their commissions were drawn up, making
their assizes official. Then they would be told of special duties
or problems. In 1176 they had to see that castles were
demolished; in early Stuart times they had to deal with the
Roman Catholics. Thus, before the Summer Assizes of 1617,

they gathered in the Star Chamber to hear the Lord Keeper, Francis Bacon, compare 'hollow church-papists' to 'the roots of nettles, which themselves sting not, but yet they bear all the stinging leaves. Let me know of such roots,' he said, 'and I will root them out of the country.' Since 1760 judges have been free of such political duties. But Bacon's opening words deserve to be better known:

'First, you that are the judges of circuit are as it were the planets of the kingdom (I do you no dishonour in giving you that name) and no doubt you have a great stroke in the frame of the government, as the other have in the frame of the world. Do therefore as they do; move always and be carried with the motion of your first mover, who is your sovereign. A popular judge is a deformed thing; and *plaudits* are fitter for players than magistrates. Do good to the people, love them, and do them justice. But let it be, as the psalm saith, *nihil inde expectantes*, looking for nothing, neither praise nor profit.'

There was a time when they got a great deal more; in Edward I's time all but two of the judges were found guilty of corruption, and were dismissed and heavily fined. It was perhaps for the same reason that Edward III ordered in 1346: 'It pleases the King that the justices [of assize] shall take nothing from the parties who have business before them, except for food and drink, and that of little value.'

The judges certainly had to provide some of their necessities; as the letter of 1262 shows, they included bread, beer, meat and so on. But the local gentry always made a handsome contribution. Here and there in books of local history one can find the Sheriff's accounts at assize time; they give a changing picture of hospitality on the grand scale from the reign of Henry VIII onwards.

At the Lent Assizes in 1528 Sir John Nevill of Chevet, Knight, the Sheriff of Yorkshire, had to provide wheat, malt, beans and hay; and the fish part of the diet included 'salt-fish; 2 barrels of herrings, 2 barrels of salmon, 12 seams of sea-fish [sic], 6 score of great pike and pickerings, 20 great breams, 12 great tenches, 12 great eels and 300 other eels, 20 great rudds, 28 great fresh salmon, a barrel of sturgeon, £2 6s. 8d.; a firkin of seal . . .'

It was a time when sturgeon was plentiful, and not a royal fish; at the Lammas Assizes 1529 the poultry he provided included many wild fowl which were not beyond the plates of ordinary people: '22 swans, £5 10s., 12 cranes, 30 heronsews [young herons], 12 shovelards [ducks], 10 bitterns, 80 partridges, 12 pheasants, 20 curlews, 32 curlew knaves [whimbrels], 6 dozen plovers, 30 dozen pigeons. . . .'

One of the judges evidently liked mulled wine: 'For ¼ lb of sugar which Sir Stephen Tempest had in wine, 5d.' Although rush-lights were probably good enough for the Sheriff and his family, the judges needed something better: 'Item, paid for 4 lb of cotton weak lights which were used when the judges were here (at Skipton) 1s. 6d.'

Richard Lowther, the High Sheriff of Cumberland, seems to have been much more frugal. His accounts begin:

THE JUSTICES' DIET

1567 the 6th day of May. An estimate of a proportion for the assizes.

A house, first prepared a house and some stuff Carlisle with a barn and horsegrease and fire. £5.

Other items include beef, £7; mutton, £6; veal, £3; 120 rabbits, and a tun of wine. One of the Bishop of Durham's servants laid in more specialised provisions:

Darlington, 29 July 1662

SIR—I am come as far as this place to meet the judge, who lay last night at Allerton, but is not come yet. We are prepared to entertain him nobly at Durham Castle.——— Pray will you go to the Woolsack in the Poultry near the Compter, Mr Turford's shop, and there buy a gallon of his best oil, and barrel of his Lucca olives, if he has any fresh and very good come in; buy them in the same long and slender barrels they came in, and tell him the last oil I had of him was none of his best. You may please to pay him out of my lord's money, and account it with me. If you can find any large good damask prunes [damsons], which are not easily got, we want some for my lord, which pray get for him.

But the Sheriffs' expenses were not confined to food and drink alone, as Sir Thomas Swinburne, Sheriff of Northumberland, found in August 1629; they are the only accounts to include a prayer, but it was appropriate under the circumstances:

A note of mine own particular private charges at this assize. I let Lanc. Augood and the Under Sheriff have the profits of the assizes, paying the judges' men and other officers their fees; yet notwithstanding I paid the judges' men out of my own purse   40s.

Item to the Judges Sir Henry Yelverton and Sir James Whitelock either of them apiece at our parting upon Benwell Hills   40s.

To the Minister of St. Nicholas Church for visiting the prisoners   10s.

For mending the town gallows and carrying the ladders   12s.

For burying 3 poor prisoners   7s. 6d.

('O let the sorrowful sighing of the prisoners come before thee; according to the greatness of thy power preserve thou those that are appointed to die.' Psalm 79, v. 12.)

                                           Total £5 9s. 6d.

The judges were entitled to a fee of £20 for going the Circuits, due to be paid before they set out. Great wrath was expressed in 1627 when the Lord Treasurer owed them a year's pay, which he promised faithfully to give them as soon as some money came into the royal coffers; but he only paid off the judges who had lent him money, until the others threatened to sue.

Mr Justice Whitelocke's accounts for that year show that the Northern Circuit cost him about £20 for the return trip, and £26 while on circuit. He took thirteen horses and ten men with him, including his clerk, cryer (a sort of usher who would proclaim the court's opening and closing), a marshall (whose duties included seeing that felons were properly branded), a butler, cook, and other servants. 16d. a day he reckoned for the upkeep of each man and horse, while he himself lived in unashamed luxury at 8s. 4d. a day. The biggest part of his income came from the official fees and fines in the cases he dealt with, some £80 in all, and each circuit town and county contributed something towards his upkeep, so that from his visit he made a clear profit of £90, a tenth of his total profit for the year. Seventy years later, however, judges were always out of pocket after their circuits, and their salaries were revised.

Once a judge reached circuit territory, he would be joined by a cavalcade of the Sheriff's men, sometimes as many as 300, and the barristers might also ride with them. It was too formidable an array to tempt highwaymen, though in 1559, the year before the Restoration, Peter de Beauvior, an officer discharged from Cromwell's army, lay in wait for Baron Thorpe as he rode through Doncaster on his way to York. The scoundrel muttered darkly that if he met with 20 or 30 men he would show them all, since he cared no more for killing a man than for killing a woodcock. He asked more questions than was healthy about the judge's route, and the money he might have with him. He was probably deranged; he would hardly have flaunted his words and weapons if he had been sane and in earnest. Nonetheless, he rode about with several armed companions, and at Doncaster stayed at the same inn as the judge, posing as one of his party. He was armed with four pistols, a carbine, a rapier and a pocket dagger; he kept his firearms loaded; but his threatening behaviour got him arrested, and he was lucky indeed to be discharged at York Assizes upon finding sureties for his good behaviour.

No other judge has been threatened while riding the Circuit; it was rare enough for violence to occur in court, as when a man threw a famous 'brickbat that narrowly missed' at a judge. His right hand was cut off forthwith, and he was hanged, it being the standard punishment for such offences, and enough to discourage them.

But there were other hazards. In 1661 the bridge over the River Tyne at Corbridge needed rebuilding, but the citizens begrudged the expense, so the people of Newcastle sent a petition to Parliament:

When the waters are high (which very often happens) all the said carriers and other persons are either stopped in their journeys or forced to ferry over the Tyne or ford it to the great hazard of losing themselves and their goods (above three-score persons being at one time drowned in ferrying over at Hexham, besides many others yearly lost in ferrying and fording the said river), the judges at one time in great danger of being drowned, and oftentimes impeded in their passage betwixt this town and the city of Carlisle in their circuit, and all for want of the repair of the said bridge at Corbridge.

It was rebuilt in 1674, and is still standing.

It is not generally recognised that a judge's wife may be something of a hazard. Lord Ellenborough's wife once offered to accompany him on circuit, and he told her that he had no objection, provided she did not clutter the carriage up with bandboxes, which particularly irritated him. On the first day, happening to stretch his legs within the carriage, his foot struck against something under the seat; he found it was a bandbox. And so, no doubt thinking some exasperated thoughts about Lady Ellenborough, he flung up the window and pitched out the bandbox. Serve her right. The coachman would have stopped to pick it up—'Drive on!' cried Lord Ellenborough, furiously, so it was left where it lay in the ditch.

When they reached the assize town, Lord Ellenborough arrayed himself in his robes, and could not find his wig. 'Where *is* my wig?' he demanded. 'My Lord,' replied his servant, 'it was thrown out of the carriage window.'

When riding the Circuits, the judges and the serjeants (who like modern Queen's Counsel were distinguished senior members of the Bar sometimes appointed to sit as Commissioners of Assize) were not dressed ostentatiously. These were their instructions in 1635:

The judges and serjeants, when they ride circuits, are to wear a serjeant's coat of good broad-cloth, with sleeves, and faced with velvet. They have used of late to lace the sleeves of the serjeant's coat thick with lace. And they are to have a sumpter (pack-horse), and ought to ride with six men at the least.

When the judges entered a county, the Sheriff was there to meet them, and the smarter the Sheriff's escort, the better they were pleased. These 'javelin men', as they were often called, wore the Sheriff's livery and followed his trumpeters to meet the judge. However, near Newcastle in about 1676, Roger North found the cortège anything but uniform:

They were a comical sort of people, riding upon 'negs' as they call their small horses, with long beards, cloaks, and long broad swords, with basket hilts, hanging in broad belts, that their legs and swords almost touched the ground; and every one, in his turn, with his short cloak, and other equippage, came up cheek by jowl, and talked with my lord judge. His lordship was very well pleased with their discourse; for they were great antiquaries in their own bounds.

When they reached an assize town, the judges might go at once to an assize service, and these were their instructions in 1635:

In the circuit the judges go to the church upon Sundays, in the forenoon, in scarlet gowns, hoods, and mantles, and sit in their caps: and in the afternoons to the church in scarlet gowns, tippet, and scarlet hood, and sit in their cornered caps.

And the first morning at the reading of the commissions, they sit in scarlet gowns, with hoods and mantles, and in their coifs and cornered caps. And he that gives the charge, and delivers the gaol, doth or ought for the most part to continue all that assizes the same robes, scarlet gown, hood, and mantle. But the other judge, who sits upon the *nisi prius* [civil cases], doth commonly (if he will) sit only in his scarlet robe, with tippet and casting-hood; or if it be cold he may sit in gown, and hood, and mantle.

And where the judges in circuit go to dine with the Sheriff, or to a public feast, then in scarlet gowns, tippets, and scarlet hoods; or, casting off their mantle, they keep on their other hood.

The coifs were the flat black hats which were part of a serjeant's rank; they survived into modern times as the black cap which judges donned before pronouncing sentence of death. In 1635, be it noted, the judges did not wear wigs. It was not until after the Restoration that they did so, following a fashion introduced from France. The barristers began to wear them too, but the judges thought this arrogant and presumptuous of them, and at first refused to listen to barristers so flashily attired: 'Who would have supposed,' wrote Lord Campbell in Victorian times, 'that this grotesque ornament, fit only for an African chief, would be considered indispensably necessary for the administration of justice in the middle of the nineteenth century?' Or in the twentieth, for that matter?

Lord Campbell, however, was a critical Scotsman; so was another eminent lawyer, Sir John Clerk, who was at the Judges' Service at Carlisle Cathedral in 1731:

> The judges were seated next to the Bishop and were in their robes of scarlet, faced with a light brown silk, with black scarfs, and sashes. They had long full-bottomed periwigs, a fashion very tenaciously kept up amongst the judges in England and the serjeants. This, they suppose, adds a great deal to their gravity though, if the thing be well considered, it seems pretty odd that judges should think themselves ornamented by the long hairs of a woman and who was perhaps likeways a whore to the bargain.

Once there, they were at the preacher's mercy; a sermon which ran to 40 or 50 printed pages was not unusual. Mr Justice Altham and Mr Justice Bromley, at Lancaster Assizes in 1610, two years before the famous witch trial, had to listen to a dismal-sounding discourse on 'The Dreadful Day, dolorous to the wicked but glorious to all such as look and long after Christ.' Judges suffered not only from long sermons, but dissident preachers too. Francis Bacon gave the judges due warning:

> Next, for the matter of religion, in particular place, I recommend both to you and to the justices the countenancing godly and zealous preachers. I mean, not sectaries or novellists [people with new ideas], but those which are sound and conform; but yet pious and reverend. For there will be a perpetual defection except you keep men in by preaching, as well as law doth by punishing; and commonly spiritual diseases are not cured but by spiritual remedies.

Thus, when in 1684 Judge Jeffreys, at Carlisle Cathedral, had to endure a sermon 'length and stuff intolerable', it was no isolated instance.

The Sheriff certainly failed to provide a suitable preacher in 1719. The sermons at Newcastle and Appleby were so inflammatory that the judges had to answer them in their words to the Grand Jury at those towns and, in 1824, the Rev. Sydney Smith, better remembered now as a wit than a humane reformer, outraged the legal profession at York by warning the judges against immoderate language:

'A Judge,' he said, 'always speaks with impunity, and always speaks with effect. His words should be weighed, because they entail no evil upon himself, and much evil upon others. The language of passion, the language of sarcasm, the language of satire is not, on such occasions, Christian language; it is not the language of a judge. When magistrates, under the mask of law, aim at the offender more than at the offence, and are more studious of inflicting pain than repressing error of crime, the office suffers as much as the judge; the respect for justice is lessened; and the school of pure reason becomes the hated theatre of mischievous passion.'

Every good judge would agree with him, and any bad one ought to have the words framed, and hung in his private room.

Sooner or later the sermon would come to an end, and the judges went to court to take their seats. It might not be easy; the court was sometimes so crowded at York that the judges had to elbow their way through the mob. But once on the Bench, according to a French observer, they reached a haven of tranquillity:

'Everything breathes a spirit of levity and mildness. The judge looks like a father in the midst of his family occupied in trying one of his children. His countenance had nothing threatening in it. According to an ancient custom, flowers are strewed upon his desk, and upon the clerk's. The Sheriff and officers of the court wear each a nosegay. By a condescension sufficiently extraordinary, the judge permits his Bench to be invaded by a throng of spectators, and thus finds himself surrounded by the prettiest women of the county—the sisters, wives, or daughters of grand jurors . . . They are attired in the most elegant negligé; and it is a spectacle not a little curious to see the judge's venerable head, loaded with a large wig, peering among the youthful female heads.'

The Frenchman obviously warmed to the array of feminine beauty; an English visitor did not:

'It is rather too much,' he wrote, 'to see the ladies putting on their bonnets in the morning, look at the judges and hear the prisoners condemned to death, and then take them off again to prepare for the dance at night. One would not expect that they should return home to eat no dinner; but, without incurring the charge of any mawkish sentimentality, one may be permitted to feel something revolting in the very name of an assize ball.'

Still, however frivolous the ladies might be, the judge had to tackle his task in deadly earnest. He had first to address the Grand Jury, not the same thing at all as the jury of twelve who try criminal cases, but a sort of committee of responsible citizens of the county. He would explain to them the state of the country and their duty as magistrates, saying something too about local problems. At York Assizes, Mr Justice Bayley's exhortation to calmness three weeks before the Peterloo Massacre was generally approved, though his analysis of economic problems and comments upon the national debt were thought naive. At any rate, the judge's weighty words would be received in a respectful silence broken only by the cries of those who found their pockets had been picked; for, even in court, the bulging wallets of the assembled Grand Jurors were a favourite target of the light-fingered.

Then the judge would begin the trials. Criminal cases started with counsel for the prosecution explaining the facts to the jury, unless he happened to be out of court, as sometimes occurred. In a shop-lifting case before Mr Justice Bayley at Carlisle in 1828, the *Carlisle Journal* said:

> The prisoner pleaded 'not guilty'. The counsel for the prosecution being out of court, the judge called upon the witnesses, and was in the act of examining the first one, when Mr Peter Hodgson of Whitehaven, the attorney for the prosecution, came into court, and stopping the business, addressed his Lordship thus: 'My Lord, Mr Coltman, the counsel for the case, is at present engaged in the other court.'
> JUDGE: Well, I can't help that.
> Mr P HODGSON (after a pause): My Lord, shall I bring him here?
> JUDGE: Don't interrupt me. Go and do your business.
> (Mr Hodgson's precipitate retreat occasioned a titter throughout the Court.)

When the judge began his ordinary work in court, it was quite usual for him to sit for 16 hours of the day; he would rise for dinner from 3.0 to 4.0 p.m., and continue late into the night. It is as well that the assizes lasted for only two or three weeks at a time, since there is a limit to human stamina. They got through a quantity of work which astonished Sir John Clerk, and astonishes us still:

> I saw in the space of six hours [he wrote], that is between four in the afternoon and ten that the court sat, 14 trials discussed, which is more than we in the Exchequer of Scotland would discuss in 20 days, according to the prolixity and loquacious janglings of our lawyers and juries. The counsellers were men of great abilities and never bestowed one word more on a cause than was sufficient for it.

He found the juries very swift and obliging: 'The jury never almost differ from the opinion of the judge and seldom go out or dispute two moments on any cause, but join their heads together and choose who shall say for them, that is given their verdict in the court which is immediately recorded.'

If the verdict was 'guilty', the judge had to pronounce sentence. When Mary Bateman, who called herself a sorceress, was convicted of murder by poisoning at York in 1809:

> . . . the judge, in a most impressive manner, passed sentence of death upon this wretched woman and, as is usual in cases of murder, ordered her body to be given to the surgeons for dissection. The prisoner, to delay execution, pleaded pregnancy, on which a jury of matrons was directed to be immediately impanelled, and to prevent the women from leaving court, all the doors were ordered to be closed. A jury being formed, and charged in the usual manner, retired for the purpose of discharging their duty, and found that she was NOT quick with child.

After a hard day's—and night's—work the judges would return for food and relaxation to their lodgings, which had to be of a high standard: 'In the first place,' Sir Daniel Fleming instructed his undersheriff at Carlisle in 1661, 'sufficient inns and quarters must be provided for the judges' entertainment, and store of wine laid in, with other furniture according to the High Sheriff's discretion, for his honour and credit.'

At each assize town the judges would be hard worked, but

well housed and fed, till the time came for them to move on, from York to Newcastle, and from Newcastle across to Carlisle on the bleakest and wildest part of the Circuit. While Durham remained an ecclesiastical enclave, they needed the Bishop's permission to pass through it, and they found hardly a hostelry worth the name till they reached Carlisle. Monks Hall marked their last stop in Northumberland, and their first in Cumberland was the Capon Tree, under whose spreading branches they could stop and picnic. Its name had nothing to do with poultry, and its fame owed something to the '45 Rebellion, for six of the convicted rebels were hanged on its branches. Still, Carlisle grew nearer now, and the Sheriff would be there to meet them with his 'javelin men' and to lead them into Carlisle; and when the assizes were over, a similar escort would see them to the border of Westmorland, where another escort awaited them.

That would be the end of the duties of the High Sheriff of Cumberland, provided he had not made the grievous error of forgetting the Clerk of Assize, whose comfort had also to be considered. It was important not only to send him a venison pasty and a bottle of wine; his fee had to be paid as well—Sir Daniel Fleming knew that to his cost:

Before the judges of assize clerk take horse [he ordered], the Sheriff must procure the calendar of the gaol from the Clerk of the Assize under his hand, and must sign the counterpart thereof, which the Assize Clerk will keep. The Clerk of the Assize will have for his fee upon the delivery of the said calendar £1 6s. 8d.; the four associates £2 . . . If the Clerk of Assizes have not his fee, he will cause you to trot to the remotest part of the county. I myself have several times ridden to Naworth before I could have the calendar of the prisoners' judgment, for until it be received, no execution can be made.

The judges would then ride to Appleby in Westmorland, and finally to Lancaster, and would then have completed their circuit, and come to no harm; and if dagger money was indeed given them for their protection, it would have served them well. But it is a myth. The fact is that, when the judges left each county, they expected a farewell gift as a fee, not to buy protection of any kind. The judges represented the King, and it was usual for royalty to be lavishly treated. York gave £100 to Henry VIII after the Pilgrimage of Grace, when there was good reason to fear his wrath, and when James I's queen came there, she was given a large silver cup with 80 gold coins in it.

When Mr Justice Whitelocke visited the Northern Circuit in 1628, he was given £1 in gold by the Sheriff of Northumberland, a spur royal (gold coin) by the Mayor of Newcastle, and a dudgeon (boxwood) dagger by the Sheriff of Carlisle. Perhaps the legend of dagger money springs from Roger North's words in 1676: 'the Northumberland sheriff gave us all arms, that is a dagger, knife, pen knife, and fork all together,' but it was hardly intended as a provision against danger. More often than a dagger, indeed, the Mayor of Newcastle gave an antique coin, and the city's accounts for 1567 show why: 'Given at Mr Mayor's commandment to the judges, two old royals, *for their fee,* 30s.'

These were Sir Daniel Fleming's instructions for Cumberland in 1662:

When the assizes are over and the judges ready to go away, according to the old custom they will expect their Scotch daggers, viz. either judge, the Clerk of Assize, the marshalls, 4 associates, 2 grooms, etc. will expect each of them one, which the Sheriff much then have in readiness . . . If it happen to be a maiden assizes (*viz.* none hanged), then the Sheriff must give with ever dagger a pair of white gloves, which may be had in Carlisle.

In one year he bought two fine daggers for the judges, costing 15s. each, and some much cheaper 'silver-rooved' and 'brass-rooved' daggers for the rest of the party. They were given, not as weapons, but as keepsakes.

It was too charming a custom to last. The Long Parliament, suspecting bribery in such gifts, banned them in 1640. But old habits die hard. The Judges' Means and Salaries Bill in 1691–92 gave judges better pay, and ruled that they should receive no fees 'other than such ancient and legal fees as have always been allowed and taken.'

Some presents were still made. 'I dined with the judges,' wrote Sir John Clerk about Carlisle in 1731, 'and found a plentiful table which is kept at their own expenses since the increase of their salaries, but there's no great expense

206

necessary at their tables since the county gentlemen send them always presents of venison, moor fowls, mutton etc. in great plenty.'

Some customs were killed off by economy campaigns. Once the railways ran between Newcastle and Carlisle in 1844 the judges usually arrived by train and large mounted retinues became a thing of the past. A committee in Newcastle decided that it was time to review some of the old customs. 'On this head,' the committee reported, 'we are of opinion that the complimentary payments to the judges' servants, namely the fee for gloves, opening courts, train bearer, butler, coachmen, porter, and further allowances for lodgings, to the judges' servants ought to be discontinued.'

And some customs the judges killed off themselves. There used to be a charming practice on a different circuit that, when the train stopped at Ludlow on its way from Shrewsbury to Hereford, the judges were offered cakes on a silver salver, and wine in a loving cup. But one of them complained of the needless delay, and the ceremony ceased.

Even in the present century the Mayor of Newcastle used to hold a Dagger Dinner when the judges were presented with a gold coin, and at York the Lady Mayoress gave the judges a silver vinaigrette, perhaps a survival from the days when they carried posies to ward off gaol fever.

Few of these customs now remain. The judges are paid by the state, and their lodgings are looked after by local authorities with a care which is modern but attentive. Liverpool only became an assize town in 1835, and the present judges' lodgings have been in use since 1867. Everything is done within reason to provide a suitable place for the judges to relax after their important labours. When they noted in their visitors book in 1923 that a set of bowls and a croquet set would be most welcome for their leisure hours, the Town Clerk pointed out gently that they were already provided.

Years of crisis and hardship were to follow: during World War II a shortage of manpower allowed Devil Weed (Polygonum) to run rampant through the flower beds at the Liverpool lodgings, a plague which was not abated until 1948.

In 1971 the assizes were abolished, being replaced by the Crown Courts, which the High Court Judges still visit in much the old way. Some of the pageantry has departed; judges are no longer regarded as deities, nor do they expect to be treated as such. Gone are the days when (in a Punch joke from World War II) a judge could ask, 'What *is* sweet rationing?' Modern judges are closer to real life, and much more approachable.

The last word shall come from a very distinguished criminal judge, at leisure on the Liverpool croquet lawn in the 1920s, living in nearly the best of all possible worlds. According to the visitors book: 'There is a G sharp in the treble of the piano which is mute. This is the only defect we have discovered in the house, and it has not seriously interfered with our comfort.'

Horace E. Avory
Autumn Assize 1924

FOURTEEN

The Young 'FE'

> 'I have been recently admitted to the Bar, and can
> only give a faint outline of my future success in that
> honourable profession; but I trust, sir, like the
> eagle, I shall look down from lofty rocks upon the
> dwellings of man.'
>
> Samuel Watson Royston,
> *The Enemy Conquered; or, Love Triumphant*

The use of initials is a mark of his greatness. More than 40 years after his death he is remembered simply as 'FE', though what the 'E' stands for is forgotten. F stands for Frederick, certainly—most people know that—but the E is for Edwin— Frederick Edwin Smith, to give him his full name. This Smith was one of the greatest advocates of all time.

He was born in 1872 of no blue-blooded family. His great-grandfather was a miner, his grandfather a teacher, and his father was a barrister whom FE reckoned was the finest speaker he had ever heard, and who set the highest standards for his sons. Young lads should read *Tom Sawyer* and penny dreadfuls, if they want to, but not if they had him as a father, for he allotted them the books they should read, and made them write an essay on them when they had read them.

His education began at Sandringham School, near Southport, and the only distinctive side of his character to emerge at that early age was his hatred of classical music in general, and piano lessons in particular. He used to say that he could only remember the National Anthem with difficulty, which means having even less of a musical ear than another member of the Northern Circuit, W S Gilbert, who said he could only remember two tunes; one of them was the National Anthem, and the other wasn't.

When FE entered Birkenhead School at the age of 13 he soon showed his rare qualities of courage, dash and determination. He needed them when cycling, for it was the age of penny-farthings, or 'high bicycles' as they were also known. His father took him on holiday to Egypt in 1881, when he was nine, and he rode one of those amazing machines—'Xtraordinary' was the trade name of a particular model—from Shepherd's Hotel in Cairo to the Pyramids, and was probably the first boy ever to do so.

I remember when I was a boy of 12 [he later recalled], I purchased one of those high bicycles which was much too big for me, and the only method of descent possible for me was to relax gradually and finally and completely the momentum of the bicycle, so I call it, and then fall over the handles to the ground. I have never been decorated for any of these performances. (Laughter). I once rode more or less continuously on a high bicycle from my native town of Birkenhead to Edinburgh, and I took part in my tempestuous youth in high bicycle races, which I consider incomparably more adventurous than riding in the Grand National.

He was not far wrong, because a book on cycling, published in 1887 when he was 15 years of age, says, 'Falling forwards from a bicycle is by no means a difficult exploit—indeed, the difficulty is to avoid doing it. The manoeuvre is so common that the peculiar form of tumble that ensues is known by the definitive name of "the cropper" or "imperial crowner".'

When FE was only nine he decided he wanted to be the Lord Chancellor some day; it was ambition high enough to meet his father's approval. At Birkenhead School he won prizes in English, Modern History and French; he was a keen debater, and at football he was regarded as 'a doughty player, clearly skilful and quite fearless—a trifle ruthless, some of his opponents thought.' But this was true of everything he did. He once said to one of the masters, 'I decline to accept the view you have taken, sir, and I offer you an open challenge to demonstrate before the form that I am wrong.'

He had no illusions about himself; at the age of 17 he described himself as 'a youth of incredible intellectual arrogance', but one must recognise that he was now a *brilliant* young man. It is a word which must constantly be applied to him. He was brilliant at sport; the misfortune of breaking an arm might have spoilt his chances of a rugger blue when he was up at Oxford, but it did not stop him from playing, regardless of the pain. He was also unlucky not to win a blue for long-distance running, and he was no mean tennis player.

'The men players then wore short flannel knickerbockers secured above the knee by elastic,' he remembered, 'with black ribbed stockings. I am like those who can talk of cricket when it was played in tall hats. Twenty or thirty years ago lawn tennis was very aptly described as pat-ball. It was a soft game played by soft people and rewarded by easy athletic success. Today lawn tennis can be claimed as one of the manly games.'

He was being a little modest. There was a time when lawn tennis was scornfully dismissed as pat-ball—up to 1880, because the rules of the game required the net to be four feet high in the middle, and five feet high at the sides. If one hit the ball high enough to clear the net and hit it hard as well, it simply went out of the court. The rallies were interminably long, sometimes lasting up to 80 returns, and it was only a question of which player could keep it up longest, but the rules were changed in 1880 so that the net was lowered to three feet in the middle, and lowered still further in 1882; hard-hitting tennis was now possible, and the modern game can be said to date from then. FE had played during this period of change, and at the age of 20 he played in a Northern County Championship against H S Mahoney, the English champion. There was nothing pat-ball about his tennis then.

At about this time he published an English translation of one of Plautus' Latin comedies under the title of *The Haunted House,* and he went, with the help of a scholarship, to Wadham College, Oxford. He continued his debating there, of course, and his maiden speech at the Oxford Union earned this praise from the undergraduate paper *Isis*: 'The speech of the evening . . . was the amazingly vivacious and brilliant performance of F E Smith, the Wadham freshman.'

He frequently debated against the young poet Hilaire Belloc, and in 1892 became President of the Oxford Union. He must have been one of the most dazzling men Oxford has ever seen. In that same year, 1892, he entered politics; his first speech was at Liverpool's Hope Hall. The *Birkenhead Advertiser* used the inevitable word about it: 'A brilliant torrent of really forensic eloquence . . . It will amuse and charm all readers to make the smashing blows that Mr Smith delivered at Liberal effrontery, and the admirable manner in which he turned the Liberal arguments against themselves.'

This was also the year in which he got a first class degree in Classics, and stayed on to obtain, not only a first class degree in Law, but also the Vinerian Law Scholarship; FE regarded it as the greatest honour he ever received, and he had plenty to choose from. He now remained at Oxford as a don at Merton College, lecturing first in Law and then in Modern History; 'modern' is a relative term in historical circles, for his favourite and chosen period was the Stuart era. He had also to correct examination papers.

In a certain examination there were six papers. Four were set by others, and two by myself. I cannot claim in my two papers that I attained a very high standard of efficiency. . . . There were some questions which I could answer myself, and I put them in because it would be less trouble for me to correct the papers. (Laughter). But the task of the examiners is a fairly easy one. We have a large field of knowledge to draw on. Not that we possess it, but we have a valuable number of works in which it is imperfectly set down. (Laughter)

He had now joined Gray's Inn; perhaps his plans for coming to the Bar were still uncertain, but in 1897 he became involved in an incident which might have wrecked them altogether. He was then an Oxford don aged 25. The Prince of Wales visited Oxford and mounted police were called out to dispel an Oxford 'rag'. FE saw the police roughly manhandling an elderly college servant and plunged into the crowd to rescue him; he was arrested and charged with assaulting the police and obstructing them in the execution of their duty. Minor though such charges are, young men convicted of them are not allowed to come to the Bar, a profession where complete integrity is essential.

When the case was heard, counsel for the prosecution suggested to FE that his explanation could only mean that the police were lying. It is a good point to make, except against a Vinerian Law Scholar. 'There are five possibilities,' said FE unhesitatingly. 'I am lying; the officer is lying; I am mistaken; he is mistaken; or we are both telling the truth, and our statements are not irreconcilable.' He was acquitted, amidst acclamation, and a future Lord Chancellor was free to be called to the Bar.

It was natural for him, with his home at Birkenhead, to join the Northern Circuit. Leslie Scott was head of a set of chambers in Liverpool, and had an enormous practice, especially in shipping cases. FE met him at Oxford, and congratulated him on some articles he had written on maritime law. Scott, for his part, was impressed by the young law don, and invited him to become his pupil, which he did in 1899.

Even Scott had to take a holiday sometimes. In August that year a Wigan solicitor, who had intended some briefs for Scott, entrusted one to his pupil instead; it is how young men at the Bar get their first opportunities. So FE rose to his feet before the Wigan licensing justices, seeking a licence for a woman to sell alcohol, and perhaps Mary McKanny's only claim to fame is that she was his first client. He conducted the case well, and more of such cases followed in the future.

He was first mentioned in the Liverpool press in February 1900, when he had a watching brief at the assizes. A barrister with a watching brief can take no active part in a case. As Edward Wooll, when sitting as the Recorder of Carlisle, once said to a young man, 'You may watch, and you may pray; but now you must sit down.'

Two days later he appeared in a case of a promissory note for £100, a dispute between two brothers; he was acting for the plaintiff, and won. The next reported case of his was in July 1900: *Lewis Pearce and Co v New Brighton Tower Company.* New Brighton is a holiday resort just across the Mersey from Liverpool. The defendants had granted the plaintiff an exclusive right to have a stall there selling gold wirework, which was presumably made into cheap souvenirs, but the defendants let someone else have such a stall there. Furthermore, during the months of July and August, the busiest months for trippers, they cleaned and scraped the ironwork on the tower, and the plaintiff claimed that it damaged his goods. FE appeared for the defendants, but lost the case; the plaintiff won £40. Nothing daunted, FE applied for a new trial on the grounds that the damages were too high. The new trial was granted, but he lost the second case as well.

The plaintiff was represented by another young Liverpool

barrister, Rigby Swift. He was two years younger than FE, but not having been a university don had been in practice four years longer and was already becoming very successful. He might well have wondered if he would ever take silk—he did so ten years later; he might even have wondered if he would ever become a High Court Judge; this lay twenty years ahead. But he could never have imagined that his opponent, FE, would be the Lord Chancellor who promoted him.

The next case of FE's in print was another licensing case; the police objected that his client should not be granted a licence to sell alcohol, because she was a loose woman, or at least allowed loose women to use her public house. FE pointed out that a landlady could hardly be expected to question the ladies about their gentlemen friends, which is a good debating point, but a practised eye can soon spot ladies of easy virtue. The case was adjourned.

His first criminal case was at the Liverpool Assizes in November 1900, prosecuting one of a gang who had robbed a sailor in the street. The man was convicted and sentenced to nine months hard labour.

1900 began with him representing brewers at the inquest on a man who had died from arsenic poisoning, which was something of a beer-drinking hazard at that time. He was also in accident claims, such as collision between a horse-drawn cab and a lady cyclist, but a much more important event that year was his marriage in April 1901 to Margaret Furneaux, the daughter of an Oxford don. Of course he was a dashing groom, and she a radiant bride; so are all young barristers and their brides; it is part of the proper order of things. The pink shirt he wore at the time was thought somewhat bold, but that was his own personality precisely.

There is very little to be said about his married life. No doubt he was a fond husband, and he was certainly faithful, but he was too strong a personality to be wholly domesticated. He liked poker sessions which went on into the small hours of the morning, and he regarded women as somewhat second-rate creatures. He opposed the granting of votes to women, and although he said, 'I do not wish to decry the claim of women to intellectual distinction,' that is exactly what he meant. Indeed, in his famous lecture on Eloquence in 1927, he described women's power of thought:

I ask this audience to remember that in these changed days when the House of Commons is open to women, the latter may find themselves engaged in a Parliamentary campaign, and that, putting the matter in its humblest form, the power of apposite concise and relevant argument will not do harm to their position, even in the domestic circle. (Laughter).

FE cannot have been an easy man to live with, but Margaret must have admired his brilliance. He could spare the time for a brief honeymoon at Brighton, but plenty of work awaited his return. A Blackpool householder wanted to stop a plumber carrying on his business next door, which was perhaps a little sensitive of him, as a palmist practised on the other side of his house and the local environment was further enriched by a fish and chip shop and a sawmill. Still, the plumber's house was covered by a covenant which banned business activities and, despite FE's best efforts on the plumber's side, the plaintiff won his case, and £35 damages.

None of FE's cases so far were important or memorable, but young members of the Bar cannot expect that class of work. He defended a dog-cart driver whom Rigby Swift claimed had caused an accident by 'furious' driving at the rate of 15 miles an hour, and he was instructed by the Musicians' Union to object to a music licence being granted to Liverpool's Royal Court Theatre on the grounds that the proprietors were sweating their labour (cries of 'Oh!' in court), since they were only paying the players 5s. or 6s. a night.

One of his cases was connected with the Boer War. The plaintiffs manufactured strawberry jam for the troops at the front, and put it into 200,000 tins made by the defendants. This consignment had only got as far as Woolwich Arsenal when the tins leaked, and 4 tons of the jam had to be reboiled before it was thought fit to send once more to the troops. The case was settled outside the doors of the court.

But most of his work was still in licensing cases. Several times that year he was led by the great Marshall Hall KC who, finding that the licensing bench refused to accept his arguments, 'threw up his brief'. It is a magnificent and futile gesture practised either by bad losers or the insufferably conceited, should there be any difference between them. 'I do not propose,' said Marshall Hall, 'to take up my own time and the Court's by addressing you any further upon the applications. I will therefore leave my learned junior Mr Smith to mention the takings and other particulars . . . I think that is the most dignified way of treating those applications under the circumstances.' He stalked out of Court; FE remained behind and did rather better than his eminent leader.

Licensing applications are hardly glamorous, but they are sometimes rich in local colour. Once, when Danny Brabin opposed the granting of an off-licence for alcohol to a grocer's shop—this would be during the 1950s—an aged gentleman entered the witness box. He was expected to give evidence that it would be the greatest possible convenience to him to purchase beer under the same roof as baked beans, but he found himself for the first time in the public gaze, and the temptation was too much for him. So, he described that great moment, 50 years before, when he had been captured during the Boer War as a spy, and was about to be shot at dawn, but at the last moment a message came from President Kruger that he had been reprieved.

Danny Brabin made the only possible comment under the circumstances. 'On behalf of the Licensed Victuallers' Association,' he said, 'let me congratulate you on a very lucky escape!'

The Boer War was reflected in FE's Conservative politics, which took up more and more of his time. He suggested to his audience that a Liberal candidate in Liverpool should answer two of those loaded questions politicians love so dearly: 'Do you believe that the Boer, or Britain, was right in the great struggle we have just carried to a close?' and, 'Do you or do you not say that Mr Gladstone was right in surrendering British control over Majuba 20 years ago?' (Voice from the hall: 'No!', and applause).

By his second year at the Bar, FE had already made a great impression. He handled libel actions, breaches of contract, and humble traffic accidents with wayward trams. In November 1901 he defended George Wise, a Protestant lecturer who addressed to large open-air meetings at Liverpool such tasteful and reasoned criticisms of a Catholic Mass as 'The Lord God is going to jump into the bread.'

Violence usually broke out, so the stipendiary magistrate bound him over to keep the peace for a year. FE went to

London to challenge his decision, arguing that it was the Catholics who started the fighting at those meetings, and not George Wise who was to blame. The appeal was dismissed; Mr Justice Darling, a noted wit, observed, 'I notice in the case that this is described as "a crusade" on the part of Mr Wise. I thought "crusades" always caused a breach of the peace.' (Laughter.) When the case was over Lord Alverstone, the Lord Chief Justice, sent FE a note congratulating him, with the inevitable adjective: 'I predict for you a very brilliant future.'

It was FE's first important case, and law students still observe it as a significant statement on the limitations on free speech. It was in that same month that The Great Liverpool Bank Fraud was committed, a case which increased FE's fame. 'It was such a chance as may make or mar a man,' he said of it.

At the Bank of Liverpool worked a clerk called Thomas Paterson Goudie, a seemingly blameless man who secretly bet on horses. One November day in 1901 he slipped quietly away from the Bank to avoid the auditors, leaving behind him a deficit of £170,000. It was more than an embezzler had ever cost a bank before.

Panic broke out on the Stock Exchange; the Bank's shares dropped two guineas in value in a single day, narrowly escaping ruin. For three weeks the nation held its breath, for Goudie had vanished off the face of the earth; he had been sighted simultaneously in Genoa, and Paris, and Brazil. But when he was traced to a quiet Bootle lodging-house it meant a trip to the Old Bailey, a plea of guilty, and FE to defend him. His accomplices argued their innocence desperately, and had the very best King's Counsel to defend them: Harold Avory, Rufus Isaacs, and Marshall Hall. But Goudie was defended by the young man of 29, whose name was quite unknown in London.

This case [said FE to a crowded court], has had the misfortune to have become very notorious—the large sums involved, the skilful way in which the frauds have been carried out, Goudie's escape and his capture having combined to attract public attention. I do not state in terms that a man's moral quality varies with the pecuniary conduct in-

217

volved, but a great deal has to be said for Goudie. At the time of his engagement he entered this employment with the highest testimonial from a small Scottish bank in which he had previously served.

Huge though the sums were that had been taken from the Bank, FE continued, none of them had rubbed off on Goudie, for he had been tricked out of his winnings time and time again by the other defendants. The speech ended in the simplest possible words: 'Goudie comes from a family in Scotland, perhaps humble, but against whom nothing has been said. He has three sisters, whose sacrifices alone have made it possible to have what legal advice he has had, who hold the sanguine view that he may yet amend his ways.' It was a speech that held the Court spell-bound, but the time had not yet come for FE to transfer his practice to London.

His first murder case came in 1902, his third year at the Bar. At Liverpool Assizes in December 1902, Mr Justice Jelf saw FE led by senior counsel in a case of murder committed during a stormy meeting conducted by John Kensit, another Protestant 'reformer'. He was also led in the prosecution of a policeman for perjury, and in the case of a 'musical' salmon; plaintiff explained that he meant that the salmon was 'humming', and gave him food poisoning. But he lost his case, and had to whistle for his damages.

The judge had another murder case to try at those assizes; three maids had smothered with a pillow the elderly drunken woman they worked for, and one of them, Ethel Rollinson, a girl of 20, was caught pawning the dead woman's watch and clothing. The death was clearly no accident, and the motive was as obvious as Ethel Rollinson's guilt. But she had nobody to defend her, so the Judge asked FE to undertake the case. He gave up an important brief to do so.

It was a small-scale sordid case, as murder cases go, and at first the court was almost empty; but the word ran round that it was being defended in no ordinary way, and the court was packed as FE made his final speech, making stylish bricks without straw:

What was the position in which the girls found themselves? They are poor girls without any money, and are only defended by the direction of the judge; and have none of the resources that have enabled the prosecution to marshal their case . . . I have no intention of contending that the prisoners did not rob Miss Marsden. I admit that. Both girls are orphans, and were practically friendless; they were sent out to make their livings amongst the temptations of a large city, and the prosecution have not been able to bring forward a single fact to the discredit of either of them, until the present charge was made.

The girls were found guilty of murder, but the jury recommended that they should be shown mercy, and their lives were spared. You can guess what the Judge wrote to FE: 'I never heard a hopeless case more brilliantly defended.'

Thus FE did not succeed in getting his client acquitted; but he had not failed in doing his best for her, and it is times such as this which justify the advocate's calling. He touched upon it in his lecture on Eloquence:

Probably few at this meeting [he said], will ever stand trial on a capital charge. (Laughter). But it must be a poignant moment for such a person when the advocate for the defence is called upon to make his closing speech. I do not know in how many instances innocent lives, endangered through formidable circumstantial evidence, have been saved by the gift of eloquence and the insight of advocates, and I look back with pride upon the long history which makes plain the large proportion of our civil liberty due to the independence and eloquence of the Bar.

Therefore I am impressed by that form of eloquence, because it produces results, and I am reminded of a conversation between a bishop and a judge:

'I am a greater man than you,' said the bishop, 'because all you can say is "You be hanged", but I can say, "You be damned".'

'No doubt,' replied the judge, 'but when I say to a man, "You be hanged," he *is* hanged.' (Laughter).

In 1903 he was chosen as the Conservative candidate for Liverpool's Scotland Division, a seat he could never hope to win against its popular member, T P O'Connor. These were his views on Home Rule for Ireland: 'If there is a way out of the difficulty,' said FE, 'and even if we have to pay 10 millions or 20 millions, or whatever it might be, we are cheaply rid of disaffected Ireland, if it secures the desired result. (The audience: Hear, hear).'

It was the year of *The Veronica*, his first famous murder case, included in the *Notable British Trials* series; that ship's crew mutinied and murdered the captain and mate. FE was led for the prosecution by A A Tobin, so it contains no examples of FE's advocacy.

It was a year in which he appeared for a Vicar of Everton, sued for slander by a curate who had kissed a choir boy, and explained that he was simply treating the boy as he affectionately treated his own brothers and sisters. He was led for the defence by William Pickford KC, who somewhat surprisingly let his junior make the final speech to the jury; but Pickford was described as 'a master of lucid and convincing statement, seldom condescending to eloquence,' which suggests that he was sound but dull, and right to leave it to FE.

It was also a year in which most of his time was devoted to cheap cigarettes.

Ogdens' Guinea Gold gaspers were not worth a guinea or anything like it, though big advertising campaigns suggested that the public demand for them bordered on frenzy. To lure tobacconists into the Guinea Gold rush, Ogdens announced that they would, for four years, distribute their entire net profits plus £200,000 a year to the shopkeepers who stocked their product. The plan went, so to speak, up in smoke; there was a take-over bid and Ogdens were put into voluntary liquidation. 800 disappointed tobacconists now sued for their lost bonus and FE had to defend each action. It was an invaluable source of experience in legal technicalities, which are often of greater value to a barrister than the ability to make a thrilling speech in a murder case:

> Every young barrister dreams of being engaged in heavy litigation [he wrote], but few can ever have had the fortune which came to me, at a time when I had been called for four years, of being retained in an unprecedented series of actions arising out of the same events, and thus of gaining in a short space of time that indispensable knowledge and experience of practice and procedure which can only be acquired by a busy junior.

To put it another way: 'from 1902 to 1906, hardly a day

passed without my being engrossed in one aspect or another of the innumerable lawsuits brought against the Company.' It meant he had to draft 800 defences, and countless other pleadings; there were many hearings in the High Court, and thereafter the Court of Appeal and the House of Lords. 'I was almost overwhelmed by the number of cases,' he recalled.

But this was only part of his practice. When passengers were injured on the Lancashire and Yorkshire Railway, he was usually for the defence. He prosecuted thefts from the docks, company frauds, and murder. Statistics might show how busy he was at this time, but not why he deserved to be.

A case in 1904, however, provides an admirable illustration of his style. George Wise was once again in court, this time as plaintiff in a libel action, for an election broadsheet had asked some pointed questions of him, such as 'If Evangelical-cummilitant Protestantism isn't one of the most paying games nowadays?' and 'Where is the £40 from the Defence Fund?'

It suggested that George Wise was a money-making hypocrite, not to be trusted with cash. This time FE was appearing for the defence, together with his first pupil, Edward Wooll; they claimed that the comment was fair, and would justify it. Small wonder that the court was packed to hear him cross-examine the controversial Mr Wise:

Q: I think, generally speaking, you are like Mr Chamberlain, Mr Wise; you do not believe in taking things lying down?

A: It is not wise to do so. (Laughter).

Q: What is your experience as an agitator in Liverpool?

A: I do not like the word 'agitator'. I call it a Crusade.

Q: Your counsel used the word, but you did not approve of it?

A: No.

A A TOBIN (for George Wise): I am afraid it was my wickedness. (Laughter).

Q: Now, your income from all sources connected with this agitation is about £200 a year?

A: No, I get no money at all from carrying on religious agitation.

Q: Then you get it for your public efforts, or whatever you call it?

221

A: I am paid as the pastor of the mission to which I belong.

Q: And you throw the rest in, I suppose?

A: I do. (Laughter).

Q: I suggest, Mr Wise, that your public work consists of an extraordinarily vulgar campaign against Roman Catholicism?

A: No, it does not.

Q: I am going to suggest that you are not the sort of man who ought to receive compensation when the defendants satirically describe you as a kind, wise and religious man . . . Did you speak of the 'lambs of Rome', but say this: 'Jesus said, Feed my lambs, but in the Revised Version it ought to be Fleece my sheep?'

A: I read that from a book. I read it to show the impeachment published by others.

Q: Do you think it was proper to utter to an ignorant rabble of this kind in the interests of religion?

A: Well, it is only fair for me to say that it was done in 1901, and since then I have regretted doing so, and have promised never to do it again. I acknowledge my error.

Q: Is it not a fact that you have been preaching against Roman Catholicism?

A: No; it was against Ritualism.

Q: Will you swear that you have not been preaching or lecturing against Roman Catholicism in the last three months?

A: No. I will not swear to it; I believe I have.

Q: Is not the real reason why you would not work with Mr Stones [another 'Crusader'] the fact that he wanted £2 10s. per week? (Laughter)

A: No, that is not the only reason. I stood on my honour as a Christian gentleman.

Q: On what, Mr Wise?

A: On my honour, sir.

Q: I see. That is where you stood. (Loud laughter).

The whole cross-examination lasted two hours; George Wise was awarded one farthing damages.

Wise had little chance against the tongue of an ex-President of the Oxford Union; but FE's learning was formidable too.

He addressed the Liverpool shipowners on the difficult international law of contraband, for at this time, during the war between Russia and Japan, ships' cargoes of food, coal, cotton and machinery were being seized.

FE could really do no wrong. Harold Jager, one of his pupils, was standing at a window in the courts looking out at Liverpool when Sir Francis Kyffin-Taylor KC, a senior member of the Circuit, asked him the name of the new building with the golden dome.

'The Royal Insurance Building,' said Jager; and so it was.

'No, no,' said the other, teasingly, 'those are FE's new chambers.'

> Life in chambers [wrote Jager], was a continual delight. FE would come in after a day's busy fighting in court. He would pace up and down his room like a caged lion, talking nineteen to the dozen, telling us how he had scored off judge, counsel and witnesses, illustrating, with vivid specimens of his speeches, cross-examinations and encounters with the Bench. A good many of these paeans of victory were the figments of his own imagination. He would invent incidents which never occurred, in order to introduce some especially neat repartee which had subsequently flashed into his mind, too late for actual use, but too good not to be retailed to his admiring audience.

FE's ambition now was to secure the greatest audience of all: the House of Commons. When Joseph Chamberlain, the Conservative leader, visited Liverpool to address a huge rally, FE merely seconded the vote of thanks:

> If I win Scotland Division [he said], for which you know I am the Conservative candidate, I will win it for the policy of Mr Chamberlain. (Cheers). The half-way house is a good place to stop, but the end of the journey is much better. (Hear, hear). Mr Chamberlain only made one mistake in his recent Glasgow speech, and that was to say that Glasgow was the second city of the Empire. (Laughter and cheers). But I suppose he received that information from an ignorant Scotsman. (Laughter).

It was hardly profound, but there was no questioning his hold over the audience. Chamberlain insisted that he had to be given a safe seat, and so he was adopted as Conservative candidate for Liverpool's Walton constituency.

At a time before the forming of the Labour Party, the Conservatives had as obvious a claim to working class support as the Liberals, and FE's constituency was a working class one. Looking back on him now, he seems to represent the aristocratic élite, the sort of man to bring true democrats out in a rash; but his constituents loved him. He meant what he said, and he took the trouble to make his meaning crystal clear.

Some politicians wrap their words or brains in cotton wool, but not FE. He did not hide the fact that he was a successful member of the Bar, and nobody taunted him for his affluent way of life which included a spacious home in the pleasant Wirral countryside near Birkenhead, and an extensive stable of horses. Many people of consequence lived like that. What mattered was that FE threw himself as vigorously into politics as he did into everything else. Voters like a man who fights for their beliefs, and they certainly chose the right man in him.

1905, his sixth year at the Liverpool Bar, was hardly a happy time for the Conservatives; their national popularity was waning fast. Still, as a local paper said, using the inescapable word, 'one may venture to assert that the most brilliant and broad-minded of all the candidates standing for Liverpool is Mr FE Smith.'

Mr Jellicoe, his Liberal opponent, attacked him by saying that he was a well-fee'd lawyer for the licensing trade. So he was. But, as FE pointed out, he had at different times acted *for* the brewers, and *against* them, it being but a small part of his practice in any event. 'If,' he riposted, 'Mr Jellicoe carries into private life the rich invective of which he appears a master, I may appear as *his* well-fee'd lawyer in the near future. (Laughter).'

In January 1906, when the general election came, a Liberal landslide was certain. The *Liverpool Daily Post,* a paper of strong Liberal views, recognised the fighting qualities of the young Conservative candidate. 'One thing is certain,' it wrote; 'it will not be a kid-glove fight in Walton.' But it had no other good words for him, and mocked his election campaign.

'The Conservative candidate,' it reported, 'cut rather a comical figure, at whose appearance the Liberals were highly amused. Dressed in a light tweed overcoat and a low bowler

224

hat, and perched on the seat of his car, he resembled nothing so much as a vendor of fancy goods at a fair.' But he won.

'Making, perhaps, the only political mistake of its lifetime,' FE recalled more than 20 years later, teasing the paper at a Liverpool Press Club dinner, 'the *Daily Post* announced immediately after the general election of 1906 that they wished to hear nothing of me any more (laughter) and they did not propose to provide me with the notoriety and advertisement which alone counted with me. (Laughter).'

In March 1906 he made his maiden speech in Parliament, an hour of dazzling invective in which he scored off both Winston Churchill and Lloyd George, who found himself for the first time within FE's gravitational pull: 'We have just listened to a very brilliant speech,' he said.

FE left Liverpool at once, and entered London chambers. From that date onwards, fond though he always remained of the Northern Circuit, he could not really be regarded as one of its members. Two years ahead of him lay silk—he was the youngest KC of his time—and the offices of privy Councillor, Attorney General, and Lord Chancellor. His youthful energy may have seemed inexhaustible and in 1928, speaking at a dinner of the Japanese Society in London, he used their traditional interest in ancestor worship to touch on the question of old age:

I am fast reaching the age [he said], when I become more and more inclined to encourage the worship of the old by the young. In our modern English world that is not a fashionable cult, but my birthday is tomorrow and in three years I shall, unfortunately—if I live—have attained the age of 60.

Well, anybody who is travelling so swiftly along the road of life becomes more and more indulgent of the worship of ancestors. At present, while you are 60 you still retain a certain degree of affectionate relationship with those who follow you; when you are 70 you become rather a bore; when you are 80 you are pointed out as an interesting relic, and when you are 90 you are wheeled about. I have wondered if there is anything in this rejuvenating idea. I have thought of this matter deeply, and I cannot see that a man of 150 would be any particular addition to the home.

There would be a promising youngster of 80 or 90 about the house, and he might think he was entitled to come into his own.

It may have seemed as if FE could carry on for ever, and that he would still seem a promising youngster at 80 or 90, but the three words 'if I live' were significant. By his unsparing efforts at everything he did he had burnt himself out and, on 30 September 1930, the life of one of the greatest advocates of all time came to an end, under the title of Lord Birkenhead, a place he was always proud to remember.

He died not a wholly popular man; the brilliance of his tongue was both to be feared and admired. He scorned soft compromises, and there are many famous stories of him putting judges in their place, but these belong to his time in London, not the seven early years he spent in Liverpool.

A portrait of him at his home on the Wirral, where he kept his beloved horses, was penned by Harold Jager:

FE would often say to [his pupils] Rutledge or Wooll, 'I want you to come out to The Grove with me tonight; we must go carefully into that such-and-such case.' They would go out together; a groom with three horses would meet them at Spital station. Arriving at Thornton Hough, they would potter about the garden; FE and Wooll would practise jumps in the field. I was often one of the party. We would then dine sumptuously, and the rest of the evening would be spent in light and airy persiflage, in chaff, and amusing dissections of various members of the circuit, and in general relaxation. Next morning we would return to chambers, without the important such-and-such case having once been mentioned.

The portrait is faded now; it does not show the tremendous effort and ability he brought to his work, for he concealed it with insolent ease. But it conveys much of the exhilaration of being young, and at the Bar, and FE Smith.

FIFTEEN

Goldiana

'I'm one of the few persons now alive who can talk
nonsense. That's why I'm so charming. Everyone
else is so deadly earnest.'

Somerset Maugham, *The Explorer*

In the select band of Great Advocates, some names remain
imperishable—of great men who dominated the court in their
day. Yet, in this firmament stars can grow pale and be lost
from view. Though he is still fondly remembered on the
Northern Circuit, the public has now forgotten a member of
the Bar whose comic genius was second to none. The late
George Robey used to be known in the music halls as 'The
Prime Minister of Mirth'; if Mirth had needed a Lord Chancellor, it would have had to be Sir Noel Goldie, KC.

Noel Barré Goldie was born in 1882, and received a gentleman's education at Rugby and Trinity College, Cambridge.
He was called to the Bar in 1905, and that same year was
elected Junior of the Northen Circuit. His chambers were in
Harrington Street, Liverpool, which meant that for one year
of superlative vintage there practised within the same building
three members of the Northern Circuit who have each earned
a chapter in this book: F E Smith, Goldie and Rigby Swift. It is
a wonder that one building could hold them all.

A Junior of the Northern Circuit is elected from the most
promising of the newcomers to the Bar; he held that office
between F Boyd Merriman and H Gorell Barnes, who became
judges of great distinction. It was a great age, and in those
marvellous years Goldie would never have been made Junior
if he had not been an obviously pleasing and talented young
man.

Nothing is remembered of his early years, because the
stories of him go back no further than the 1920s. Some of them
are to be found in the newspapers; others are part of circuit

legend, and if Goldie did not say the words attributed to him, no-one else would have dared to. Most of the best stories were recorded by Goldie's Boswell, the young Fred E Pritchard, who heard many of them with his own ears.

No doubt in those Edwardian days he built up a practice with ability and charm, and a noted sense of humour. But war came. Between 1914 and 1918 he served as a Staff Captain in the Royal Artillery in France and Belgium, and after the Armistice returned to rebuild his practice. He would have to, for practices do not mind themselves, and reputations have to be earned anew, so there was nothing to be done but settle down to work again, and put a cheerful face on it—and nobody had a merrier countenance than Goldie. In 1920, then, he was back at the Bar, now 38 years of age, conducting a prosecution at the Liverpool Quarter Sessions for the prosaic crime of stealing tinned Government rations. So he rose to his feet and said, 'Gentlemen of the Jury, Napoleon once said that an Army marches upon its stomach . . .'

It was said of a certain army officer that his men would follow him anywhere, if only out of curiosity. Goldie shared that gift; one either followed him like that or not at all, because some of his utterances had the logical force of Groucho Marx when he announced that if you cook apple sauce like cranberries, it tastes more like stewed prunes than rhubarb does. Here is Goldie proving inexorably that his client was not to blame for a car accident in which someone was killed. It comes from the official shorthand note:

GOLDIE: Now I want to ask you this, and this is my last question, You have told us you had an old model Chrysler, and you admit you were going at this speed of 50 miles an hour on this broad road. If there were not these little bumpy things there, could you drive a car, if you were fool enough to try to do it, at 75 to 80 miles an hour on that road without anything being likely to happen at all, if you were an expert driver and fool enough to risk it?

ACCUSED: That is right.

GOLDIE (triumphantly): Then if there is any bend at all, it is very slight! Are those objects, which I ventured to draw the Jury's attention to, a sort of, shall we say, wave, to which you referred?

228

ACCUSED: Yes.
GOLDIE: Thank you. That, my Lord, is the case for the Defence.

In his final speech to the jury in that case he explained what the crime involved: 'As regards dangerous driving, my Lord will direct you; but I tell you now, that dangerous driving must consist, so to speak, of doing something with the intention of doing it.'

Nobody knew what Goldie was going to say next, and juries hung upon his every word. 'Then, members of the jury, my client commenced to suffer from a most distressing complaint which, for the purposes of this case, I propose to call "pimples".' Goldie would never call a spade a spade if it paid no dramatic dividends—or a bus a bus, for that matter.

'There, members of the jury,' said Goldie, 'was my client quietly crossing this great open space of a cross-roads on his motor cycle, and there, rushing towards him, came this great Juggernaut of a bus called, members of the jury, appropriately enough, a Leyland Tiger!' He won the case, of course—juries ate out of his hand; so much so that in 1928 he took silk, at the age of 46.

Those were great years for Noel Goldie, KC; one important privilege of being a silk is that judges allow him more scope to be incorrigible, and Goldie went from strength to strength. He was made Recorder of Burnley in 1929, and of Manchester in 1935, positions hardly granted to men of straw; and in 1931 he became the Conservative member for Warrington. In those days, the letters NBG were used in common parlance as short for 'No Bloody Good', but at the hustings Goldie exploited it: 'My opponent may try to make merry with my initials,' he proclaimed, 'so he may as well know they stand for "Nobody Beats Goldie"!' The rival candidate failed. Not many of Goldie's opponents in court succeeded, either.

There were times when he must have seemed the silly-ass type of Conservative. In his next election campaign in 1935, a time of mass unemployment, he said:

While I have been the member for Warrington it has always been said that when returned I promised that I will try and bring work to the town. I am now permitted to disclose that a new works is coming to Warrington connected with the paper-making industry.

I honestly believe that the new works will mean employment for hundreds of Warrington men and women. I claim no merit for it whatever; but I would like to point out to the people of Warrington that if the Socialists are returned to power no firm would be such blithering fools as to erect a factory in Warrington.

But it was always a mistake to underestimate him. He did not often speak in the House of Commons, but confined his speeches to subjects on which he was well informed; it is not a habit to be discouraged among politicians. During a debate on prison reform in 1937, years before Risley Remand Centre was opened within his old constituency, he saw the need for such an institution: 'I wish to draw the Home Secretary's attention to one or two points to which I think improvement is desirable. I cannot see why a man who is sentenced to hard labour should have to sleep on the first 14 days of his sentence on bare boards without a mattress. That is a relic of barbarism. (Cheers).'

The *Liverpool Daily Post* recognised his merits as an MP after that speech:

There was the spirit of the genuine reformer in Mr Goldie's speech in the House today on prison administration. The member for Warrington is one of those (too few in number) who speaks only on subjects on which they have a special information, and he produced an excellent impression by the views he expressed from his experiences as Recorder. His views fell in with the sympathetic temper of the House, and with that of the Home Secretary who has an inherited interest in prison administration, and who found a good subject for it in his début in Parliament as Home Secretary . . . The testimony of the Home Secretary and Mr Goldie justified and encouraged still further the humane treatment of prisoners.

Goldie could certainly be serious when he needed to be. But he is best remembered for his fun, and during a House of Commons debate in 1938 on the Administration of Justice he reverted to type. Sydney Silverman suggested that every Quarter Sessions should have a legally qualified chairman.

Goldie wondered whether this was really necessary, but drew on his experience of Quarter Sessions where a little more legal expertise would not have come amiss:

I recall the days, rather before my time, when things were not as they might have been, and the clerk put the question, 'Guilty or not guilty?' The accused said 'Not guilty', and the clerk said, 'We shall see.' (Laughter).

Or the aged chairman who said to the accused, 'Do you wish to say anything to the jury before they find you Guilty?' (Renewed laughter).

Goldie was not cleverer than his colleagues; his was not the keenest of the logical analytical minds so often found at the Bar. Comedy was his forte, and a conjuror's sleight-of-hand for producing rabbits out of a hat which anyone else would have found empty. He was especially valuable in cases which nobody else could have won; and part of his technique was to assert a thing boldly until people came to believe it. In one case he was acting for a boiler-maker who was probably drunk when a motor car knocked him down. This is how Goldie opened the case:

GOLDIE, KC: My Lord, my client is a boiler-maker, and though the thirst of boiler-makers is notorious, it is hard to believe that the effect of four half-pints of beer on a Saturday night would be such as to render a boiler-maker so intoxicated as to be unfit to be on a pedestrian crossing.

F A SELLERS, KC: It was Sunday.

GOLDIE: I am so much obliged to my friend. That makes my case all the stronger.

With advocacy of that order Goldie should certainly have won the case, but some clients put themselves beyond all rescue.

GOLDIE: Would four half-pints of beer make a boiler-maker drunk?

PLAINTIFF: No. *The barrel it was brewed in* would not make a boiler-maker drunk.

Sellers, in cross-examination, extracted the information that the plaintiff was a Scotsman, who had been unemployed until the weekend of the accident, when he was paid the handsome sum of £4:

PLAINTIFF: But I was not drunk!

SELLERS: Is not that an occasion when you might let your-self go?

PLAINTIFF: No. The only three occasions on which a Scots-man is likely to get drunk are New Year's Eve; January 25th—the anniversary of the greatest poet ever produced, Robbie Burns; and the Football International, when England plays Scotland. (Laughter).

SELLERS: Do you always comply with that standard?

PLAINTIFF: Yes.

SELLERS: Don't you have any other days *by way of rehearsal*?

PLAINTIFF: No.

After the plaintiff's evidence, a doctor from Bootle hospital gave evidence that the plaintiff was very excited and drunk, and Goldie did his best to shake his evidence:

GOLDIE: Did you apply any test for drunkenness? Did you ask him to say, 'British Constitution' or anything like that?

DOCTOR: No.

GOLDIE: You could not ask him to walk. You simply said, 'Get thee hence. Bootle Hospital is no place for you,' and sent him to the workhouse. Did you know that for a month later he was kept in hospital?

DOCTOR: I did not know.

Despite Goldie's best endeavours, the plaintiff lost his case.

In another similar case Goldie's turn of phrase made the defendant's careful driving seem quite unthinkable: 'Is it not a fact, Sir,' asked Goldie, 'that the left-hand clog worn by the pillion rider came into such contact with the road that sparks, if I may put it this way, flew, with the result that Cheetham Hill Road looked for the moment as though it was part, so to speak, of the Infernal Regions?'

It is very much the conjuror's trick of 'forcing' a card on a member of the audience. When he wished to establish that a bottle of milk contained ammonia, he asked a doctor called on behalf of the Defence: 'Now, doctor, I want you to imagine please, because so far you have been so fair with me, that you are at a dinner party, and that the hostess is suddenly seized with an attack of, shall we say, *mal-de-mer* (because that's what they call it in polite society), and a gentleman friend picks up the cream jug and says, "My God, ammonia!" What would you say she was suffering from?'

He often used the phrase 'because you are so fair' when charming a witness into saying that two and two made five; but it became something of a habit: 'Now, doctor, come if you will—for I know you are always so fair—to Tuesday.' The technique did not always work, even with his own witnesses.

'Now, doctor, tell us if you will, for I know you are always so fair, does or does not, yes or no, this lady suffer, so to speak, from arthritis?'

'No.'

'But, Mr Goldie,' asked the Judge, 'I thought it was part of your case that she *does* suffer from arthritis?'

'I'm much obliged to your Lordship,' said Goldie; 'I'll just clear that up. Now, doctor . . .'

Counsel are not supposed to ask their own witnesses 'leading questions' which suggest the desired answer, but here is Goldie proving where an accident occurred: 'Bearing in mind that there is a furniture shop, a tobacconist's shop, and a draper's shop, can you tell his Lordship which *furniture* shop he was opposite? I beg your pardon, which shop of any kind he was opposite?'

'The furniture shop,' said the witness, by some happy chance.

Such leading questions were rather naughty, and his opponents would naturally object, so Goldie would assume an angelic expression and refuse to ask a direct question even on matters beyond dispute. He asked a little girl:

'You, I think, go to St Luke's School?'

'Yes,' said she.

'And St Luke's School has I think a *Girls'* department and a *Boys'* department. Which department were you in, Marjorie?'

There would be laughter in court, after which he would ask another outrageous leading question. Many of Goldie's opponents found to their dismay that while they were still laughing he had won the case. Members of the Northern Circuit knew his tricks, and could beware of them, but others who met Goldie departed sadded and wiser.

There was a very complicated Treasury case about a will. Goldie started by telling the judge it was a 'friendly action' involving no real dispute, and kept on saying it. By the time his distinguished opponent from London had a chance to suggest otherwise, it was too late.

Then there was the famous encounter with G O Slade, KC in a libel case. Slade was a great expert in these cases, learned, sonorous, and slow in his delivery. He was making his final speech to the jury when, reaching what he considered an important point, he paused, heavily.

'Now, members of the jury,' said Goldie, springing to his feet, 'it is *my* turn to address you . . .'

'I haven't finished yet,' said Slade angrily.

'I do so beg the pardon of my learned friend,' said Goldie, blandly, adding in an undertone, 'They don't teach you *that* one on the South Eastern Circuit, old boy.'

It was a wicked thing to do, but pompous advocates are fair game. Bearcroft was the victim of the famous trick in the Carlisle salmon case and seems to have been a sitting target.

He was once at Bar Mess on the Oxford Circuit, and was sitting next to a young barrister who was rather full of himself, as young men at the Bar tend to be. After listening to him for a while with mounting disgust, Bearcroft growled, 'I suppose there's nothing you think you can't do.'

'Oh yes there is,' said the young man, 'I can't afford to pay for my dinner, but *you* can.' And Bearcroft had to.

Goldie would have greeted as a kindred spirit the young John Scott, who attended Carlisle Assizes for seven years before he got his first brief, with a fee of one guinea. His client was an old woman who had tipped another out of her armchair; John Scott said it was only fair that the plaintiff should tip *his* client out of her chair, then adding that as the plaintiff's attorney was a Mr Hobson it was almost 'Hobson's Choice!'

The jury, laughing heartily, awarded the plaintiff only one penny damages. This joke of his attracted further work at the same assizes worth 70 guineas, 'which proves,' noted Scott, 'that a lawyer may begin to acquire wealth by a little pleasantry, who might long wait before professional knowledge introduced him into notice and business.'

There was this marked difference between John Scott and Noel Goldie, however; you knew when Scott was joking, but with Goldie you could never be sure. Even connoisseurs of Goldiana might find it hard to say which of these sayings was by accident or design:

234

In this case, my Lord, my client fell, so to speak, in a sense forwards, and in a sense backwards.

And the next thing, Members of the Jury, that my unfortunate client knew of this, he was unconscious in the butcher's shop.

Now, Sir, imagine if you will that you are a hound or a dog rushing towards me and I'm standing where you are.

Now, let us get this clear. The light was in darkness, was it not?

Or the most famous saying of them all:

Members of the Jury, so disfigured has my client's jaw become that never again will he be able to bite his bottom with his top teeth.

However, it is equally certain that it made no difference. If Goldie said something wrong he would cancel the mistake by ignoring it:

GOLDIE: My client, Members of the Jury, is a stonemason; and those of us who know the House of Commons know the great heights at which these stonemasons have to work.
W GORMAN, KC: Your client is a plasterer's labourer.
GOLDIE: My friend is always helpful.

One of his clients was injured when a falling bale knocked him off his cart.

GOLDIE, KC: Were the bales at the back of the lorry standing on end, and the bales in the middle lying down?
MR JUSTICE WILLMER: What size are these bales, Sir Noel?
GOLDIE: Four feet by four feet by four feet, my Lord.
JUDGE: Sir Noel, if they are four feet square, what is the difference between standing up and lying down?
GOLDIE: My Lord, I'll leave that to my expert.

Sometimes Goldie was playing the fool, but those who knew him well never underestimated him. Much of what he did was instinctive, and some of it was carefully planned. He was once defending a defamation case brought by a 'vexatious litigant', one of those tragic but tiresome figures who pursue a myriad fancied wrongs in hundreds of sheets of tortured writing. The documents in the case mounted high—Goldie's junior had a full-time job managing them all—and when Goldie cross-examined the plaintiff it was in a rambling, aimless sort of way. The jury may have wondered if Goldie had lost his senses, but they were quite sure that the plaintiff had, and they stopped the case.

This story is not widely known, and contains no quotable turns of phrase; but it demonstrates Goldie's great ability. Those who have to cross-examine deranged witnesses find it impossible to make them admit the absurdity of their beliefs; their obsessions wind like tentacles around a submerged rock, and there is no shifting them. Yet, seldom learning by experience, they try to shift the witness from his position by a direct attack, and hours can go by in futile endeavour. Goldie knew better, and his different approach worked like a charm.

Of course he had his faults. He could salvage a hopeless case, but it might not be wise to leave in his hands a simple case which his eccentricity could spoil. His strength lay with juries and witnesses, and his weakness with technical arguments and knotty legal points. It was said of him that he won more cases before juries, and then lost them in the Court of Appeal, than any other advocate. In that court he was once asked, 'Mr Goldie, have you considered the case of *Smith v Jones*?'

'If your Lordship pleases,' said Goldie, 'with the greatest possible respect, the case, if I may say so, can be easily distinguished from the present.'

'That's a pity, Mr Goldie,' said the Lord Justice of Appeal, 'because I thought it was in your favour.'

Sometimes when taxed with a difficult legal point he had to decline to argue it altogether. And there is a story of him appearing in the Court of Criminal Appeal for a client convicted of murder: 'The first point, my Lords,' he said, 'is that the learned Judge never dealt with the burden of proof at all.'

The three judges turned aghast to the transcript of the Judge's summing-up, because if he had failed to make it absolutely clear to the jury that in a criminal case the burden of proving the guilt of the accused lay on the prosecution, the conviction would have to be quashed; one cannot have a jury thinking that it is for a man to prove his own innocence. At last one of the three looked up: 'But, Mr Goldie,' he said, 'if you start at page 139 of the transcript, you will see that the Judge

236

dealt with the burden of proof admirably and at length over several pages.'

'My second point . . .' continued Goldie, imperturbably.

This legend is certainly untrue, but it illustrates the fact that Goldie was not at his best in the Court of Appeal, yet could survive a forensic disaster unruffled, as in a final speech to the jury:

GOLDIE, KC: With regard to that £70, Members of the Jury, I ask you to remember that the prosecution have not produced the paying-in slips. *Where* would I have been— where would my client have been—if the paying-in slips had been produced to show that he paid that money into the bank?

NEVILLE LASKI, KC: The paying-in slips *have* been produced, and are an exhibit.

GOLDIE: I'm so much obliged to my friend. That makes my point all the stronger.

One case above all which shows Goldie's style to perfection is *Stewart v Silcock Brothers* in 1935, still an age when civil cases had juries to try them. Liverpool's Royal Southern Hospital had a money-raising fête, which included a funfair organised by Silcock Brothers, a well-known fairground firm. Goldie's client, Mr Stewart, was injured whilst riding on one of the funfair amusement machines. It might easily have been a helter-skelter, or a bumper-car, but it was in fact a 'Noah's Ark', and Goldie surpassed himself:

Even in the dullest assize in your Lordship's court,' said Goldie to Mr Justice Porter, 'there comes a moment of merriment. I, my Lord, am the glad messenger of that moment. My Lord, this case arises out of a most unfortunate accident which befell my client while riding upon a pleasure machine known as a Noah's Ark. And, my Lord, if the original ark had proceeded as fast as this one went, it would have arrived on Ararat before the first dews had fallen from heaven and, if the animals, going in two by two or three by three, had had to go into this ark, they would undoubtedly have been drowned before they succeeded in getting through the doors. (Laughter).

The absurd nature of the case was enhanced when part of it,

a jazz-coloured swan, was produced in court, and the usher sat on it by way of demonstration. 'I am sorry we have not the organ here, my Lord!' said Goldie. (Laughter). He went on to explain that the animals moved forwards and sideways while the ark was moving very fast both sideways and up and down. 'Those unfortunate animals have to carry two persons. (Laughter). In most cases the lady sits in front, and the gentleman who has the gallantry to go on these animals has nothing to hold onto but the lady's waist. With your arms around the lady, you trust in providence and the proprietors.' (Laughter).

One witness said that, 'the animals had a bucking motion and sort of pendulum effect from side to side.'

Goldie: 'Like an Isle of Man boat!' (Laughter).

Another witness said that the only warning notice of any kind he saw was that part of the proceedings would be given to the Royal Southern Hospital.

Goldie: 'There was nothing about the *Outpatients Department,* was there?' (Laughter).

Another witness said the only way he could keep on a horse on the machine was by wrapping his legs round its neck: 'The only time I fell off it was when I sat on it properly and was looking round. I went on it again after I had fallen.'

Goldie: 'Sportsman!' (Laughter).

After all this the judge decided that the defendants should clearly have foreseen that persons standing on the machine were on risk, and awarded the plantiff £120.

A photograph of Goldie in the 1930s shows him still looking young, with a pleasant and intelligent face; you might almost take him to be shy and sensitive. Perhaps, deep down, he was; but on the surface he had the technique and attack of a top-notch music hall comedian. He was not one of those diffident barristers who almost apologise for speaking, and thereby deserve to; he had a great booming voice which led Edward Wooll to nickname him 'Vox', from the Latin quotation: *Vox magna et praeterea nihil,* which means, 'a great *voice* and nothing more.'

But there was something more, and it explained why people could not help hearing him, and had to listen as well. His sense of humour was often quite outrageous, and although there are many other barristers with a sense of humour, there were none greater. It is perhaps easy and obvious, when a witness said, 'I saw the plaintiff's motor cycle collide with the horse—just before the collision the motor cycle backfired', for Goldie to ask, 'Are you sure it was the *motor cycle* that backfired?'

But it was not at all easy or obvious to say to Mr Justice Hawke, who had just passed sentence of death in the previous case, which was a murder case, 'My Lord, this accident occurred at the new Liverpool Abattoir at Stanley, which is situated, if I may say so with the greatest possible respect, not very far from your Lordship's lodgings.'

In 1939 Goldie was appointed to sit for several weeks as an Assize Commissioner, which gave him the temporary position of a High Court Judge. Some verses were written about it:

> *Goldie's enriched a Bench that's growing dumber—*
> *Alas, one swallow doesn't make a summer—*
> *But, as his wisdom one attempts to follow*
> *Goldie's a summer-up who makes one swallow.*

He was remarkable, too, when required to try divorce cases. If a petitioner gave her address as Puddleby-in-the-Marsh, Goldie would enquire about those rustic scenes he knew and loved, and then grant her a decree of divorce without necessarily having heard any evidence. And he was readily distracted by thoughts of his regiment or public school. If some woman from Bethnal Green explained proudly that both her sons were at good schools, Goldie would assume she meant Eton or Harrow.

But it is as the Recorder of Manchester that he is best remembered, and Manchester Quarter Sessions used to be known to the profession as 'Goldie's Circus'. One has to make many allowances; the court had far more work to do than it could cope with.

Goldie dealt with—or more often dismissed—cases with breathtaking rapidity, not least if they came before him on a Saturday morning while the races were on. Only the prosecution lost out in the process when he stopped cases short, for he never denied the accused a fair hearing. Though under pressure, he did not lose his temper in court, and his approach to punishment had much to commend it. He believed in treating a first offender with leniency, if he could; giving him a second chance, if he offended again; but for a third offence, sharp

239

punishment was inevitable. An offender could hardly complain, if he had misused two chances given to him; and as rules of thumb go, it was probably better than most.

When Goldie retired as Recorder of Manchester, a full-time judge was appointed to do the work he had tackled part-time, but it was not Goldie's rapidity which gave his Sessions their legendary reputation. On the Bench, he had more scope than ever before; there was no judge to suppress him. His turns of phrase were as splendid as ever. He was much vexed by offences in public lavatories committed by male mutual misbehavers, and announced, 'The public lavatories of Manchester have got to be cleaned up, and I propose to make a start.' And when sentencing two culprits he said, 'You two men have to take yourselves in hand and pull yourselves together.'

In those days welcome assistance to those in trouble was given by some nuns in Manchester, and Goldie once said, 'My advice to any young men in Manchester is this. If you ever feel the urge to do something wicked, go straight to Sister Angela!'

The years were drawing on. When World War II ended in 1945, Goldie was 63. His great successes had been in civil cases heard by juries, but such cases had come to an end. The Labour Party swept to power and Goldie lost his seat in Parliament, though he was given a knighthood. An era was over.

He had been a silk now for almost 20 years, and if the old magician had lost a little of his dexterity, and fumbled some of his tricks, it was not his fault. In 1949 there was a murder trial in Liverpool, the famous 'Cameo Case', so called because the two accused robbed the manager of the Cameo Cinema, and shot him dead. When Goldie asked a witness, 'Was the door *closed*, or was it *shut*?' he was on familiar form. But when he said to the jury that the defences of the two accused 'more or less hung together', it was an unhappy phrase, for the noose awaited both of them. It was in itself a harmless error, but when he turned to the two accused with a charming smile and said, 'I beg your pardon, gentlemen,' he plunged the court into horrified silence.

In the years that followed, Goldie gradually appeared less and less in court, but was often to be seen at Bar Mess, an honoured figure on the Circuit he loved. Yet in this late period his advocacy acquired a new and almost surrealistic quality:

GOLDIE: Are you a member of the Master Builders' Federation?
ACCUSED: I am.
GOLDIE: You am? (Laughter).
JUDGE: You said 'you am'.
GOLDIE: I thought perhaps I'd missed out the 'd'. At any rate, you were, are, am a member?

He died on 6 June 1964 at the age of 81. He once said of himself, 'I have achieved a measure of success solely by means of eccentricity,' and the *Liverpool Daily Post* wrote of him:

He was not a profound lawyer; that rather deadening distinction was denied him. But he was a remarkable, and in some respects a unique personality. Strangers visiting his court might have observed a certain unconventionality—perhaps they might even have thought it a lack of dignity. Obviously he was interested not so much in the letter of the law as in men and women.

Since his death, a new generation of barristers has joined the Northern Circuit, knowing him only by name. Posterity must form its own opinion. Meanwhile, let it be recorded that, in the year 1979, his name was still a by-word for warmth and good humour. It is easy to look at his jokes and take him for a fool; but his opponents did not make that mistake twice. It is natural to wonder what sort of personality lay behind the buffoon's mask, but it was no mask. Goldie was the same in court as out of it, and whenever he created laughter, he revelled in it.

At the Bar, James Boswell showed brilliance unmatched by stamina; James Losh was a humourless plodder; but Goldie was a dazzling success; a happy marriage, service for his country in war and in peace, in Parliament and on the Sessions bench, coupled with a knighthood and the enduring affection of his colleagues, are the hallmarks of it.

As judges go, Judge Jeffreys had a marvellous acuteness of mind and most of his decisions were entirely right, but his manner towards others has made him hated unto eternity. Goldie was often wrong, but is still remembered and loved. It is easy to understand why. There is something of Goldie in all of us—seldom perhaps enough; he is, so to speak, the patron saint of those who put their foot in it, as we all do at times. One can take an affectionate farewell of his genial shade as he does precisely that:

> My Lord, I have considered the whole of the proofs of the witnesses for the defence in this case, and though I have, with the greatest possible respect to your Lordship, a large number of most important bus drivers and conductors from the Manchester Corporation whom I have the honour to represent, there is only one witness whom I have decided to call, as his statement, which I have so to speak tooth-combed, will decide the whole case in my favour. His evidence is so important that I have decided to rely upon him entirely:
> —Battersby! [A silence.]
> —BATTERSBY! [A profound silence. Goldie looks at his brief.]
> —Davenport! [The witness enters the box.]

SIXTEEN

A Breath Of The North

'He had a ready kind of rough Lancashire eloquence, arising out of the fulness of his heart,
which was very stirring to men similarly circum-
stanced, who like to hear their feelings put into
words.'

Mrs Gaskell, *Mary Barton*

Mr Justice Swift was trying a case on the Western Circuit, and
a very long case it seemed to be. Three times he tried to speed
counsel up, and three times he failed, so he leaned back in his
chair. 'Oh, for a breath of the North!' he sighed.

One does not have to come from the North to be shrewd and
blunt, but it helps, and these were two of his notable traits. He
is remembered as one of the great characters from the
Northern Circuit, and the only one to qualify as such by his
career on the Bench. Generally speaking, a Judge's career has
no place in a history of the Circuit; for, even though a barrister
may have spent all his life on the Circuit, once he becomes a
High Court Judge he is lost to it. He ceases to be a fixed star on
the Circuit, and instead becomes a judicial planet in orbit
round the whole country.

But Rigby Swift was different from all the rest in that he
carried his northern qualities around with him wherever he
went. He was a Northerner through and through. Until he
became a High Court Judge and, as he put it, 'a commercial
traveller in justice,' he had spent almost his whole life in
Lancashire. He never acquired the impersonal Oxbridge
accent usual among lawyers; his speech was not exactly
Lancastrian, but very like it, with the same flattened vowels,
and a curious habit of stressing the end of his first name, so that
Rigby became Rig-*bah*! It was so much his trademark that the
Hon. Mr Justice Rigby Phillip Watson Swift was known
universally as Rigby.

He was born in St Helens on 7 June 1874. He went to school and university in Liverpool, and then, since his father was a Liverpool barrister, joined him in chambers at the age of 17, where he practised until, just before taking silk in 1911, he moved to London.

At the Bar he worked extremely hard, and built up an enormous practice, but there is only one story about him in those days. A bus crashed into a wall, and when an injured passenger sued for damages, the bus driver claimed that he had swerved to avoid a dog. Rigby rose to cross-examine him.

'Was it a *nice* dog?' he said, and sat down. The plaintiff won his case. It is a classic example of what a good cross-examination should be.

F E Smith knew Rigby well at the Liverpool Bar—they had chambers in the same building—and when FE became the Lord Chancellor, he appointed Rigby to be a High Court Judge at the rather young age of 46. This is what *The Times* had to say about it:

> No appointment could meet with greater approval—we might even say enthusiasm—in the legal profession and among the public than that of Mr Rigby Swift. His qualifications for elevation to the judicial Bench are undeniable. A good lawyer, with what might be called a dainty and good-humoured style of advocacy, elegant without being flamboyant, tactful without being sycophantic, firm without bitterness, no man ever accepted one of the most difficult of professional positions with greater promise of success. He should make at once a scholarly, business-like and human judge. His was an obvious choice for promotion. It was generally expected.

The prophecy was fulfilled. It is always easy to criticise judges, and some of them deserve it from time to time; but it is even easier to underestimate the difficulty of their task, and to take their successes for granted. No member of the Bar pretends to understand every branch of the law. Before he went onto the Bench, Rigby had many criminal cases, and commercial disputes between business men, and claims for negligence, and other wrongs; if a solicitor sent him a case involving difficult questions of bankruptcy law, or of wills and trusts, he would probably recommend the solicitor to pass the papers to another barrister with a more specialised knowledge of that class of work. But a High Court Judge, especially when he goes on assize, has to deal with any sort of case which comes before him. The predicament was wittily explained by Lord Sterndale, the Master of the Rolls, at a Liverpool Law Society dinner soon after Rigby was appointed to the Bench:

> Look at our judges; I don't suppose there is a steadier lot of men in the kingdom—(laughter)—hard working, regular, and respectable. (Laughter). You never hear of them ever threatening to go on strike. If the divorce business is a bit congested with orders, and the foreman (the Lord Chancellor) likes a man from some other line that is a bit slack to help out, does that man apply to the union and say, 'My job is Chancery,' and lay down his wig? (Loud laughter). Not he. He just goes and does his bit of divorcing, and then goes back to his own particular job.' (Laughter).

Once on the Bench, Rigby had to try cases of landlords and tenants, rating, town and country planning, as well as the line of work he was used to; but in no case did he seem to be out of his depth. A judge must be able to tackle all sorts of unfamiliar problems, and Rigby managed to.

Many other judges, of course, have been models of fairness and ability, without making the impact that he did on the general public. The explanation does not lie in the *Law Reports,* where one can read his decisions on the acceptance of Spanish walnuts by the buyer before he had seen them, or the validity of regulations about the illuminated rear number plates of cars. His greatest value lay in jury trials, where he had a gift for putting things in a way that could be immediately understood, with a pleasing touch of humour into the bargain. Thus, in a slander case:

NORMAN BIRKETT, KC: It is highly defamatory to say to an employer that he ought to get rid of an employee.

RIGBY: Suppose a man were to go into a grocer's shop where there was a red-haired employee, and say to the shopkeeper, 'I don't like red-haired men. I am not going to come back until you get rid of him.' Is that any slander?

BIRKETT: I should submit it was defamatory. I hope it would not be said of *any* red-haired man. (Laughter—Birkett had red hair).

RIGBY: Oh, Mr Birkett, for the moment, of course, you are wearing a wig. You realise, of course, more than anyone that I did not intend any reference to you.

It is very important that a judge should seem impassive, not to be openly disgusted with the disgusting. There was the 'Trunk Trial' in 1923, *R v Robinson,* so called because the accused murdered a woman and then cut her into little pieces and put them in a trunk; indeed, the murdered woman's husband could only recognise her from her front teeth, small ears, and the crooked forefinger of her right hand. The details were ghastly, but Rigby made the jury concentrate on the only issues in the case which mattered:

Robinson's conduct towards the body is of the greatest importance, for the Crown contends that no-one who has not committed a murder, no-one who is not in fear of his own life, would do such terrible things. Mr Vine has quite rightly pointed out, however, that Robinson is not being tried for the way in which he disposed of the body, or for concealing the fact of the woman's death. You must therefore take into consideration the manner in which the body was dealt with, but you must not allow it unduly to influence your judgment.

Sometimes witnesses may be exasperating, but the judge must keep his temper. I doubt if Rigby sympathised with a major who claimed damages from another man for enticing away his wife. The major not only sent his wife love letters, but kept copies of them as well. It seemed a coldly calculating move.

RIGBY: I have never heard of anything so extraordinary in my life as a man copying his own love letters. Do you mean to say that he kept a copy of this letter beginning, 'My dearest darling,' and going on for two pages, saying, 'Baby, I am so unhappy about you, as I love more than my life?'

MALCOLM HILBERY, KC (for the wife): Yes. In all cases he kept copies of his letters and in some cases drafts in addition.

RIGBY: There is a page and a half more of it. Can you imagine a man writing that sort of thing and then sitting down and copying it?

A JURYMAN: We can not, my Lord, unless it was a carbon copy.

Rigby stopped the case.

A judge can only be judged in the context of his times. The twenties are remembered for the Charleston and the General Strike. It was also a time when Progressive Whist was deemed to be an illegal form of gambling. The prosecution of the OK Social Club in 1929 is certainly illuminating. Glynn Blackledge appeared for the Club, appealing against a conviction in the Magistrates Court, and argued that although the losers in any hand of the game changed partners, it was still a game of skill:

Mr JUSTICE AVORY: Two good players might go through the evening getting bad partners. Nothing upsets a good player so much.

BLACKLEDGE: But nothing pleases a good player so much as to get rid of a bad partner as soon as possible.

RIGBY: But how can you eliminate chance from any game of cards? Do you suggest that the cards were cut and dealt with skill?

The appeal was dismissed, which was right under the law as it then stood. It is not a judge's job to be ahead of his times. Indeed, to be very much ahead of one's time may be positively dangerous.

In 1925, Rigby tried Harry Pollitt and eleven other Communists for sedition; they and their sympathisers were and still are his sternest critics. 'In my view,' said Walter Citrine, then Secretary of the TUC, 'a most unsuitable judge had been selected.'

'The sentences,' added Col. Wedgwood Benn, MP, 'are perfectly iniquitous. The judge's summing-up was extremely biassed.'

Rigby had been a Conservative MP for St Helens for several years, but to be a Tory MP is hardly the mark of Beelzebub, even now. Harry Pollitt conducted his own defence, and wanted to read out some Conservative speeches by Lord Birkenhead, Lord Carson, and Sir William Joynson-Hicks, the Home Secretary:

'No,' said Rigby, 'I cannot give you permission for that. I do not see how seditious speeches by them can be of the slightest assistance to the jury or have anything to do with this case. You could have preferred a bill of indictment against them if you wished to do so. We cannot have their seditions mixed up with yours.' (Laughter).

Here is part of his 'biassed' summing-up, where he defines sedition:

'What is meant by overthrowing the Government,' he said, 'is a complete change in the constitution, the abolition of the King and the House of Commons and a substitution of some form of government by a committee of workers. It would be laughable if it were not so serious to suggest that anyone could persuade sailors and soldiers not to carry out orders. What would happen if they allowed that? There would soon be a revolution. As one of the defendants' passages said of Moscow, 'four regiments of guards disobeyed their officers. The revolution had begun.'

All the defendants were convicted, and sentenced to six or twelve months imprisonment. They asked to be allowed to see their wives before they were taken to prison, but the warders objected that this would be inconvenient. Rigby's response was typical of him: 'Let the inconvenience be overcome,' he said. 'I desire that their wives may see them.'

In 1930, the *Daily Worker* was guilty of Contempt of Court by describing Rigby as a 'bewigged puppet', and one of its staff declared that 'the whole career of Mr Justice Rigby Swift has been completely anti-working class.' But only four months earlier he had tried a case where a working-class woman had been killed in an accident, and her husband claimed damages for her loss. Scholefield Allen, for the defendants, quoted a case which said that such damages ought to be small, because a wife's services were given free:

RIGBY: How long ago was that?
ALLEN: 1915.
RIGBY: I am not accepting the idea that the wife of a working man, who runs his house and looks after the children, is not of great, substantial and really important use. To my mind the pecuniary value cannot be the money actually put down at the end of the week on the kitchen table. Even supposing that she never brings a penny into the house, at any rate she is preventing pennies from going out.

So he granted fairly substantial damages, and was perhaps going further than other judges had gone in the same direction. But he put less value on wives who had left their husbands, when their husbands claimed damages for the loss: 'Wives cannot be assessed on their cash value. They are not chattels.'

He was always sympathetic towards ordinary people who seemed hedged in by inhuman rules or laws. Railway tickets, for instance, had small words printed on the back greatly restricting the right of a passenger to sue if he was injured by the railway company's negligence.

In 1923 Rigby heard a case called *Nunan v S E Railway*. Mr Nunan was killed in a railway accident, but the words on his ticket limited the damages to £100; Rigby thought his widow should have received £800. He got over the difficulty by pointing out that the widow had not bought the ticket; she had made no bargain with the railway, so she was not bound by the £100 limit. So she got the £800.

Rigby always hated the hypocrisies of the Divorce Court, such as a Judicial Separation, which grants one spouse a separation from the other, yet preserves the marriage bond, thus ensuring that the other is not free to remarry. A P Herbert called such stalemates 'Unholy Deadlock', and this is how Rigby expressed himself on the subject in 1937:

> If she believes that her husband who has left her is living in adultery, what a farce to come to this court and say she does not believe in divorce because those whom God hath joined together should not be put asunder. I do not know whether the fault is on her side or on his, and I do not care. Something happened to separate them. It might be her fault, it might be his; but long before they came to this court they were divorced. Those whom God has joined together *were* put asunder. They only come here to have the label of matrimony removed, and this woman comes here and tells me she does not want the legal tie removed. She wants to have some control still over her husband. And so she shall. She shall remain married to him so far as I am concerned.

So her application for a judicial separation was dismissed.

He also hated the system of Professional Co-Respondents, which now belongs firmly to the past. If a husband and wife were tired of each other but had no valid grounds for a divorce, they could fake a case of adultery. The husband would do the 'decent thing' and spend the night in a hotel with another woman, signing her into the hotel register as his wife. When the chambermaid brought in the early morning tea, the husband would be in bed with the other woman. They might well not have committed adultery at all, but the judge would be bound to infer from the chambermaid's evidence that they had.

It did not appeal to Rigby. Once, when a chambermaid gave the usual evidence, he passed her a photograph which had been handed in: 'Is that the person you saw in bed?' he asked.

'Yes,' she said.

'That's odd,' said Rigby, 'I've accidently handed you the photo from the previous case!'

He expressed himself more seriously on the subject in 1925:

If, instead of registering at a hotel, and committing, or pretending to commit, an act of adultery with some strange woman, who is merely brought in for the purpose of completing the machinery to obtain a divorce—if that could be avoided by some such declaration as I have suggested, the court would still inquire into all the circumstance, would still exercise the discretion as to whether it granted a divorce or not, would still maintain full control over the custody and maintenance of the children and would, in fact, exercise every power and discretion that it does now. There would be the substitution of a declaration before a responsible officer in place of a declaration and physical exhibition before a hotel reception clerk and chambermaid.

These reforms were not carried out until 50 years later. It is not a judge's job to be ahead of his times, and such outbursts are only justified if he is proved right. Indeed, to be very much ahead of one's time may be positively dangerous. In a case at Leeds, a child climbed on to a heap of soil and was injured. The question was whether, in legal terms, the heap of soil was an 'allurement' to children to climb on it, and the jury wanted to know what it meant:

RIGBY: The best thing I can do is to give you an illustration. If you put a piece of cheese upon a little wire in a mouse-trap that would be an allurement for the mouse to enter. Allurement is something seductive—an attractive invitation.

Clear-minded lawyers can be bad judges if they cannot keep order in court, but this was the least of Rigby's problems. Despite frequent moments of humour, his court was no place for clowning. He ruled the court with a rod of iron, and three slow taps with his pencil on the edge of his desk was a warning not to be ignored. When a member of the Bar incurred his displeasure, there would come the tap—tap—tap. 'Let me give you some advice,' Rigby would say ominously, 'and do not forget it.'

Counsel was once cross-examining a witness who seemed to be telling lies. 'Don't tell lies to the jury,' said counsel. Rigby's pencil went tap—tap—tap: 'That is not a proper observation to make.'

COUNSEL: Then I withdraw it.

RIGBY: You should never have made it. It is preposterous for counsel to tell a witness not to tell lies. Most irregular and most improper. I hope I shall never hear it again.

COUNSEL: I do not make observations without foundation.

RIGBY (terrifyingly): That makes it worse. If you say anything more I shall tell you to sit down. I rebuke you for your conduct.

It was very unwise to take liberties with him. A young member of the Bar got more than he bargained for and, perhaps, deserved:

RIGBY: When are the next City Quarter Sessions?

W T FIELDING: I understand it will be held about the beginning of April.

RIGBY: If there are no City Quarter Sessions until the beginning of April, that may be a good reason for sending Quarter Sessions cases to the Assizes. Does that occur to you?

FIELDING (blissfully unaware of the wrath to come): I have not given the matter one thought.

RIGBY: Why not?

FIELDING: I have so many other things to attend to.

251

RIGBY: I do not understand that. If you attend to a case of this sort, you should attend to it properly. If you cannot attend to it you should return your brief.

FIELDING: I hope to do my best in regard to this case.

RIGBY: Then you ought to be able to tell me, without being impertinent to me, why a Quarter Sessions case has been sent to the Assizes.

FIELDING: I must apologise if you think I was being impertinent. I had not the slightest intention of being impertinent.

RIGBY: When you told me you had too much to attend to, to look after this case properly, you were impertinent to me.

FIELDING: What I wished to say was not that I had no time for this case, but that I had other matters to attend to.

RIGBY: I dare say you have. I have nothing to do with other matters. All I have to do is to attend to this case, and the first thing that strikes me about it is that it ought to have been sent to Quarter Sessions. I am asking you why, and I do not expect to be met with the answer that you have not got time to think about it.

FIELDING: As your Lordship pleases.

That was Rigby at his worst. At times he could be simply impossible, but quite impartially; impossible with anybody. A distinguished KC came up from London to appear in front of him: 'I didn't quite hear what you said,' observed Rigby at one stage.

'I am so sorry,' said the Silk, pleasantly; 'I am afraid the acoustics are not very good in here.'

'Oh!' said Rigby, outraged. 'You come up here from London to criticise the conditions in my court?' and with that he leant back in his chair, and obstinately shut his eyes.

There were times when his outspoken comments caused resentment. Motorcyclists were not flattered when he said, 'A motorcycle is driven by a hot-headed youth without a hat, and everybody except himself and the young lady sitting on the pillion behind him hates him.' And women could hardly be gratified when he said, 'I never knew a woman who would not buy a coat cheaply if she could get it.'

Nobody minds judges laying down the law—that is their job; if only they would not insist on laying down the facts, as well!

252

There was a road accident case in 1930 when a woman and her husband were injured. Her first words after the accident were, 'My God, he's killed. I told him not to cross too soon.' Rigby regarded these words as very important. 'When a man is drunk,' he said to the jury, 'he tells the truth. Similarly, people tell the truth in moments of great distress, pain, and agony, and you may think Mrs Argent did so after the accident.'

It sounds very wise; but on the very next day he tried another road accident case in which the police had gone to the bedside of an injured girl as soon as possible to get her account of the accident. This time he took the opposite view: 'I cannot understand,' he said, 'why policemen go to hospitals and worry people who are very ill and suffering from considerable pain, as obviously this poor girl must have been at the time. I wonder that doctors and nurses allow policemen to go and play about in a hospital. I wouldn't if I were a matron!'

Rigby's most striking feature was his broad red face, as full of bluff common-sense as a Yorkshire farmer's. It often shone with good humour, and he loved having his leg pulled on suitable occasions. Goldie certainly met with his approval when, discussing a racehorse, he asked a witness, 'I believe it is a very *swift* horse?'

Like all strong judges, he respected advocates who stood up to him. He once asked the young Fred E Pritchard, 'Where are we getting to now?'

'About half-way through my cross-examination,' said Pritchard, in all innocence, and Rigby was quite delighted.

The most famous story about him comes from Manchester Assizes, where a young man was floundering through his final speech. Rigby did his best to make it clear that he needed no further persuasion in the young man's favour. J C Jackson, KC happened to be in court, and passed the young man a note; the young man read it, but went floundering on. Rigby's curiosity was aroused, and he insisted on the note being passed to him. One could have heard a pin drop, while he studied it impassively: it read, 'Sit down, you fool, the old bu . . . .'s with you.'

'Have you read this note?' asked Rigby.

'Yes, my Lord,' said the young man.

'Then read it again,' said Rigby. The young man took the hint, sat down, and won his case.

Four cases in particular illustrate his abilities and style as a judge. The first was an election petition which he heard in 1929, a year before the *Daily Worker* described him as a 'bewigged puppet'. An election petition is a complaint by some of the electorate that an election was so irregular it should be set aside.

The Conservatives alleged that Mr Moses, a very popular Labour candidate for Plymouth's Drake Division, had been elected because a rich friend of the candidate had offered the members of a boys' club all sorts of treats if their parents voted for Mr Moses. Stafford Cripps, KC who was acting for Mr Moses, argued that the election was not invalid.

RIGBY: Is it not a corrupt practice for Mr Ballard to say to the boys, 'Go and tell your fathers and mothers to vote for Mr Moses and if he gets in I will give you a fireworks display?'

CRIPPS: It might be, but I am calling rebutting evidence by calling Mr Ballard, who will say that it is an ordinary method of his, and that he was anxious, in the interests of his institute, to promote the candidature of Mr Moses.

RIGBY: Surely it is corrupt treating if he links the result of the election and fireworks display in the same sentence?

CRIPPS: There have been a number of cases of treating on a most generous scale held not to be a corrupt practice. At Aylesbury, Lord Rothschild gave a party to 7000 people. It was held that that was not corrupt treating.

RIGBY: Did they talk about votes?

CRIPPS: I do not know, but he was a candidate.

RIGBY: It makes a difference if you mix up votes and tea. (Laughter). It is not in the eyes of the law as bad for a man to say, 'Here is a cup of tea; vote for So-and-so, than to say, 'If so-and-so gets in I will give you a cup of tea.'

It must surely be a foregone conclusion that when a Labour candidate is elected under such circumstances, the election will be held invalid by a judge who has not only been a Tory MP, but is also a bewigged puppet. But Rigby decided that although Ballard had made the promises, there was no evidence that they had influenced any voters and he upheld the election as valid.

In 1934, the case of *Crowley v Hammett* caused a tremen-

254

dous sensation. Aleister Crowley sued Nina Hammett for defamation because she alleged that he was practising Black Magic; her defence was that it was true. Malcolm Hilbery, KC established, in a devastating cross-examination, that Crowley called himself 'Beast 666', and showed him a number of newspaper articles in which he was described as 'the King of depravity', 'the wickedest man in the world', and so on. Rigby had some questions to ask about this.

RIGBY: It is said of you 'it is hard to say whether he is man or beast.'

CROWLEY: It was said of Shelley that he was sent from hell.

RIGBY: I am not trying Shelley. I am trying your case. When that was said in the public press did you take any steps to clear your character?

CROWLEY: I was 1500 miles away. I was ill and penniless.

RIGBY: I do not ask about the state of your health. Did you take any steps to clear your character?

CROWLEY: I wrote to my solicitors, and then it was impossible.

RIGBY: The answer is that you took no steps to clear your character?

CROWLEY: Yes. I did not take any action then because I was advised that my action would last 14 days, and I would have to find £10,000 to fight it.

RIGBY: Now you see how absurd that advice was, because this case won't take anything like 14 days. I imagine you have not found £10,000, have you?

CROWLEY: No.

After further evidence of Crowley's blasphemous and sexual practices, Rigby delivered to the jury the strongest summing-up he ever gave:

I have nothing to say about the facts except this. I have been over 40 years engaged in the administration of justice in one capacity or another. I thought that I knew of every single form of wickedness. I thought that everything which was vicious had been produced at some time or another before me. I have learned in this case that we can always learn something more if we live long enough . . . I have never heard such dreadful, horrible, blasphemous and abomi-

255

nable stuff as that which has been produced by the man who describes himself to you as the greatest living poet . . .

The jury's verdict was for the defendant.

There are not many barristers now who can remember Rigby on the Bench. They speak of his last years when he was a sick man, and was something of a holy terror; young men quaked in their shoes at the thought of him. Others can only know him from the printed page, where his great northern qualities of directness and good humour still shine out, especially in the case of *Joyce v Lord Revelstoke* in 1935.

Angela Joyce was the stage name of Ivy Dawkins, who was Miss England in 1930, and a starlet after that; Rupert Baring was a young Cambridge undergraduate when he met her, and proposed marriage to her, but when he reached the age of 21, he became Lord Revelstoke and changed his mind about marrying her; Angela sued him for breach of promise of marriage. It was then the law that a young man who proposed marriage before the age of 21 could not be held to that promise unless he repeated it after becoming 21. Angela Joyce claimed that he had repeated it, and this was the only issue in the case.

Rigby's first task, as in so many cases, was to ensure that the jury did not get carried away by their feelings. He began his summing up of the case by saying:

If this had been an action even for breach of promise of marriage in which the plaintiff had been Miss Ivy Dawkins a shop assistant, and the defendant had been Rupert Baring a gas inspector, or something of that kind, little interest would have been taken in the case; but because the plaintiff is Miss Angela Joyce, a film actress and writer, and because Rupert Baring is Baron Revelstoke, considerable interest appears—as you may observe by looking round the court or reading newspapers—to be taken in the matter.

Whatever Rigby's own feelings were about film stars and aristocrats, he suppressed them, and warned the jury that if a breach of promise had occurred, they had to consider the appropriate damages in a business-like way:

You may have to assess what damages she sustained by reason of her position, if she was entitled to it. She lost the society and position of being a married woman, and the

256

position of being the wife of a member of the peerage. You must put that into pounds, shillings and pence, if ever it comes to a question of assessing damages in this case. You are not here to punish the defendant.

But was there, in fact, a breach of promise? Had he renewed that promise to marry after he became 21? Here Rigby appears at his very best: wholly sincere, and admirably sensible:

It is all very well for you and I—some of us in middle life—to talk of the folly and extravagance of youth and the language which they indulge in. If we want to be honest with ourselves we had perhaps better not cast our minds back too searchingly to the time when we were 19. Boys do fall in love and they do write letters which in the cold light of this court sound very different. Read by Mr Laski [for the plaintiff] they sound like poetry; read by Mr Birkett [for the defendant] they sound rubbish (laughter), but there is not one word in any letter about marriage. Does that look as though marriage was being contemplated by him?

This letter writing, this 'die if I cannot see you tomorrow,' this telephoning to her every night, went on for six or seven months, and then it stopped. There are—and you will choose between them—two reasons given why it stopped. According to Lord Revelstoke it stopped because they both cooled off. You may think that that is not an unnatural explanation. Those sort of infatuations do cool off, as your experience of the world must have taught you. Very few men, I imagine, marry the woman that they first tell they love. I am told [here he had a twinkle in his eye] that they always tell the woman they marry that she is the first woman they have ever loved.

There are no such phrases in the letters as 'Oh my darling, I am looking forward to the time when we shall be together always,' or 'won't it be delightful when we have a house of our own?' Nothing of the sort. Simply the vapourings about love and affection which do not amount to corroboration of a promise to marry.

The vital question in the case was the date on which the promise of marriage was made. It so happened that the letters were all undated; and it was remarkable that Angela Joyce had kept none of the envelopes, which would have shown the postmark:

> If the letters were written in 1932, how fortunate it would have been if they had been in envelopes bearing a date after April 1932. But how unfortunate it would have been if they had been in envelopes stamped August 1931!

The jury retired for half an hour, and then found in favour of Lord Revelstoke. The case was so clearly explained that nobody could fail to understand it. This was Rigby's supreme quality.

When not on circuit, he lived at Crowborough on the Sussex Downs. Here he played golf, and pottered about; his beloved wife Beatrice kept pigeons and dogs, and was a leading light in the village activities. Rigby was very fond of expressing his views on married life in court.

In March 1937, at Birmingham Assizes, he declared: 'You cannot assess the value of a wife as though she were a chattel. She is not a piece of furniture. You can not treat her as though she were a piano, and ask yourself how much a leg you pay for it. You have got to ask yourselves, what did he lose when a woman who could no longer live with him went away and left him? He lost nothing—nothing.'

A month later Lady Swift was struck down by a brain haemorrhage. For three days she remained unconscious; Rigby hardly left her bedside. Then she died, and Rigby lost almost everything in the world that he cared about, for he had no children.

But nobody could have guessed it from reading the newspaper accounts of his last great case, *Jackson v Paramount Pictures*, heard in London in June 1937. The case certainly had a star cast. Counsel for the Plaintiff was H C Leon, better known to the reading public as Henry Cecil, the author of *Brothers-in-Law*. Marlene Dietrich was present, at least in spirit, because the plaintiff was an English journalist who went to Hollywood to write her life story.

He claimed that the defendants had promised to let him interview her, and had broken that promise; as a result, he had been unable to write her life story:

RIGBY: How old is Miss Dietrich?
H C LEON: 32.
RIGBY: Not a very long story!
LEON: In the life of an actress of such distinction it might be longer than it would be if someone wrote *my* life story.
RIGBY: It may be full, but not very long.
LEON: The approach to a film star by a journalist is a matter of some delicacy. It is not easy for a journalist to approach film stars, and still less to be allowed to write their life stories.
RIGBY: You are upsetting all my preconceived notions, but it does not matter. (Laughter) . . . What does he call the story?
LEON: The Mona Lisa of the Movies. (Laughter).
RIGBY: I wonder why everyone was so anxious to secure the life story of Miss Dietrich, who is only 32 years old. Shall I tell you the answer given by Shakespeare many years ago? It is, 'Sweet are the uses of advertisement!' (Laughter).

His judgment was simple, but not unkind.
'The heading of Mr Jackson's article about Miss Dietrich,' he said, 'is: Why I Do Not Live with My Husband, and on reading the article, one discovers that the reason is because Miss Dietrich works in Hollywood and her husband lives in Paris. (Laughter). I am satisfied that Mr Thomas [Paramount's publicity manager] never did more than say he would *do his best* to get Mr Jackson an introduction to Miss Dietrich. There was no evidence of a contract in what happened between Mr Thomas and Mr Jackson. I am sorry for Mr Jackson, who has had bad luck in the matter.'
A month later he went to Birmingham Assizes again, and was ailing rapidly; he had to be helped in and out of court. He sat for the last time in August 1937, and must have known he would never sit again. 'I'm finished,' he said to his clerk, and went home. Only a year before, there had been mention in a case of undertakers:

COUNSEL: Undertakers do not usually come to this court.
RIGBY: No, we go to them. We are usually *their* clients. We make one application: there are no adjournments, and one application is often quite enough.

One was enough for Rigby. He died in October 1937, aged 63. His faults were the faults of a strong judge, who at times did not know his own strength. After his death, the Lord Chief Justice paid tribute to his virtues: 'He was known as an independent, humane, learned and direct judge. He never left in doubt what his opinion was. He never took refuge in words of ambiguity. It was never Mr Justice Swift's way to steer a safe middle course in the channel of no meaning between the Scylla and Charybodis of Yes and No.'

A thousand years separate Mr Justice Rigby Swift from King Alfred the Great, one of whose laws was: 'A man can think of this one sentence alone, that he judges each one rightly; he has need of no other law books.' Rigby's common sense was of the highest order. But he knew his law books as well.

SEVENTEEN

Revelry By Night

'They are (as shall be seen anon) agreeably low,
delightfully disgusting, and at the same time
eminently pleasing and pathetic.'
W M Thackeray, *Catherine*

When the Circuit began in 1176, there were no barristers at all. Later when attorneys were first allowed to represent their masters, cellarers were often the spokesmen for the monasteries who went to law. Perhaps even in those early days there grew up a fraternity who, when the court rose, would gather together over a posset of wine to exchange uninhibited views about the judge, and cap each others' stories of triumph and defeat.

It is almost impossible for a layman to understand how two members of the Bar who have been fighting each other hammer and tongs all day can be the greatest good friends by night, but it is rather like tennis: the best games are fought against good players, not duffers.

This spirit exists whenever barristers meet out of court, but it exists particularly when they gather for Bar Mess. James Boswell found his colleagues rough, unpleasant company, but he was too sensitive to appreciate a joke at his own expense. He was not alone in this. A senior member of the Circuit in those days was once addressing a jury when a spectator in the gallery fell from it in his sleep, and was killed. Other members of the Circuit indicted him for murdering the victim with a blunt instrument, to wit his speech, but he regarded the joke as being in rather poor taste.

The Northern Circuit is not generally so fastidious. In 1828, Dr Brown prosecuted some body-snatchers for conspiring to steal 20 dead bodies. Courtenay, for the defence, objected to the form of the indictment; Dr Brown pointed out that it was a

261

form regularly used for coining offences: 'I took it from the Mint Prosecutions,' he said.

'You have no right to serve up *Mint Sauce,*' retorted Courtenay.

The Bar was much more robust in those days. It was considered fair game to insult witnesses with personal remarks. At Lancaster Assizes in 1818, as James Parke wrote to his wife:

There was an assault case yesterday of a trifling nature. A man with red whiskers was witness for the plaintiff. Topping, in cross-examination, said to him, 'Well, friend, I suppose they called upon you as a witness, because you happened to have such large whiskers?'

'I believe so.'

'Well, then, friend, I should advise you to shave them off, that you may not be brought to Lancaster upon the same errand.'

'I think I shall, sir.'

Today a letter came from the man to Topping, by the post, enclosing his whiskers, and telling him he had taken his advice.

At Newcastle in 1847, the Bar were pleased to acclaim that rare phenomenon: a perfectly honest witness:

Mr WATSON: Now, witness, answer the question that I shall put to you 'Aye' or 'No'.

WITNESS: Oh, nonsense!

THE JUDGE: Witness, how can you use so uncivil an expression to the learned Counsel?

WITNESS: My Lord, I am upon my oath, Sir.

But it was Mr Addison at Durham in the following year who received the most crushing reply. He was questioning a clergyman aged 73 whose memory, he suggested, was beginning to fail:

Mr ADDISON: How long ago can you recollect anything?

THE WITNESS after some thought: I can remember when *you* were a little boy.

These anecdotes were gleefully recounted at Grand Court, and due action taken; Courtenay was congratulated on his Mint Sauce joke and fined two gallons of wine, which he had to supply to the Mess. It was a harmless way of levying contributions, and is still practised in theory today, though the fines are never enforced.

Grand Court was always the Circuit's night of nights. James Losh thought it 'a scene of folly, a mixture of coarse humour, envy and insolence, which though it may amuse some minds, appears to be only fit to excite disgust.' But the great historian Thomas Babington Macaulay, who was a member of the Circuit in 1826, enjoyed it immensely. One of its features is the pair of speeches which makes fun of the silks (Queens Counsel) and the stuffs (the junior members of the Bar who wear stuff gowns). He wrote one of those speeches, a macaronic poem in Greek and English, describing the feast at which Alexander murdered Clitus:

When at first I did come back from ploughing the salt water
They paid me off at Salamis, three minae and a quarter.

It would be over the heads of the Bar now, but he would have been delighted to know that, in the 1930s, his famous poem of Horatius keeping the bridge was adapted by Fred E Pritchard, one of the masters of Grand Court speech-writing, to describe Rigby Swift's visit to Liverpool Assizes:

Sir Rigby Swift of Liverpool
By his black cap he swore
That the great Northern Circuit
Should live in peace no more
By his black cap he swore it
And named Commission Day
And bade Bill Graham give it forth
That he was shortly coming North
And with Macnaghten J.

. . . On seeing Schofield Allen
Sir Rigby's noble brow
Frown'd such a frown that in my dreams
I seem to see it now—
Before a word was spoken
He issued a decree
That Allen should be taken far
Beyond the lightship at the bar
Where sharks and monster fishes are
And hurled into the sea.

263

Grand Court did not exist only for fun and games; it enforced the rules of the Circuit. Young Macaulay had been given letters of introduction to an attorney at York, of great value to a member of the Bar still unbriefed. It was, however, a rule that such letters should on no account be presented personally. As Macaulay wrote to his father:

Even to take a meal with an attorney is a high misdemeanour. One of the most eminent men among us brought himself into a serious scrape by doing so. But to carry a letter of introduction, to wait in the outer room while it is being read, to be then ushered into the presence, to receive courtesies which can only be considered as the condescensions of a patron, to return courtesies which are little else than the blessings of a beggar, would be an infinitely more terrible violation of our professional code. Every barrister to whom I have applied for advice has most earnestly exhorted me on no account whatever to present the letters myself. I should perhaps add that my advisers have been persons who cannot by any possibility feel jealous of me.

The Circuit has always had its strict conventions. In 1846, three members of the Circuit were fined for writing to Appleby to order post-horses, presumably because they should have waited their turn when they got there, in order of seniority. It was also a Circuit rule that, in travelling from one Circuit town to the next, a junior should not presume to pass his senior:

'In coming from Appleby to Penrith,' declared Knowles, the Circuit's Attorney-General in 1848, 'I myself was first, Matthews 2nd, and Dykes 3rd in order. Dykes having shown a disposition to pass me was warned not to do so but with a laugh of triumph he drove past, leaving us in the dust or, as we would say after the trial of today, in a backwater. I move that Dykes be fined.'

Breaches of discipline are fairly rare. But Grand Court has its regular ceremonies. It begins after dinner when the dishes have been cleared away. The Junior of the Circuit, who has charge of the proceedings, bids the Cryer proclaim Grand Court in almost the same words that opened Arthur Mangey's trial in 1696:

CRYER: Oyez, oyez, oyez: All manner of persons that owe

264

suit and service to this Grand Court of the Northern Circuit, draw nigh and give your attendance.

It used to be the bounden duty of every member of the Circuit to be present, save for the most compelling reasons. When Mr Maude was absent in 1827, the Messenger, another Circuit officer, was sent to fetch him:

The door being opened, the Messenger and his assistants entered with Maude in custody. The Messenger stated that they had been to pretty Mr Maude's lodgings and there were informed that he had gone to dine with the judges. Thither they immediately repaired, and took pretty Mr Maude into custody in the act of drinking a glass of wine at the judges' table.

Those who were absent without cause were fined the cost of a gallon of wine, and the Cryer announced their names with embellishments: 'Cold Bath Roebuck', 'Cork Murphy', 'Fat Murphy', 'Silly Warren'.

In Victorian times, Crompton evolved from 'Clumsy Crompton' to 'Crafty canvassing clumsy Crompton', and Farside became 'Fomenting fiddling fidgetty Farside'. Today the alliteration has become almost an art in itself. Buffins is absent; only last week he was seen with a black eye, and said he had walked into a lamp-post by mistake. So:

Buffins, come into Court. Beautiful, black-eyed Buffins, come into Court. With a beautiful black eye from bumping his bonce on a bollard, Buffins come into Court.

Bumped his bonce on a bollard be blowed! Buffins was bloody well with a bird when her boy-friend broke into the bedroom and battered him; but what the bird can behold in Buffins is beyond me. Buffins, come into Court.

When the Cryer has finished with the absentees, the two speeches are read which make fun of the silks and the stuffs. To keep the old circuit traditions alive, there is a reading from some old part of the circuit records, such as are set out here. To keep in touch with the present, the Attorney-General inquires whether any member of Circuit has had a son and heir since last Grand Court? And whether any member of the Circuit has received any official appointment since last Grand Court? Such good fortune is warmly applauded, though not always from disinterested motives.

When James Parke was made a judge in 1828, a colleague wrote, 'the Liverpool lads are not a little rejoiced, not because Parke has got much honour, but because he is taken out of court and his business goes among the young ones.'

When these formalities are over the company amuses itself. Ballcock may tell one of his jokes, even with ladies present, for they are used to him by now, and Fizzwig will burst into song, unless forcibly restrained. Such, broadly speaking, are the proceedings at Grand Court, when the greatest and most pompous figures on the Circuit are open to ridicule. What might the Trades Union Congress not become—or the General Synod of the Church of England, for that matter—if only it had Grand Court!

The basic tradition of Grand Court is the same as it always was, twice a year, at York and Lancaster. But its geography was radically altered when it was clear that the Circuit was to be divided into two separate Circuits, to cope with the pressure of work which followed the rise of the big manufacturing towns. From 1876, Yorkshire, Durham and Northumberland became the North-Eastern Circuit and, the Northern Circuit comprised Lancashire, Westmorland and Cumberland alone. Mr Justice Ridley described in his Memoirs the last Grand Court of the old Circuit. A new Junior had to be sworn in, and Ridley was appointed Cryer for this occasion:

'After haranguing the new man on his general duties to the Circuit,' he wrote, 'I ended with:

> And should she ere the winter months be flown
> Twin Circuits bring to life and lose her own,
> Yours shall it be her dying hours to tend
> Her hopes to cherish and her rights defend

which was received with applause. And so ended the Northern Circuit as I knew it.' Though a hundred years have passed since that occasion, the Northern and North-Eastern Circuits still share a common feeling, and carry on the same traditions.

The twentieth century brought no immediate changes to circuit life. In 1914, many members of the Bar went off to the War. F E Smith's pupil, Edward Wooll, was one of them and when the Armistice came it was his duty to accept the keys of

266

the surrendered city of Cologne from its then Mayor, Konrad Adenauer. After the Nazis came to power, Wooll made one of those gestures typical of him. He visited Germany, and had to complete a questionnaire which asked whether he had ever visited Germany before, and if so, in what capacity. 'Yes' wrote Wooll to the first question—'as Conqueror', to the second one. The Nazis cannot have been amused.

Once, at Bar Mess, Wooll offered a guest a glass of port. 'I do like port,' said his guest, declining it, 'but I'm afraid port doesn't like me.'

'I've always had a high regard for its opinion,' said Wooll, drily.

During the 1930s the port-loving members of the Circuit perpetrated a Falstaffian deed at Carlisle; after a particularly good mess they packed Bill Graham, the Clerk of Assize, into a laundry hamper and put it onto the Newcastle train.

The circuit hospitality of these years was much appreciated by the Undersheriff of Westmorland at Bar Mess at Appleby. 'We had such an excellent dinner,' he recalled, 'and heard such witty stories afterwards, that it was late before we reluctantly bade our jolly hosts farewell. The stories they told us were wonderful and made us ache with laughing.' This is the only rib-tickler he quotes:

A newly-arrived court attendant was asked by a chairman of Quarter Sessions, who was making his way to the magistrates' room before going into court, 'Where can I find the agenda?'

'The last door on the right down the passage,' whispered the man.

It must have been a very good dinner.

In 1939, the younger members of the Bar went into the forces, and were only seen in chambers when on leave. But, as far as wartime conditions allowed, the old spirit still survived.

In 1943, for instance, a barrister serving in the RAF had to go to Buckingham Palace to be awarded the Distinguished Flying Cross. He called in on his chambers at lunchtime, and of course celebrations took place. In the midst of it a Bar Clerk unexpectedly appeared: 'A brief's just come in for this afternoon, sir,' he said to a young member of the Circuit; 'you can read it in the taxi on the way to court.' The young man finished his drink and set off, but the ride seemed unusually bumpy, and the brief struck him as having been typed with an unsteady hand. Still, by the time he got to court he knew that his client was charged with drunken driving. The case began.

The first witness gave evidence that the defendant's car had mounted the pavement of a straight road and had attempted to climb a tree. The young barrister felt that there must be one or two questions he should ask, but they escaped him for the moment, so he sat silent. With each witness it was the same, until the prosecution case was closed.

'Now,' said the magistrate, 'is there any legal submission you wish to make?' The young man rose to his feet. It was no mean achievement, for the earth's gravitational pull was particularly fierce that afternoon. And still he could think of nothing to say.

'I suppose,' said the magistrate, 'you want to submit that there is no case for your client to answer?' The young man nodded; it seemed the best thing to do.

'Well,' said the magistrate, 'I think you're right. Case dismissed.'

The client was overjoyed. 'You were brilliant,' he said to the young member of the Circuit, 'simply brilliant; I've never heard of a case being handled like that before.'

The prosecuting police inspector was somewhat sourer. 'You know why you won that case, don't you?' he snarled. 'The magistrate was bloody well drunk!'

When the War was over the barristers returned to make a living at the Bar. It was not easy; counsel for the Defence in a murder case which lasted for several days, was paid the princely sum of £5, for which he had undertaken a 'Poor Person's Defence', and £5 was the fixed fee for it. The defence solicitors were £500 out of pocket and sent their figures to the Lord Chancellor; soon afterwards, in 1948, Legal Aid was introduced for poor litigants in High Court and County Court cases.

It was an event of the greatest importance to the Bar, though it does not make gripping reading. Still, until it took its full effect, there continued the extraordinary ritual of the 'Dock Brief', which gave a prisoner the right to retain any barrister in court, prosecuting counsel apart, provided he had two guineas for the fee in his pocket.

One day at the Liverpool Crown Court, a prisoner pointed to one of the wigs and said, 'I'll have that gentleman.'

'I think he means you, Miss Blank,' said the Recorder; 'I'm afraid he can't tell your sex from behind.'

'You can't tell her sex from the front, either,' muttered an ungallant colleague.

There were few lady barristers in those days; Liverpool's Rose Heilbron, however, was a household name; she took silk in 1949, and appeared in many famous murder cases. Many people still believed that women did not have the right sort of brains for the Bar—too much intuition, and not enough thought. Besides, the language in some cases was perfectly dreadful! There was a story about one young lady prosecuting a burglary case:

> On the night of January 13th [she explained to the Recorder], PC Dogberry, who is stationed at Bootle, went to the warehouse of Messrs Warbeck and Simnel, where he heard a noise. Taking a torch from his pocket, PC Dogberry (who is stationed at Bootle) shone it up at the roof, and there he saw the accused looking down at him.
>
> 'Come down,' called out PC Dogberry—who, I think I mentioned is stationed at Bootle—and the accused shouted back: . . .
>
> 'I don't think we need go into *that* detail,' [said the Recorder hastily, to spare her blushes.]

It would not happen today. The ladies at the Bar can deal as resolutely with unpleasant topics as a lady surgeon can perform a delicate operation. Lady barristers are now fully accepted by the public, and certainly by their male colleagues, a number of whom have married them. At the Liverpool Bar alone there are eight married couples, and very happily married they are. But it can lead to difficulties. One couple who got engaged were in the same chambers, and their clerk realised that some of their work might have to be rearranged.

'Good heavens,' he said anxiously, 'they're not both going to be away on their honeymoon *at the same time,* are they?'

Lady members of the Circuit never came to Bar Mess during the 1950s—it was thought to be much too robust for them, and the ladies for their part thought that if the men wanted to keep their rude little jokes to themselves, they could. I can still remember the sensation on the Circuit in the early 1960s when the rule was first broken. Rose Heilbron, QC was in Lancaster for the assizes, and was sitting over her dinner alone with an Agatha Christie thriller, when the genial Alex Karmel, QC invited her to join the Mess.

'But I've just finished my dinner,' she exclaimed.

'Never mind,' said Alex; 'come and have another.' And she did.

Grey heads were shaken, to be sure; there was no knowing where it might end—women might even come to *Grand Court*! And in the end, they did. Some of the jokes are a little more restrained, which is no great loss, but the proceedings have gained charm. The worst forebodings were unfounded.

When I joined the Circuit in 1957 things were much more difficult for young ladies at the Bar; but they were much more difficult for young men too. It was a time when more people were leaving the Bar than were joining it. Indeed, on my first day in Chambers, a well-meaning colleague advised me to leave the Bar at once. The great Goldie was more affable:

'Well, Hamilton,' he said when I was introduced to him at Bar Mess, 'what university did you go to?'

'Oxford,' I said.

'Ah yes,' he said, nodding sagely, and walked away; he was a Cambridge man.

It was an age when young men at the Bar could not hope to live off their fees for several years. Indeed, in my second month at the Bar I only had two briefs: a very minor prosecution and a Dock Brief.

It did not come entirely as a matter of luck. Most people are right-handed, and we used to reckon that the most propitious place to sit in court was just in front and to the right of where the prisoner stood in the dock, almost within reach of his pointing index finger. There was keen competition for that seat a full hour before the court sat, and the occupant would not dare to vacate it. When I was chosen it meant two crumpled pound notes and a florin in my hand; it paid for my bed and breakfast for half a week. But when my luck was out, I spent the day listening to the Recorder sentencing criminals and I was at one in spirit with all the young barristers who had ever ridden round the Circuit empty-handed.

We went round the Circuit too, catching the early train to

Lancashire towns for the first day of Quarter Sessions, when small briefs were handed out to those who were first in the queue; and we also gave law lectures. One dark day I realised that I was doing hardly any lecturing, and even less at the Bar; but I inherited a course of talks on that heart-warming topic 'Current Affairs', which brought in 30s. a night. I arrived at the Ladies Guild—they met in a room over a grocer's shop—and was fiercely accosted by the Chairwoman.

'Who are you?' she demanded.

'Mr Hamilton,' I said nervously.

'Not *the* Mr Hamilton, you're not,' she said decisively, and indeed, I wasn't; I'm still not, for that matter.

A turning point in my career came during some lectures I was giving in 1960 on 'English and Clear Thinking.' The more clearly my class thought about it, the more they reckoned they could do without me, and my lecturing career came to an end. But by this time Legal Aid had been extended to cases in the Magistrates Court, and from that time onwards, newcomers to the Bar were able to earn a reasonable living. The Bar became much more attractive as a profession; there were 2000 barristers in 1957, but there are more than 4000 now. A serious problem now is to know how to find room for them all, because one does not wish to turn talented youngsters away.

By 1957 wartime restrictions had completely disappeared and the Circuit had resumed its convivial ways, not least in the person of the late Charles Elliott, of Manchester. He was everything a good Circuiteer should be: courteous, witty, extremely able in court, and excellent company out of it. He was once briefed in a case at Lancaster Assizes but, as the afternoon wore on, there seemed no prospect of the case starting, so he and his genial opponent were discussing an excellent bottle of brandy when his clerk dashed in. 'You're *on!*' he cried.

A few moments later Charles was on his feet before the judge, explaining that his client had been run down in the street by a slew balloon.

'A blue saloon,' corrected the judge.

'Quite so, my Lord,' said Charles, 'I said a blue saloon, and I meant a slew balloon.'

Bar Mess was always particularly convivial at Appleby Assizes, because there was very little law business to interrupt the celebrations; which is why the efficient administration of the law led to Appleby ceasing to be an assize town. It was at Appleby Assizes in the 1950s that the incident occurred of Charles Elliott's teeth. Bar Mess had been unusually lively, even by Appleby standards, and the party was about to disperse when Charles discovered that there were twelve bottles of champagne in the hotel cellar. It seemed a shame to waste them.

At last the hotel lay wrapped in slumber. Charles and a young colleague had adjacent bedrooms. At dead of night both doors opened, and two shadowy figures emerged in search of bathrooms; a little later the figures returned, and both doors were shut again. By the wrong occupants; in the haggard light of dawn the young man woke to find his room strangely unfamiliar, and Charles' teeth grinning at him from a washstand tumbler.

The Bar was never a more drunken profession than any other. Because of the modern breathalyser laws, members of the Circuit are necessarily more restrained, unless they happen to be staying overnight at the hotel. One morning at Carlisle, after a good Mess, a young man at breakfast was trying to balance a fried egg upon his knife. 'I want to swallow it all in one go,' he explained anxiously, his complexion an ominous olive, 'because if it breaks and all the yellow runs out, I shall be terribly ill.' The thought struck a colleague also as very grave, and he left the room.

Members of the Circuit stay at hotels in circuit towns less often than they used to, because of the motorway, which has greatly changed circuit life. A journey round the whole of the old Circuit that used to take three weeks, can be done in a single day. It is possible to commute to Carlisle; there is no Bar Mess at Lancaster now at night. But still the old legends and new jokes circulate with the port at Grand Court.

But time is drawing on, and the Junior orders the Cryer to close Grand Court:

CRYER: Oyez, oyez, oyez. All manner of persons that owe suit and service to this Grand Court of the Northern Circuit, depart hence and give your attendance at another place. God save the Northern Circuit and the Queen.

The company disperses. Some festive souls go in search of

272

pubs and clubs, for the night is yet middle-aged; some climb their stairs on tip-toe, lest their son and heir, born since last Grand Court, be woken out of slumber. And some go to burn the midnight oil, for there is a difficult case in the morning.

The great mirrored room stands empty, reflecting tables beyond tables beyond tables, on which stand the Circuit bells graved with the names of the Juniors of the Circuit, many of them famous names in the law; the silver tongues are silent now. There will be an ordinary Bar Mess here next week, and Grand Court again next term; old tales re-told and new faces. There are young people coming to the Bar who will be as good as any that went before them, and the great days of the Northern Circuit are not over yet.

Acknowledgements, Further Reading and Notes

My particular gratitude is due to three sources. In alphabetical order: The Athenaeum, Liverpool, whose library contains much not readily available elsewhere, and Mr. John Henshall ALA.

Miss Margaret Brander JP, ALA, the Reference Librarian of Tullie House Carlisle, who made available to me the James Losh diaries, and placed in my hand many books and pamphlets I should never have found for myself.

Sir Fred E. Pritchard for *Goldiana,* much help on Rigby Swift, and a continuing tradition of Circuit wit.

Many members of the Northern Circuit provided anecdotes and information; other sources are given under the relevant chapters.

Chapter 1: ALFRED AND AFTERWARDS

P. J. Helm's *Alfred the Great,* an excellent and lively book for the general reader.

English Historical Documents Vol. 1, in most public libraries, gives King Alfred's laws and a useful summary of the period.

H. C. Lea's *Superstition and Force* (1878), long out of print, is the best book on Trial by Ordeal, but Paul Vinogradoff's article on *Ordeal (Christian)* in the *Encyclopaedia of Religion and Ethics* (1917) Vol. IX p. 519 is in most public libraries.

On the Saxon period and law see also

Pollock and Maitland's *History of the Common Law* (1895)

F. M. Stenton's *Anglo-Saxon England* (1943)

Dorothy Whitelock's *The Beginnings of English Society* (1952)

T. F. T. Plucknett's *Concise History of the Common Law* (1948)

D. P. Kirkby's *The Making of Early England.* (1967)

Robert Baldick's *The Duel* (1965) deals with Trial by Battle.

Other sources include:

p. 1: The Mirror of Justices, ed. Andrew Horne (1768); also Selden Society (1895) Vol. 7. Bishop Asser's *Life of Alfred* is in *Six Old English Chronicles* ed. J. A. Giles (1896), or ed. Dorothy Whitelock (1959).

p. 7: Gilbert the Goose's case: G. Neilson's *Trial by Combat* (1890) Elias Piggun: *Select Pleas of the Crown* ed. Maitland, Selden Soc. Vol. I p. 192

Wiliam Pygun: *Gesta Abbatum* (Rolls Series) I. 221

p. 9: The Border Quarrel, Nicholson and Burn's *History of Cumberland and Westmorland* (1777) I. 595

The Lilburn feud: *Pauline Gregg's Free-born John* (1961); *Calendar of State Papers (Domestic) 1636–7* pp. 136, 181; and especially *Some Old Forms of Law* by James Clepham, *Arch. Aeliana* (O.S.) IX pp. 180.

p. 11: a modern edition of *Bracton,* a key work, is by Samuel E. Thorne (1968). The statute is 32 Henry VIII c.12; Baines' *History of Lancashire* (1870) II.574 comments on it.

p. 5: The bleeding corpse: WHD Longstaffe's *History of Darlington* (1854) pp. 232–3

p. 12: Alan and the Scythe: *Rolls of the Justices in Eyre for Yorkshire 1218–9* (Selden Society Vol. 57, p. 662). Deodands are summarised in Blackstone's *Commentaries* (ed. Chitty) I. 300–2.

Chapter 2: THE CIRCUITS BEGIN

English Historical Documents Vol. 2 (in most public libraries) quotes the Assizes of Clarendon and Northampton. Dorothy M. Stenton's *English Justice 1066–1215* (1964) and her introduction to *Rolls of the Justices in Eyre for Yorkshire 1218–19* (Selden Society Vol. 57) are important; the latter sets out in English translation many typical cases. Likewise *Pleas before the King and Justices 1198–1212* (Vols. 67–8, 83–4). But this chapter is based on *Northumberland Assize Rolls* (ed. William Page, 1891; Surtees Society Vol. 88); all the cases for 1256 come from it, but are in Latin. See also J. S. Cockburn's *The Northern Assize Circuit* (Northern History Vol. 3, 1968)

p. 13–4: the territory and instructions for the Assizes of 1176 and 1189 are in the Latin chronicle of Roger of Hoveden (Rolls Series) II.87–8

p. 16: Modern Assizes are described in Sir Basil Nield's *Farewell to the Assizes* (1972), giving a High Court Judge's view of them. The clergymen's strike is described by Roger of Hoveden III.261.

Chapter 3: THE JEWS AT YORK

The best books are Michael Adler's *The Jews of Mediaeval England* (1939) and Cecil Roth's *History of the Jews in England* (1941); other important sources are H. G. Richardson's *The English Jewry under the Angevin Kings* (1960) and the introduction to J. M. Rigg's *Selected Pleas Starrs and Records of the Jewish Exchequer* (1902, Selden Society Vol. 15). More general background is given by John T. Appleby's *England without Richard* (1965) and Agnes Strickland's *Lives of the Queen of England* (1864), especially concerning Eleanor of Provence and her extravagance.

Richard I's coronation is described by Roger of Wendover, *Flores Historiarum,* and Roger of Hoveden I.8 et seq (Rolls Series). William of Newburgh (Rolls Series) IV.294 describes the massacre with a vividness which needs no extra colouring.

p. 35: The Phantom Jury, in Sir Herbert Maxwell's translation of *The Chronicles of Lanercost* (1913) p. 58.

p. 37: 'Unless I am cheated out of my property.' See *Certain Starrs* by the Rev. J. T. Fowler, Yorks Archaeological and Topographical Journal 1873–4, Vol. III.

Chapter 4: FOUL BILLS ON THE BORDER

An excellent modern book in paperback is George Macdonald Fraser's *The Steel Bonnets* (1971). As he says, the best way of meeting the Border raiders at first hand is to read (or rather dip into) the two massive volumes of the *Calendar of Border Papers* (1560–1603), to be found at public libraries and Record Offices. See also Godfrey Watson's *The Border Reivers* (1974), equally good. The other basic sources are:

The Hamilton Papers (1532–90)

Calendar of State Papers (Domestic) from Henry VIII to James I.

George Ridpath's *Border History* (1848)

R. R. Reid's *The King's Council in the North* (1921)

Howard Pease's *The Lord Wardens of the Marches of England and Scotland* (1913)

But almost everything in this chapter can be found in the *Calendar of Border Papers,* through its index.

p. 38–9: Bernard Gilpin: see C. S. Collingwood's *Memoirs of Bernard Gilpin* (1884) *p. 40–50: Sir Robert Carey's Memoirs* (reprinted 1808)

p. 40–41: The Foul Bills procedure: see Bishop Nicholson's *Border Laws* (1705), or Nicholson and Burn's *History of Cumberland and Westmorland* (1777), especially its introduction.

p. 50: Mungo Noble's acquittal: a famous story told by Roger North. The Earl of Leicester's Journal is in the *De L'Isle and Dudley MSS* Vol. 6 p. 590.

Chapter 5: IN TIME OF PESTILENCE

The best books are Philip Ziegler's *The Black Death* (1969) and Professor F. F. D. Shrewsbury's *A History of the Bubonic Plague in the British Isles* (1970), with John Howard's *The State of the Prisons* (1777), reprinted in the Everyman Library. Most Archaeological Societies have articles about the plague in their transactions. Other sources include:

pp. 54–5: 1597, and Arrowsmith's fate: Robert Surtees' *Durham* (1816) IV.5. Volume I.xcii describes Thomas Morton's courageous deeds.

p. 56–7: The outbreak at Preston: R. Sharpe France's *A History of the Plague in Lancashire* (1939), and *Lord Kenyon MSS* (Historical MSS Commission 1894, Appendix 4.)

p. 57: The lawyers in Oxford: letter from Denis de Repas to Sir Edward Harley, quoted in Walter G. Bell's *The Great Plague in London* (1924).

p. 58: The Earl of Clarendon's letter, *Verulam MSS* (Hist. MSS) pp. 59–60. Lord Campbell's experience: *Lives of the Chancellors* IV. 345n.

p. 59: The Black Assize: C. S. Collingwood's *Memoirs of Bernard Gilpin* (1884) p. 326.

p. 61: John Heystrom's *Jail Fever* (1781) is in the Jackson Library, Tullie House, Carlisle.

p. 62–3: Notes of Visit to the Prisons in Scotland and the North of England in Company with Elizabeth Fry, by Joseph John Gurney (1819).

Chapter 6: THE LANCASHIRE WITCHES

The one indispensable book is Potts' *Discovery* (1613), reprinted by the Chetham Society Vol. VI., or by G. B. Harrison with an intro-duction (1929). Edgar Peel and Pat Southern's *Trials of the Lancashire Witches* (1969) considers all the available evidence excellently. Alan Macfarlane's *Witchcraft in Tudor and Stuart England* (1970) concentrates on witchcraft in Essex, but shows that individual regions must be considered separately. Other sources include:

p. 65: The Papal Bulls: J. R. Tanner's *Tudor Constitutional Documents 1485–1603* (1922). 'A thousand pulpits covered in dust': Christopher Hill's *Change and Continuity in 17th Century England* (1974). Kentucky hill-billies: Wallace Notestein's admirable *History of Witchcraft in England* (1911), not easily found. Pendle in 1673: Richard Brome's *Britannia* (1673).

p. 66: Sir Richard Molyneux's reports: *Salisbury MSS* (Hist. MSS) Vol. 8, p. 213

p. 67: James I's wedding-night: see James I's *Daemonologie* (1597), and Agnes Strickland's *Lives of the Queens of England* (1865) Vol. IV. Agnes Sampson's trial is in *News from Scotland,* reprinted in the *Gentleman's Magazine* Vol. 49, p. 393.

p. 68: James I's tests of a witch: Sir R. Filmer's *Advertisement to the Jurymen of England touching Witches* (1679).

p. 69: James I and witch soup: Victor Hugo's *Toilers of the Sea!.*

p. 78–9: the 1633 witch trial and its consequences are to be found in T. D. Whitaker's *History of Whalley* (1872); the *Calendar of State Papers (Domestic) 1634–5* pp. 26, 77–9, 98 and 129; *The Farington Papers* (Chetham Society Vol. 39, p. 27). Harvey and the toad is a story told in Notestein's *History of Witchcraft.*

No witches were convicted in Yorkshire at this time; see *Yorkshire Witchcraft Prosecutions 1567–1640* by P. Tyler (Northern History IV 84–109); the Yorkshire people had more sense.

Chapter 7: JUDGE JEFFREYS' JAUNT

My favourite book is P. T. Helms admirable *Jeffreys* (1965); G. W. Keeton's *Lord Chancellor Jeffreys and the Stuart Cause* (1965) gives a good account of his visit to the Northern Circuit, and assesses his genuine merits as a judge. See also H. Montgomery Hyde's *Judge Jeffreys* (1940) and Lord Birkenhead's *Fourteen English Judges* (1926); Lord Campbell's *Lives of the Chancellors* Vol. IV is most lively, and greatly underestimated. The sources include:

p. 81: leapfrog: I can find no authority for this legend, even in the important writings of Roger North: *Life of Lord Keeper Guilford,* and Autobiography (ed. Jessop, 1890).

pp. 83, 85–6: The trial of Titus Oates is in the *State Trials* series.

p. 85: His BROW and his TONGUE: in a pamphlet of 1764.

p. 87: The Earl of Sunderland's letter: *Calendar of State Papers (Domestic) 1684–5.*

p. 80: At York: Sir John Reresby's *Memoirs* (ed. 1875) p. 305.

p. 88–90: At Newcastle: *The Memoirs of Ambrose Barnes* (1866, Surtees Society Vol. 50); biassed but lively. At Carlisle: *Bishop Nicholson's Diaries* (Cumberland and Westmorland Archaeological Society, Vol. I p. 15; *Sir Daniel Fleming's Account Book* Historic MSS Commission Vol. 12 part 7, p. 40).

p. 90: At Durham: Robert Surtees' *Durham* (1816) I. cxvii; J. Nichols' *History of Leicestershire* IV. 830.

p. 92: At Kendal: Richard S. Ferguson's *History of Westmorland* (1894) pp. 178–9. At Lancaster: Robert Halley's *Lancashire: Its Puritanism and Nonconformity* (1869) II.181, 271; and *Calendar of State Papers (Dom.) 1685,* No. 496.

Chapter 8: A COINERS' TRIAL

The Mangey trial is reprinted verbatim from the transactions of the Thoresby Society (1899) Vol. 9 pp. 205–227, with their kind permission. The activities of Daniel Awty and other Yorkshire coiners are described in *York Castle Depositions* (Surtees Society Vol. 40 p. 215), H. Ling Roth's *The Yorkshire Coiners* (1906), John Marsh's *Clip a Bright Coin* (1971) and John Leyland's *Coining in Yorkshire* (Old Yorkshire V. 116). Macaulay's *History of England* Chapter XXI describes the havoc wreaked by coining in 1685; Sir John Craig's *The Mint* (1953) runs from Saxon times. The Leeds Mace is described by Llewellyn Jewitt, *Corporation Plate and Insignia of Office* (Art Journal Vol. 42 p. 301); Mangey's secret room in *Old Yorkshire* Vol. III pp. 200–2; and the murder of Mr Deighton in the *Annual Register* 1771, Jan 4th.

Chapter 9: A LITTLE TRIP ROUND THE CIRCUIT

There is no adequate account of a barrister's day-to-day life. The chief sources are Lord Eldon's *Anecdote Book,* ed. Lincoln and McEwen (1960), and H. Twiss' *Life of Lord Chancellor Eldon* (1846); even better are James Parke's letters, never before published, in the Northumberland County Record Office, North Gosforth, Newcastle upon Tyne. Daniel Defoe's *Tour through the Whole Island of Great Britain* (1724–6), Thomas De Quincey's *The English Mail Coach* (1849) and the Rev. William Macritchie's *Diary of a Tour through Great Britain in 1795* are very helpful, but there are many good books on stage-coach travel: Joan Parkes' *Travel in England in the 17th Century* (1925), Thomas Burke's *Travel in England* (1942), and Edmund Vale's *The Mail Coach Men in the late 18th Century* (1960), for instance. Other sources include:

p. 119: Crossing the Humber: *Memoir of Rokeby J.,* (Surtees Society Vol. 37)

p. 121: Wordsworth's buttered toast: De Quincey's *Recollections of the Lake Poets* (1834–40) pp. 196–7.

p. 122: George Gray's dentifrice: Robert Surtees' *Durham* (1816) II.16

pp. 127–8: the body-snatchers: W. H. D. Longstaffe's *History of Darlington* (1854)

p. 132: Charles Dickens: *A Lazy Tour of Two Idle Apprentices,* in his *Christmas Stories.*

pp. 136–7: Lancaster Assizes: from a shorthand transcript.

Many of the Lord Eldon stories are also to be found in Lord Campbell's *Lives of the Chancellors,* where it describes his career.

Chapter 10: THE GALLOWS ON HARRABY HILL

For the '45 Rebellion in general, Sir Walter Scott's *Tales of a Grandfather* (1929), Sir Charles Petrie's *The Jacobite Movement* (1932), John Prebble's *Culloden* (1961) and Tomasson and Buist's *Battles of the '45* are most useful. The fate of the prisoners at Carlisle is given in amazing detail by Sir Bruce Seton and Jean Gordon Arnot's *The Prisoners of the '45* (Scottish History Society, 3rd Series Vols. 13–15), and I have drawn heavily upon it. Baron Clarke's notebook, with a typescript, is at Tullie House, Carlisle, but parts are reprinted in Rupert C. Jarvis' *Collected Papers on the Jacobite Risings* (1971–2). Pamphlets on the trials of Thomas Cappoch and Col. Towneley are also at Carlisle; see also M. Creighton's *Carlisle*

(1889), Mounsey's *Carlisle in 1745* (1846), J. A. Wheatley's *Bonnie Prince Charlie in Cumberland* (1903) and the *Fitzherbert MSS* (Hist. MSS Commission). Other sources include: pp. 138–9: John Wesley's *Journal,* September 22nd and 29th, October 8th 1745.

Chaper 11: POOR BOZZY

The principal sources are Boswell's *Letters* (ed. C. B. Tinker), Boswell's *Journal,* his *Life of Johnson,* and the Northern Circuit Records, the latter being unpublished. Background books include Hesketh Pearson's *Johnson and Boswell* (1958), Johnson's *Letters,* and *Johnson's England* (1933).

Chapter 12: A MODEST SUCCESS

The Diaries of James Losh, 1799–1833, are at Tullie House Carlisle. Selections from the years 1811–33 are printed by the Surtees Society, Vols. 171 and 174, with useful notes. But I have used my own selection for the whole period; the typescript is at Tullie House. Mentions of his cases in the *Carlisle Journal* and *Newcastle Courant* are disappointingly few. Other sources include:

p. 177: Wordsworth in 1800: See *Journals of Dorothy Wordsworth* ed. Mary Moorman (1971) pp. 37, 39.

p. 179: George and Weedon Grossmith's *Diary of a Nobody,* Everyman's Library or Penguin Books.

p. 180: Robert Southey's opinion: his *Life and Correspondence* (1850) III.224–5. George Stephenson: see Samuel Smiles' biography of him.

p. 183: De Quincey's recollection of Buttermere and the Hatfield case, in his *Recollections of the Lake Poets* (1834–40). Coleridge shouting 'Dinner!': his own *Notebooks* (ed. Kathleen Coburn, 1957) No. 1432.

P. 192: Wordsworth's view of Losh: *The Letters of William and Dorothy Wordsworth (The Later Years),* I.727.

Chapter 13: THE TRUTH ABOUT DAGGER MONEY

A monumental account of the Assize system is J. S. Cockburn's *A History of English Assizes 1558–1714* (1972); for modern times, Sir

Basil Nield's *Farewell to the Assizes* (1972), and, over a wide period, E. S. Turner's *May it Please Your Lordship* (1972). But a picture of a judge's daily life can only be pieced together from widely scattered sources. They include:

pp. 193–4: The letter in 1262: *The Royal Letters of Henry III* (Rolls Series, 1886) part II pp. 222–3; a remarkable document.

pp. 194–5: Bacon's instructions: Spedding's *Life and Letters of Bacon* VII. 211–3.

pp. 195–8: Provisions for the judges: sturgeon, see Whitaker's *History of Craven* (1812). Horse-grease, *Lonsdale MSS* (Historical MSS), No. 1. Mr Justice Whitelocke's accounts, in his *Liber Famelicus,* 70 Camden Society 106, often quoted.

p. 198: Peter de Beavoir, *York Castle Depositions* (Surtees Society, Vol. 40, 32–6). Corbridge, *County History of Northumberland* X.227–9.

p. 199: Lord Ellenborough's wig, Lord Campbell's *Lives of the Chief Justices* IV.303. Costume in 1635, W. Dugdale's *Origines Juridiales* (1666–80) Chapter 34.

p. 201: Sir John Clerk's observations, his *Journey to Carlisle and Penrith in 1731,* ed. W. A. J. Prevost, Cumberland and Westmorland Archaeological Society, 2nd Series, Vol. 61, pp. 202–37.

p. 202: The French and English observers, quoted by E. Halevy, *England in 1815* p. 112.

p. 204: Mary Bateman's case, *Carlisle Journal,* 25th March 1809. Sir Daniel Fleming's instructions are reprinted in Cockburn's *History of English Assizes* (1972) Appendix 3.

Chapter 14: THE YOUNG 'FE'

The sources for this chapter are Harold Jager's *Brief Life* (1934), a collection of FE's *Speeches* (1929), his son's biography of him (1933), his own *Famous Trials of History* (1926), and above all the *Liverpool Mercury* for the years 1899–1906. Towards the end of his life he spoke amusingly at many luncheons and dinners; press reports provide his views on marking exams (2.8.1923), Eloquence (22.2.1927), tennis (20.6.1927), bicycling (1.11.1927), 28.1.1928), his election campaign (24.2.1928) and old age (12.7.1928). They have not since appeared in print.

Chapter 15: GOLDIANA

This chapter could not have been written without relying heavily on Sir Fred E. Pritchard's *Goldiana,* which he compiled with Glyn Blackledge. I have added some Circuit legends of Goldie not in that collection, and some of his political speeches from the *Liverpool Daily Post* and *The Times.*

Chapter 16: A BREATH OF THE NORTH

Strenuous research in the pages of the *Liverpool Daily Post, The Times* and the *Times Law Reports* for the period 1920–37 produced the alarming fate of W. T. Fielding (pp. 251–2), the election petition (p. 254) and the case of Marlene Dietrich's life story (p. 258–9), but very little else that is not also in E. S. Fay's *The Life of Mr. Justice Swift* (1939) or Sir Fred E. Pritchard's monograph on him.

Chapter 17: REVELRY BY NIGHT

The stories in this chapter come from Circuit legends, Circuit records, Lord Eldon's Anecdote Book, and James Parke's letters; Sir Fred E. Pritchard's verses on Rigby Swift are from his monograph. Macaulay's letter to his father (p. 264), dated April 2nd 1826, is from G. O. Trevelyan's edition of his *Life and Letters* (1876) p. 108 et seq. The birth of the North-Eastern Circuit (p. 266) is in Mr Justice Ridley's *Memoirs* (Northumberland Record Office; unpublished). The story of the agenda (p. 267) is from Alexander Pearson's *The Doings of a Country Solicitor* (1947).

Index

291

Jury—*cont.*
   risk of plague 56

Kean, Edmund as Hamlet 181
Kendal 92
Kidnapping by Border raiders 44
'Kinmont Willie' Armstrong 46–57
Kirkby Lonsdale 134–5
Knaresborough,
   1262, Castle 194
   1777 prison conditions 61

Lancashire
   1176 part of the Northern Circuit 13,
      16
   1348 during the Black Death 52–3
   1786 its ladies liked by Boswell 164
   1795 its black-stockinged girls 131–2
   Catholics 65–6, 78
   ignorance and superstition 65–6
   witches 27, 65–80
Lancaster
   1612, 1633–6 witches in castle 72, 78–9
   1684 Judge Jeffreys' visit 92
   1745 the rebels barbarously treated
      141
   1786 Boswell's visit 163–6
   1818 fire in stables 133
   1819 prison conditions 63
   Dickens' view 132
   its liberties 11
   suspicious of good coins 97
   the sea-shore route 120
Lancaster Assizes
   1612 first Lancashire witches trial 69–
      80
   1633 second Lancashire witches trial
      78
   1786 Boswell's role 163–6
   1818 a witness' whiskers 262
   a slew balloon 271
   barrister plays for time 136–7
Lanercost, Chronicles of 35–6
Leeds,
   1694 its mace made by Arthur Mangey
      98
   1832 Mangey's secret room discovered
      117–8
   1846 its cellar slums 64
Liberty, where king's writ does not run
   11
Liddesdale, and its 'Great Bill' 40, 46–8
Lilburn family feud, trial by battle 9–10
Lincoln, its Jews and riots 30, 32

Liverpool
   1835 becomes an Assize town 207
   1846 cellar slums 64
   1867 judges' lodgings opened 207
   1901 great fraud on Bank 217–8
   1923–4 comforts at judges' lodgings
      207–8
   George Wise's Protestant crusade
      216–7, 221–3
   rats 64
Lloyd George, David 225
London
   1189 coronation of Richard I 28–9,
      31–2
   1262 wine in chambers 194
   1633 horse-driven mill at Mint
   1665 Great Plague
   1706 stagecoach to York 120–1
   1798 inhibits James Losh 175–6
   1802 Davy's lectures 185–6
   1906 F. E. Smith moves from
      Liverpool 225–6
   Judges gather before going on Circuit
      194–5
Lonsdale, Lord (Sir James Lowther)
   168–72
Losh, James
   1768 born 192
   at Cambridge 175
   1789 joins Lincoln's Inn 175
   1794 joins Northern Circuit 175
   1795–1833 friendship with William
      Wordsworth 176–8, 181, 183,
      187–8, 191–2
   1799 starts practice in Newcastle 176
   1800 holiday with Lake Poets 177–8
   1801 prosecutes highwaywomen 178
   1802 Humphrey Davy's lecture 185–6
   1808 house struck by lightning 184
   1813 an isolated indiscretion 188
   1820 cajoles rich uncle 188
   1821 a smuggling case 184–5
   1824 a jury wavers 182
   1825 helps launch Carlisle-Newcastle
      railway 189–90
   1828 stage-coach to London 186–7
   1832 visits Brougham and Grey 190
   1833 Recorder of Newcastle; dies
      190–2
   Diary of a Nobody 179–80
   Newcastle Literary and Philosophic
      Society 176, 179–81, 191
   passion for information 184–7, 191
Lottery 1746 for trial of rebels at Carlisle
   142–3

293